תקעו שופר

TIKU SHOFAR

A MAḤZOR AND SOURCEBOOK FOR STUDENTS AND FAMILIES

Shoshana Silberman

THE UNITED SYNAGOGUE OF CONSERVATIVE JUDAISM
נר ה' נשמת אדם

Published by
The United Synagogue of Conservative Judaism
Commission on Jewish Education

Dr. Shoshana Silberman is the author of *A Family Haggadah, The Whole Megillah (almost!)*. Presently the educational director of the Jewish Center of Princeton (NJ), she has been involved in Jewish education as a teacher, principal, workshop leader, and curriculum writer. Dr. Silberman received a B.S. from Columbia University and a B.H.L. from Gratz College. She holds a M.S.T. from The University of Chicago and an Ed. D. from Temple University.

10 9 8 7 6 5 4 3

International Standard Book Number: 0-8381-0166-6

ACKNOWLEDGEMENTS

The Spiritual Life of Children by Robert Coles. Copyright © 1990 by Robert Coles. Reprinted by permission of Houghton Mifflin Company. All rights reserved. pp. 75, 145, 255.

Anne Frank: The Diary Of A Young Girl by Anne Frank (translated by B.M. Mooyaart—Doubleday). Copyright © 1952 by Otto Frank and the American Jewish Committee. Reprinted by permission of Random House, Inc. (Modern Library). All rights reserved. p. 278.

A Family Haggadah by Shoshana Silberman. Copyright © by Shoshana Silberman. Reprinted by permission of Kar-Ben Copies, Inc. All rights reserved. pp. 8, 12-15.

Design and typography by Schaffzin & Schaffzin

Dedication

To my husband Mel

A man of valor, where can he be found?

Teaching and learning,

Supporting and nurturing.

He is a just person with a forgiving nature

Whose worth is above every treasure

and whose love is beyond measure.

With gratitude for your encouragement and assistance in preparing Tiku Shofar.

Shoshana

Table of Contents

PREFACE

When we began discussions of *Tiku Shofar* at the Publications Committee of the United Synagogue of Conservative Judaism's Commission on Jewish Education, chaired by Dr. Ruth B. Waxman, we set two goals for a new children's *maḥzor* . It had to help children (and parents) have a prayerful experience and be educational. Dr. Shoshana Silberman took up the challenge. In developing *Tiku Shofar*, she used her many talents and her educational experience to create what we trust will be a contribution to the prayer life and education of our children.

One approaches the development of a *maḥzor* with a sense of *yirah,* reverence — reverence for our tradition and reverence for the possibilities in each of our children. Our work was aided by a fine Readers Committee, chaired by Rabbi Marim D. Charry. Through their astute comments and suggestions, the members of the committee — Mr. Barry Amper, Ms. Karen Ashkanase, Rabbi Scott L. Glass, Rabbi Susan Grossman, and Ms. Saralee Shrell-Fox — contributed much to the development of *Tiku Shofar*. Of course, in the final analysis, the responsibility for the work remains with the author and editor.

An additional word of appreciation goes to the staff of the Department of Education, Rabbi Shelley Melzer and Kay Pomerantz, Assistant Directors, Dorothy Sachs, Coordinator, and Dorothy Nathan, secretary. In a myriad of ways, they contributed to the development of this work. Their eyes, minds and hearts nurtured the making of *Tiku Shofar*. Rabbi Joshua Elkin and Dr. Miriam Klein Shapiro have chaired the United Synagogue Commission on Jewish Education during the period when *Tiku Shofar* was conceived and developed.

Robert Abramson, Director
Department of Education
United Synagogue of Conservative Judaism
20 Sivan 5752

INTRODUCTION AND GUIDE

Why *Tiku Shofar*?

Compiling a *maḥzor*, whether exclusively for children or for family use, presents several challenges. The needs of congregations can vary greatly. Some, for example, hold services geared to one age level. Others span several grades. Some students (and their parents) in many congregations are not well acquainted with the prayers or even basic holiday concepts, while others come with extensive preparation. Finally, some congregations hold a separate junior congregation or youth service and others prefer family services.

This *maḥzor, Tiku Shofar,* has been designed for different groups and circumstances. It appeals to most children above eight years of age (once the basics of Hebrew reading have been taught), including teens. It allows parents to be active participants, too—not just visitors or guests. It also is designed so that a High Holy Day service experience can vary from one time to the next while maintaining the traditional framework.

Tiku Shofar achieves this flexibility because of certain unique features. You will find an abridged service text in Hebrew. Some verses are transliterated so children new to Hebrew (and many parents!) can also participate. The English translation is simple, gender-neutral, and age-appropriate without being condescending. The translation was done with both a deep respect for the authentic meaning of the prayers and a commitment to their reaching modern minds and hearts. In most instances, prayers were not translated verbatim. The goal was to capture their essence. Occasionally, with a prayer that contained multiple themes, the sub-theme is not voiced if it confuses the focus and is a major theme in another prayer or prayers in the service.

At several points, the English is presented with unusual graphics to heighten interest and suggest the prayer's intention. Interspersed in the service text are thoughts, commentaries and questions as well as holiday stories. These resources are included so that service leaders can actively involve the children (and parents if present). There is also a section with suggested activities that teachers and/or parents can do with children prior to the High Holy Days.

The thoughts, commentaries and questions, as well as the stories, can also be used by teachers and parents to prepare children beforehand. Often students come to services knowing facts about the High Holy Days but they don't come spiritually prepared. These resources are meant to help children reflect on the meaning of the Days of Awe. Rather than shying away, *Tiku Shofar* challenges children with theological questions geared to their cognitive level of development.

Based on the 1990 decision of the Committee on Jewish Law and Standards of the Rabbinical Assembly, the Commission on Jewish Education decided that *Tiku Shofar* should offer the first *b'raḥah* of the *Amidah* in the traditional version and an alternate version that includes both the forefathers and mothers. To permit congregations to maintain consistency with their practice and educational approach, it was determined that each version should be self contained on alternate pages.

How should this *maḥzor* be used? Obviously, the person responsible for leading the service must be familiar with the prayers and translations included in *Tiku Shofar*. However, it is most important that the service leader study the text **in advance** to decide which of the commentaries, questions and stories he or she wants to use at the service. Material can be added or deleted depending on the interest or ability level of the group assembled. However, the leader is urged not to attempt to make these decisions on the spot. Doing so may result in poor choices that interrupt the flow of the service.

The leader must select which prayers to do in Hebrew and which to do in English. This will certainly vary, depending on the background of the participants. I would recommend that if they know a prayer in Hebrew, they should do it in Hebrew (especially if it is sung). However, even if they know a lot of the prayers in Hebrew, the leader should also include the reading of selected translations so students can focus on the meaning of these prayers.

Advance planning is especially needed for the *Amidah* or the service could fall apart at this point. I would recommend that the opening blessings and the *Kedushah* be said aloud by the leader, with the congregation joining in. For those with a great familiarity with the text, a silent reading of the rest of the *Amidah* could follow, after which the leader and the congregation would do all or selections from the *Amidah* following the *Kedushah*. Where there is a limited knowledge of prayer, a quiet moment for each to say a personal prayer from the heart would be more suitable. Then, the leader would, together with the congregation, do all or selections from the *Amidah* which follow the *Kedushah*.

In selecting what should be read following the *Kedushah,* it would be important to include the special prayers for the Days of Awe. In *Shaḥarit* this includes *u-v'ḥen ten paḥdeḥa, u-v'ḥen ten kavod,* and *u-v'ḥen tzadikim.* For *Musaf* on *Rosh haShanah*, the *Amidah* also includes the special sections of *malḥuyot, ziḥronot and shofarot.* These sections should be introduced with stories and or commentaries, keeping in mind that some of the text may be unfamiliar. On *Yom Kippur*, of course, you will also want to include the *ashamnu* and *al ḥet.*

It is also recommended that the leader find alternatives to large group discussions. Whenever possible, the service leader should have students share their thoughts and feelings in pairs or in small groups. These can be homogeneous, multi-age or parent/child groupings. Usually, just talking to the person next to you works fine. (In fact, my own congregation of 1200 had people talk in pairs on the High Holy Days and it proved to be an exciting experience.) To do this with children, I would suggest having other adults present to assist. Teens who have been exposed to cooperative learning techniques would also be excellent facilitators for small group activities.

It is the goal of this *maḥzor* to help children pray, enable them to wrestle with Jewish texts, learn the High Holiday liturgy and grapple with important issues. The Days of Awe challenge us to learn and to change. I hope *Tiku Shofar* will help in this process.

Special thanks to Rabbi Robert Abramson for his careful editing of this manuscript. His clear thinking and helpful suggestions were most appreciated. His cheerful disposition also made the task easier.

May you be inscribed for a healthy, happy and sweet new year!

Shoshana Silberman

TO THE LEADER

•Graphics were developed by Howard Jacobson. Adapting an old tradition of using the word to decorate liturgical works, he created a style that will engage today's young people.

•In placing Hebrew and English translation we have tried to keep the *maḥzor* "user friendly." We have sought to provide both flexibility and enhance the flow of the service. Most often the English follows the Hebrew but when deemed appropriate, it precedes it.

•To enhance aesthetics and the leader's ability to direct the eyes and minds of participants to specific content, we have limited the amount of text found on any one page.

•To further aid in the use of this *maḥzor* we have used the following visual cues:

- •Hebrew prayers and their translations appear in black.
- •Stories are boxed and are lightly shaded in burgundy. At the top of the box is a graphic symbol.
- •Some supplementary materials are also in burgundy and boxed, but do not have a symbol nor are they shaded.
- •Thoughts, explanations and comments appear in burgundy.
- •In transliterating, we have used the "ḥ" for both ח and כ. The "ḥ" is pronounced as in Ḥanukkah. The letters "ei" are pronounced like the long "a" in "state." An apostrophe between vowels indicates that the vowels are each pronounced separately.

A MESSAGE TO CHILDREN

Days of Awe

Rosh haShanah begins on a very joyous note. Even before the holiday arrives, greeting cards wishing us a happy and healthy new year come in the mail. New clothes hang in our closets and the aroma of delicious foods hangs in the air. Sometimes a grandparent will come to visit or an older sibling will come home from college. Perhaps you've been invited by friends for the holiday meal. In the synagogue, people greet each other in an especially friendly way.

As *Yom Kippur* approaches, adults seem to get more serious. You can sometimes feel left out when you're not fasting or sitting for hours at services in the synagogue like the adults. And there are really no special "fun" activities organized for kids.

The Days of Awe (High Holy Days) are not like some of our other holidays. We don't get presents or dress in costumes. We don't plant trees or go on picnics or drink four cups of wine. Yet the Days of Awe (*Yamim Noraim*) can have a special meaning for kids, too. They are a time to think not only about what you want but about what God wants. Each new year is a gift from God. It is a time to celebrate getting a new start. You are given time to grow and learn, to explore and enjoy! This may be the year you finally master soccer or learn how to read from the Torah. Maybe you will visit a new place or make a new friend. And, maybe you'll be able to stop those things about yourself that you don't like, such as losing your temper or being lazy about chores. You have a chance to turn things around. This is called *TESHUVAH*. You can learn to be a better friend, improve your math scores, participate in healthy activities, or let your parents know how much you love them.

When you start to turn things around, you feel good inside — really proud. This is the best feeling in the world. The Days of Awe can give you this feeling — just like they do for adults.

Justice and Mercy

Tzedek and *Raḥamim*

"It's not fair!" children frequently complain. At home, parents hear, "Her piece of cake is bigger than mine" or "He got to watch more TV." At school, teachers hear, "She got more lines in the play" or "Why was I punished; I wasn't the only one talking?" When friends cheat, we don't like having them in our games. If they take our pencils or lunches, we boil with anger. We expect that people who break rules should be punished. This is what we mean by JUSTICE (*tzedek*).

A parent cannot always cut cake exactly evenly but the parent would be unjust to give one child dessert and the other one none. At school we do expect our teachers to give us grades based on merit, not favoritism. We also expect the principal to have the same rules for each class.

We expect the police to arrest all thieves, not just some. We expect judges to make sure that all who are brought to court receive a fair trial. We recognize that a store clerk who takes money from the register or a person who shoplifts not only hurts the owner but also the other customers who ultimately have to make up the loss.

The Torah teaches us to be concerned with *tzedek*. We are instructed not to spread false rumors or tell lies in court. If we use scales in our business, they must tell the true weight. They must be correctly balanced. People should be punished if they hurt someone. On *Rosh haShanah* and *Yom Kippur*, we are most aware of *tzedek* (justice) as we think about our behavior during the past year.

But being Jewish means not only demanding *tzedek* for ourselves and acting fairly, it means helping to make the world a more just place. We must have special concern for those less fortunate, such as the poor and the homeless. We also need to help the deaf, the blind and those with other handicaps.

Rosh haShanah and *Yom Kippur* also teach us that we need to do even more than be fair or just. We are also asked to be forgiving and especially kind. This is what we mean by MERCY *(raḥamim)*.

During the Days of Awe (*Yamim Noraim*), we think about the past year and consider how we can be better in the future. Perhaps we can help a younger brother with his homework, or mom with the groceries, or dad with making dinner, or the elderly neighbor on the block by shoveling her walkway. Maybe we can stop gossiping about a certain friend or end teasing a classmate.

We are also asked to forgive others for the hurt they've caused us. If they're sorry, we need not hold a grudge. By forgiving, we not only make them feel better but we also regain their friendship.

On *Rosh haShanah* and *Yom Kippur* we praise God for both *tzedek* and *raḥamim*. We are grateful for an ordered world and for the Torah which helps us to create such a world. We know we may not always be as successful at improving as we should, but we also know that God forgives our errors, and we are grateful for that. We are thankful, also, when those closest to us are able to forgive us, as well, and pray that we will also be forgiving to them.

BEFORE *ROSH HASHANAH*

Each morning during *Elul*, the Hebrew month preceding *Rosh haShanah*, the *shofar* is blown to rouse and remind us to do *teshuvah* (repentance). Psalm 27 is also said each morning and in the evening at the end of the service.

At a time when we are measuring our own lives, we try to remember the lessons and love of those who have died. During *Elul*, it is customary to visit the cemetery where loved ones are buried.

It is also appropriate to greet people and wish them a "*Shanah Tovah*," a good year. Many people also send homemade or store-bought holiday cards to family and friends.

At midnight on the Saturday before *Rosh haShanah*, a special *Seliḥot* (forgiveness) service is held at the synagogue. The *paroḥet* (ark curtain) and the cover for the reading tables are changed from the usual color to white, symbolizing the purity of this holy time.

EREV ROSH HASHANAH

On the eve of *Rosh haShanah*, before sunset, candles are lit at home using the following blessing: (On *Shabbat*, we add the words in brackets.)

בָּרוּךְ אַתָּה יְיָ אֱלֹהֵינוּ מֶלֶךְ הָעוֹלָם, אֲשֶׁר קִדְּשָׁנוּ
בְּמִצְוֹתָיו וְצִוָּנוּ לְהַדְלִיק נֵר שֶׁל (שַׁבָּת וְשֶׁל) יוֹם טוֹב.

We praise You, *Adonai* our God, Ruler of the Universe, Who makes us holy by Your *mitzvot* and commands us to light the [Sabbath and] festival lights.

Baruḥ atah Adonai Eloheinu Meleḥ ha'olam asher kid'deshanu b'mitzvotav v'tzivanu l'hadlik ner shel [Shabbat v'shel] Yom Tov.

בָּרוּךְ אַתָּה יְיָ אֱלֹהֵינוּ מֶלֶךְ הָעוֹלָם, שֶׁהֶחֱיָנוּ וְקִיְּמָנוּ
וְהִגִּיעָנוּ לַזְּמַן הַזֶּה.

We praise You, *Adonai* our God, Ruler of the Universe, Who has kept us alive and well so that we can celebrate this special time.

Baruḥ atah Adonai Eloheinu Meleḥ ha'olam sheheḥeyanu v'ki'yemanu v'higi'anu laz'man hazeh.

At the dinner table, it is customary to bless the children in the family. The parent(s) place both hands on head of each child. The traditional blessings are:

For girls:

Y'simeḥ Elohim k'Sarah,	יְשִׂימֵךְ אֱלֹהִים כְּשָׂרָה,
Rivkah, Le'ah v'Raḥel.	רִבְקָה, לֵאָה וְרָחֵל.

May you be like Sarah, Rebecca, Rachel and Leah.

For boys:

Y'simḥa Elohim	יְשִׂמְךָ אֱלֹהִים
k'Efrayim v'ḥiM'nasheh.	כְּאֶפְרַיִם וְכִמְנַשֶּׁה.

May you be like Ephraim and Manasseh.

It is also appropriate for parents to add their own wishes and blessings.

Parents conclude blessing all children with the threefold blessing:

Y'vareḥeḥa Adonai v'yish'mereḥa.	יְבָרֶכְךָ יְיָ וְיִשְׁמְרֶךָ.
Ya'er Adonai panav eileḥa viḥuneka.	יָאֵר יְיָ פָּנָיו אֵלֶיךָ וִיחֻנֶּךָּ.
Yisa Adonai panav eileḥa	יִשָּׂא יְיָ פָּנָיו אֵלֶיךָ
v'yasem l'ḥa shalom.	וְיָשֵׂם לְךָ שָׁלוֹם.

May *Adonai* bless and protect you.
May *Adonai* shine upon you with graciousness.
May *Adonai* look upon you with favor and grant you peace.

We recite the *Kiddush,* blessing for the wine:
(On *Shabbat,* add the words in brackets.)

(וַיְהִי עֶרֶב וַיְהִי־בֹקֶר יוֹם הַשִּׁשִּׁי. וַיְכֻלּוּ הַשָּׁמַיִם וְהָאָרֶץ
וְכָל־צְבָאָם. וַיְכַל אֱלֹהִים בַּיּוֹם הַשְּׁבִיעִי מְלַאכְתּוֹ אֲשֶׁר עָשָׂה,
וַיִּשְׁבֹּת בַּיּוֹם הַשְּׁבִיעִי מִכָּל־מְלַאכְתּוֹ אֲשֶׁר עָשָׂה. וַיְבָרֶךְ אֱלֹהִים
אֶת־יוֹם הַשְּׁבִיעִי וַיְקַדֵּשׁ אֹתוֹ, כִּי בוֹ שָׁבַת מִכָּל־מְלַאכְתּוֹ אֲשֶׁר
בָּרָא אֱלֹהִים לַעֲשׂוֹת.)

(On the sixth day, the heavens and the earth were completed. On the seventh day, God finished the work of creation and rested. God blessed the seventh day and called it holy, because on that day God rested from the work of creation.)

(Va'y'hi erev va'y'hi voker yom hashishi. Va'y'ḥulu hashamayim v'ha'aretz v'ḥol tz'va'am. Va'y'ḥal Elohim bayom hash'vi'i m'laḥto asher asah. Vayishbot bayom hash'vi'i mikol m'laḥto asher asah. Va'y'vareḥ Elohim et yom hash'vi'i va'y'kadesh oto, ki vo shavat mikol m'laḥto asher bara Elohim la'asot.)

בָּרוּךְ אַתָּה יְיָ אֱלֹהֵינוּ מֶלֶךְ הָעוֹלָם, בּוֹרֵא פְּרִי הַגָּפֶן.

We praise You, *Adonai* our God, Ruler of the Universe, Who creates the fruit of the vine.

Baruḥ atah Adonai Eloheinu Meleḥ ha'olam borei p'ri hagafen.

בָּרוּךְ אַתָּה יְיָ אֱלֹהֵינוּ מֶלֶךְ הָעוֹלָם, אֲשֶׁר בָּחַר בָּנוּ מִכָּל־עָם
וְרוֹמְמָנוּ מִכָּל־לָשׁוֹן וְקִדְּשָׁנוּ בְּמִצְוֹתָיו. וַתִּתֶּן־לָנוּ יְיָ אֱלֹהֵינוּ בְּאַהֲבָה
אֶת־יוֹם (הַשַּׁבָּת הַזֶּה וְאֶת־יוֹם) הַזִּכָּרוֹן הַזֶּה, יוֹם (זִכְרוֹן) תְּרוּעָה
(בְּאַהֲבָה) מִקְרָא קֹדֶשׁ, זֵכֶר לִיצִיאַת מִצְרָיִם. כִּי בָנוּ בָחַרְתָּ
וְאוֹתָנוּ קִדַּשְׁתָּ מִכָּל־הָעַמִּים, וּדְבָרְךָ אֱמֶת וְקַיָּם לָעַד. בָּרוּךְ אַתָּה
יְיָ מֶלֶךְ עַל כָּל־הָאָרֶץ מְקַדֵּשׁ (הַשַּׁבָּת וְ)יִשְׂרָאֵל וְיוֹם הַזִּכָּרוֹן.

We praise You, *Adonai* our God, Ruler of the Universe, Who has chosen us and made us holy through Your *mitzvot*. You lovingly have given us this [*Shabbat* and this] Day of Remembrance, a day for remembering the *shofar* sound, a holy time to recall our going out of Egypt. We praise You, *Adonai,* Ruler of the whole world, Who makes holy the [*Shabbat*, the] people Israel and the Day of Remembering.

Baruḥ atah Adonai Eloheinu Meleḥ ha'olam asher baḥar banu mikol am, v'rom'manu mikol lashon, v'kid'deshanu b'mitzvotav. Vatiten lanu Adonai Eloheinu b'ahavah et yom [haShabbat hazeh v'et yom] hazikaron hazeh, yom [ziḥron] t'ruah [b'ahavah] mikra kodesh zeḥer li'tziat Mitzrayim. Ki vanu vaḥarta v'otanu kidashta mikol ha'amim u'dvarḥa emet v'kayam la'ad. Baruḥ atah Adonai Meleḥ al kol ha'aretz m'kadesh [haShabbat v'] Yisrael v'yom hazikaron.

(On Saturday night only, we add *Havdalah.*)

בָּרוּךְ אַתָּה יְיָ אֱלֹהֵינוּ מֶלֶךְ הָעוֹלָם, בּוֹרֵא מְאוֹרֵי הָאֵשׁ.
בָּרוּךְ אַתָּה יְיָ אֱלֹהֵינוּ מֶלֶךְ הָעוֹלָם, הַמַּבְדִּיל בֵּין קֹדֶשׁ לְחֹל
בֵּין אוֹר לְחֹשֶׁךְ, בֵּין יִשְׂרָאֵל לָעַמִּים, בֵּין יוֹם הַשְּׁבִיעִי לְשֵׁשֶׁת יְמֵי
הַמַּעֲשֶׂה. בֵּין קְדֻשַּׁת שַׁבָּת לִקְדֻשַּׁת יוֹם טוֹב הִבְדַּלְתָּ, וְאֶת־יוֹם
הַשְּׁבִיעִי מִשֵּׁשֶׁת יְמֵי הַמַּעֲשֶׂה קִדַּשְׁתָּ, הִבְדַּלְתָּ וְקִדַּשְׁתָּ אֶת־עַמְּךָ
יִשְׂרָאֵל בִּקְדֻשָּׁתֶךָ. בָּרוּךְ אַתָּה יְיָ הַמַּבְדִּיל בֵּין קֹדֶשׁ לְקֹדֶשׁ.

Praised are You, *Adonai* our God, Ruler of the Universe, Who makes a distinction between the holy and ordinary, light and darkness, the Jewish people and other peoples, the seventh day and the six days for work. You have made a distinction between the holiness of *Shabbat* and the holidays. Praised are You, *Adonai,* who makes a distinction between holy times.

Baruḥ atah Adonai Eloheinu Meleḥ ha'olam, borei m'orei ha'esh.

Baruḥ atah Adonai hamavdil bein kodesh l'kodesh.

בָּרוּךְ אַתָּה יְיָ אֱלֹהֵינוּ מֶלֶךְ הָעוֹלָם, שֶׁהֶחֱיָנוּ וְקִיְּמָנוּ
וְהִגִּיעָנוּ לַזְּמַן הַזֶּה.

We praise You, *Adonai* our God, Ruler of the Universe, Who has kept us alive and well so that we can celebrate this special time.

Baruḥ atah Adonai Eloheinu Meleḥ ha'olam sheheḥeyanu v'ki'yemanu, v'higi'anu laz'man hazeh.

The *Motzi* (blessing for bread) is recited over two round *ḥallot:*
We wash our hands for the meal and say this blessing:

בָּרוּךְ אַתָּה יְיָ אֱלֹהֵינוּ מֶלֶךְ הָעוֹלָם, אֲשֶׁר קִדְּשָׁנוּ בְּמִצְוֹתָיו וְצִוָּנוּ
עַל נְטִילַת יָדָיִם.

We praise You, *Adonai* our God, Ruler of the Universe, Who has made us holy by Your *mitzvot* and commands us to wash our hands.

Baruḥ atah Adonai Eloheinu Meleḥ ha'olam asher kid'deshanu b'mitzvotav v'tzivanu al n'tilat yadayim.

Then we say:

בָּרוּךְ אַתָּה יְיָ אֱלֹהֵינוּ מֶלֶךְ הָעוֹלָם, הַמּוֹצִיא לֶחֶם מִן הָאָרֶץ.

We praise You, *Adonai* our God, Ruler of the Universe, Who brings forth bread from the earth.

Baruḥ atah Adonai Eloheinu Meleḥ ha'olam hamotzi leḥem min ha'aretz.

Some say that the round shape of the *ḥallah* is used because it reminds us of God's crown of sovereignty. Others say it is used to wish us a round year — a smooth time without difficult bumps or curves.

We dip the *ḥallah* (and apples, too) into the honey and say:

יְהִי רָצוֹן מִלְּפָנֶיךָ
יְיָ אֱלֹהֵינוּ וֵאלֹהֵי אֲבוֹתֵינוּ וְאִמּוֹתֵינוּ,
שֶׁתְּחַדֵּשׁ עָלֵינוּ שָׁנָה טוֹבָה וּמְתוּקָה.

Y'hi ratzon milfaneḥa
Adonai Eloheinu v'eilohei avoteinu v'imoteinu
shet'ḥadesh aleinu shanah tovah u'metukah.

May it be Your will,
God of our ancestors,
for this new year to be sweet and good.

On the second evening, some eat a new fruit (one not eaten recently).

ראש השנה

ROSH HASHANAH
SERVICE

SOME THOUGHTS IN PREPARATION FOR *ROSH HASHANAH*

On *Rosh haShanah* and *Yom Kippur* we use a prayer book called a *maḥzor* which means cycle. It was part of a cycle of prayer books used for all the Jewish holidays. This word comes from the Hebrew root *"ḥzr"* חזר which means "to review." Why was this a good choice for the name of the High Holy Day prayer book?

In the synagogue, the Torah Scrolls, the ark and the reader's tables are all dressed in white. Usually there are white flowers and the rabbi and cantor wear white robes. This gives us a clean and new feeling, like a sheet of paper before we write on it.

We often wish each other a "Happy Holiday" but the exact translation of *"Shanah Tovah"* is "A Good Year." Is there a difference in the two wishes?

What good things happened to you this past year? What wishes do you have for the new year to come?

Did you know that *"shanah,"* the Hebrew word for "year," also means "change"? What changes happen during the course of each year? What changes happened in your life last year?

On *Rosh haShanah*, we think about how we have failed others, ourselves and God. We regret these failings and promise to improve.

We go to synagogue a little fearful because we know we have done things that are wrong. Yet, at the same time, we feel certain it will all work out.

We are thankful that our God cares about justice, yet judges us with mercy.

The Lesson

One year on Rosh haShanah, *Rabbi Levi Yitzḥak of Berditchev told the following story:*

Once he came to an inn where many Jews were lodging because it was a market day. The famous rabbi joined these businessmen for an early *minyan*. However, he was shocked at how fast they rushed through their prayers and how badly they mispronounced so many of the words.

At the end of the service, he marched up to them and began uttering nonsense syllables such as "Ba...sha...boo...." The merchants were so astonished they could not speak. Finally, Rabbi Levi Yitzḥak explained to them: "The way I spoke to you is the way you just spoke to God!"

At first, they all stood there very ashamed. Then one of the men answered the rabbi: "When a baby utters syllables that have no meaning to anyone else, the mother and father seem to know what the infant needs. Even if you, Rabbi, didn't understand our prayers, we feel confident that God knows our true thoughts and feelings."

"This merchant was right," Rabbi Levi Yitzḥak declared. "He showed more faith in God than I did. He taught me something that I now want to teach you: On this holy day, even the prayers of those who are unable to say them properly will be heard if they come from the heart...."

Scales, Balance and Rain

In a far-away town, there was a terrible drought. No rain had fallen for several months and so food was scarce and there was little to drink. Not only did the rabbi of the town pray for rain but the entire congregation joined him in chanting and fasting. One night, this rabbi had a strange dream. He heard a voice whisper to him. "Only one man, Moisheh the shopkeeper, can bring rain. He alone must lead the congregation in prayer."

"Why should Moisheh the shopkeeper lead the service? He's an ignorant man who does not even know how to read. There must be some mistake," the rabbi thought.

However, the dream returned to him a second time and then a third. The rabbi finally decided that he would obey the voice. On the following day, he announced to the astonished congregation, "Moisheh ben Yitzḥak will lead us in the service."

The shopkeeper replied in a pleading voice, "Please, no. How can I do this when I hardly know the prayers?" The rabbi also pleaded. "Moisheh, you must do it, for you are the only one who can end the drought. God will accept your prayer if it is from the heart."

To everyone's surprise, Moisheh left the synagogue. The congregants sat silently, waiting to see what would happen next. Five minutes later they had their answer. Moisheh returned with the balance scale from his shop, marched up to the front of the synagogue and began to speak.

"Holy One of blessing, I am not a learned man. All I can show You is the good name and the honest scales I use in business. I have never lied or cheated anyone. If by being honest I have followed Your commandments, then be merciful and bring us rain."

The grateful congregants not only said prayers of thanks to God but also went home to adjust their scales. No one knows for sure if this is the reason they never had another drought. But no matter. They all felt that if their scales were in balance, the world was in balance, too.

מַה טֹּבוּ אֹהָלֶיךָ יַעֲקֹב, מִשְׁכְּנֹתֶיךָ יִשְׂרָאֵל.
וַאֲנִי בְּרֹב חַסְדְּךָ אָבוֹא בֵיתֶךָ,
אֶשְׁתַּחֲוֶה אֶל הֵיכַל קָדְשְׁךָ בְּיִרְאָתֶךָ.

How beautiful are your tents
O people of Jacob
And your dwelling places
O Israelites!
Through Your lovingkindness, I enter Your house to pray.
Here in this special place, I will bow before You.
Accept my prayers, *Elohim,* and answer me with mercy.
Teach me Your ways of truth.

After the Exodus from Egypt, the Jewish people spent forty years wandering in the desert before they entered the Promised Land. Towards the end of their journey, they needed to pass through Moab to reach Israel. Balak, the king of Moab, was so against their passing through his country that he hired a magician named Balaam to stop Israel by cursing them.

Balaam climbed a mountain and looked down on the Israelites' encampment. Their peaceful dwellings and beautiful Sanctuary touched his heart. Instead of a curse, words of blessing came out of his mouth.

These words became the *"Mah Tovu"* prayer that we recite when we enter the synagogue. We say it to inspire us to live in a way that will continually draw praise from others and make ourselves proud.

Ma tovu ohaleḥa Ya'akov, mishkenoteḥa Yisrael.
Va'ani b'rov ḥasdeḥa, avo veiteḥa,
eshtaḥaveh el heiḥal kod'she'ḥa b'yirateḥa.

Thank You, *Adonai* our God, Source of blessing

For letting me see a new day.

For making me a Jewish person.

For giving me freedom.

For forming me in Your image.

For providing me with all my needs.

For creating heaven and earth.

For opening our eyes to all that is around us.

For strengthening those who are tired or afraid.

For offering us guidance and hope.

בָּרוּךְ אַתָּה יְיָ אֱלֹהֵינוּ מֶלֶךְ הָעוֹלָם, אֲשֶׁר נָתַן לַשֶּׂכְוִי בִינָה
לְהַבְחִין בֵּין יוֹם וּבֵין לָיְלָה:

בָּרוּךְ אַתָּה יְיָ אֱלֹהֵינוּ מֶלֶךְ הָעוֹלָם, שֶׁעָשַׂנִי בְּצַלְמוֹ:

בָּרוּךְ אַתָּה יְיָ אֱלֹהֵינוּ מֶלֶךְ הָעוֹלָם, שֶׁעָשַׂנִי בֶּן־חוֹרִין:

בָּרוּךְ אַתָּה יְיָ אֱלֹהֵינוּ מֶלֶךְ הָעוֹלָם, שֶׁעָשַׂנִי יִשְׂרָאֵל:

בָּרוּךְ אַתָּה יְיָ אֱלֹהֵינוּ מֶלֶךְ הָעוֹלָם, פּוֹקֵחַ עִוְרִים:

בָּרוּךְ אַתָּה יְיָ אֱלֹהֵינוּ מֶלֶךְ הָעוֹלָם, מַלְבִּישׁ עֲרֻמִּים:

בָּרוּךְ אַתָּה יְיָ אֱלֹהֵינוּ מֶלֶךְ הָעוֹלָם, מַתִּיר אֲסוּרִים:

בָּרוּךְ אַתָּה יְיָ אֱלֹהֵינוּ מֶלֶךְ הָעוֹלָם, זוֹקֵף כְּפוּפִים:

בָּרוּךְ אַתָּה יְיָ אֱלֹהֵינוּ מֶלֶךְ הָעוֹלָם, רוֹקַע הָאָרֶץ עַל הַמָּיִם:

בָּרוּךְ אַתָּה יְיָ אֱלֹהֵינוּ מֶלֶךְ הָעוֹלָם, שֶׁעָשָׂה לִּי כָּל־צָרְכִּי:

בָּרוּךְ אַתָּה יְיָ אֱלֹהֵינוּ מֶלֶךְ הָעוֹלָם, אֲשֶׁר הֵכִין מִצְעֲדֵי־גָבֶר:

בָּרוּךְ אַתָּה יְיָ אֱלֹהֵינוּ מֶלֶךְ הָעוֹלָם, אוֹזֵר יִשְׂרָאֵל בִּגְבוּרָה:

בָּרוּךְ אַתָּה יְיָ אֱלֹהֵינוּ מֶלֶךְ הָעוֹלָם, עוֹטֵר יִשְׂרָאֵל בְּתִפְאָרָה:
בָּרוּךְ אַתָּה יְיָ אֱלֹהֵינוּ מֶלֶךְ הָעוֹלָם, הַנּוֹתֵן לַיָּעֵף כֹּחַ:
בָּרוּךְ אַתָּה יְיָ אֱלֹהֵינוּ מֶלֶךְ הָעוֹלָם, הַמַּעֲבִיר שֵׁנָה מֵעֵינַי
וּתְנוּמָה מֵעַפְעַפָּי:

Holy One of Blessing, help us follow Your kind and loving ways.

A Thought on Praising God

Why do we praise God? Some Jews believe that God wants our prayers as a way of connecting with us. Others feel that we need to pray because when we say words of blessing we are changed for the better. Some feel the need to speak to God. Others feel that prayers help us think about following God's ways. What do you think?

בָּרוּךְ שֶׁאָמַר וְהָיָה הָעוֹלָם, בָּרוּךְ הוּא,
בָּרוּךְ עוֹשֶׂה בְרֵאשִׁית, בָּרוּךְ אוֹמֵר וְעוֹשֶׂה,
בָּרוּךְ גּוֹזֵר וּמְקַיֵּם, בָּרוּךְ מְרַחֵם עַל הָאָרֶץ,
בָּרוּךְ מְרַחֵם עַל הַבְּרִיּוֹת, בָּרוּךְ מְשַׁלֵּם שָׂכָר טוֹב לִירֵאָיו,
בָּרוּךְ חַי לָעַד וְקַיָּם לָנֶצַח,
בָּרוּךְ פּוֹדֶה וּמַצִּיל, בָּרוּךְ שְׁמוֹ.

בָּרוּךְ אַתָּה יְיָ אֱלֹהֵינוּ מֶלֶךְ הָעוֹלָם, הָאֵל הָאָב הָרַחֲמָן
הַמְּהֻלָּל בְּפִי עַמּוֹ, מְשֻׁבָּח וּמְפֹאָר בִּלְשׁוֹן חֲסִידָיו וַעֲבָדָיו.
בָּרוּךְ אַתָּה יְיָ מֶלֶךְ מְהֻלָּל בַּתִּשְׁבָּחוֹת.

Blessed is the One Who spoke and the world was created.
Blessed is the One Who cares for the earth and all its creatures.
Blessed is the One Who keeps promises.
Blessed is the One Who judges and rewards.
Blessed is the One Who lives forever.
Blessed is Your Holy Name.

Your faithful ones will bless You, *Adonai*, and will sing hymns to Your glory.

Dear God,
You are the one that makes miracles. You help everyone, and worked so hard to make the earth and keep it alive. You made people, rainbows, the sun, moon, and stars. You made the sun to rise and set. You made all living things. Thank you so much, so very much.

Love from one of your
many creations,
Melissa Sands
Princeton, N.J., age 8

הַלְלוּיָהּ. הַלְלוּ אֵל בְּקָדְשׁוֹ, הַלְלוּהוּ בִּרְקִיעַ עֻזּוֹ.

הַלְלוּהוּ בִגְבוּרֹתָיו, הַלְלוּהוּ כְּרֹב גֻּדְלוֹ.

הַלְלוּהוּ בְּתֵקַע שׁוֹפָר, הַלְלוּהוּ בְּנֵבֶל וְכִנּוֹר.

הַלְלוּהוּ בְּתֹף וּמָחוֹל, הַלְלוּהוּ בְּמִנִּים וְעֻגָב.

הַלְלוּהוּ בְצִלְצְלֵי־שָׁמַע, הַלְלוּהוּ בְּצִלְצְלֵי תְרוּעָה.

כֹּל הַנְּשָׁמָה תְּהַלֵּל יָהּ. הַלְלוּיָהּ.

כֹּל הַנְּשָׁמָה תְּהַלֵּל יָהּ. הַלְלוּיָהּ.

HALLELUYAH!
Praise God in the Holy Place.
Praise God in the heavens.
Sing praises for mighty acts.
Blast the shofar.
Strum the strings.
Toot the flutes.
Clang the cymbals.
Beat the drums.
Let everything that breathes sing praise.

Halleluyah!
    Praise God in the holy place.
    Praise God in the heavens.
    Sing praises for mighty acts.
        Blast the *shofar* —
        Strum the strings —
        Toot the flutes —
        Clang the cymbals —
        Beat the drums —
Let everything that breathes sing praise.

Hal'luhu v'tziltz'lei shama, hal'luhu b'tziltz'lei t'ruah.
Kol han'shamah t'halel ya, haleluyah.

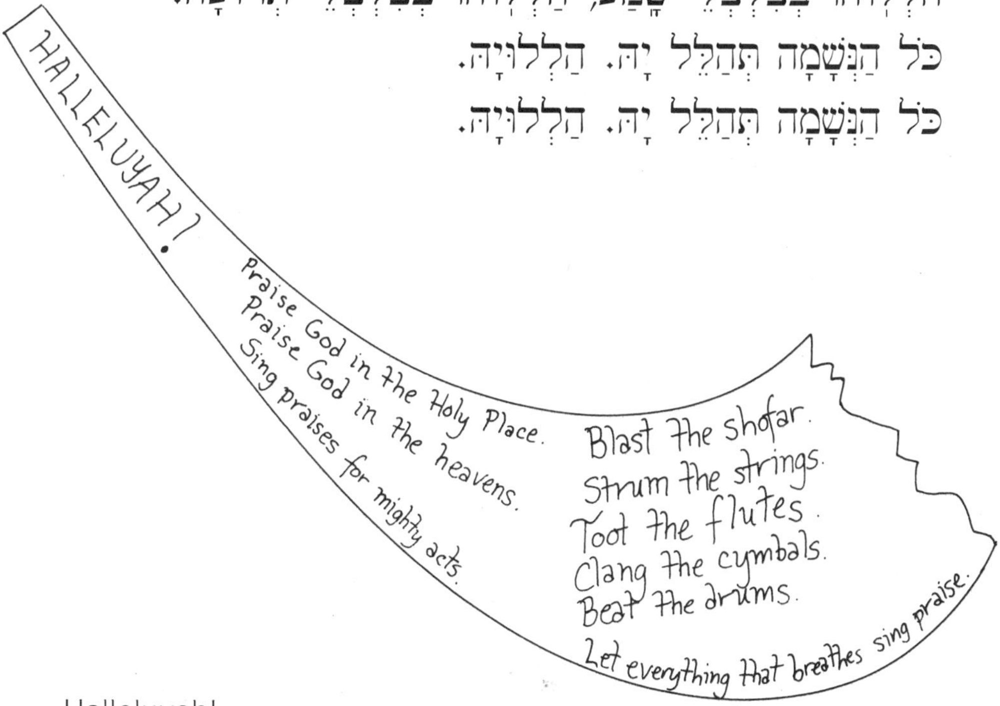

נִשְׁמַת כָּל־חַי תְּבָרֵךְ אֶת־שִׁמְךָ יְיָ אֱלֹהֵינוּ, וְרוּחַ כָּל־בָּשָׂר
תְּפָאֵר וּתְרוֹמֵם זִכְרְךָ מַלְכֵּנוּ תָּמִיד. מִן הָעוֹלָם וְעַד
הָעוֹלָם אַתָּה אֵל, וּמִבַּלְעָדֶיךָ אֵין לָנוּ מֶלֶךְ גּוֹאֵל וּמוֹשִׁיעַ,
פּוֹדֶה וּמַצִּיל וּמְפַרְנֵס וּמְרַחֵם בְּכָל־עֵת צָרָה וְצוּקָה. אֵין
לָנוּ מֶלֶךְ אֶלָּא אָתָּה.

The breath of all that lives shall bless Your name, Adonai, and shall sing of Your greatness. Since the beginning of time to the end of days, You are our God; we have no other. You help us when we are in trouble, and guide us in times of stress. God of all generations, to You alone we give thanks.

Even if our mouths were filled with as much song as the oceans hold water, and even if our lips could form enough words to fill an endless sky, we would still be unable to thank You for all the good You have done for our ancestors and for us. Stay with us, Adonai, and we will bless Your Holy name.

אִלּוּ פִינוּ מָלֵא שִׁירָה כַּיָּם
וּלְשׁוֹנֵנוּ רִנָּה כַּהֲמוֹן גַּלָּיו
וְשִׂפְתוֹתֵינוּ שֶׁבַח כְּמֶרְחֲבֵי רָקִיעַ
וְעֵינֵינוּ מְאִירוֹת כַּשֶּׁמֶשׁ וְכַיָּרֵחַ
וְיָדֵינוּ פְרוּשׂוֹת כְּנִשְׁרֵי שָׁמָיִם
וְרַגְלֵינוּ קַלּוֹת כָּאַיָּלוֹת
אֵין אֲנַחְנוּ מַסְפִּיקִים לְהוֹדוֹת לְךָ יְיָ אֱלֹהֵינוּ וֵאלֹהֵי
אֲבוֹתֵינוּ וּלְבָרֵךְ אֶת־שְׁמְךָ עַל אַחַת מֵאֶלֶף אֶלֶף אַלְפֵי
אֲלָפִים וְרִבֵּי רְבָבוֹת פְּעָמִים הַטּוֹבוֹת שֶׁעָשִׂיתָ עִם
אֲבוֹתֵינוּ וְעִמָּנוּ.

God Is More

What is it about "the breath of all that lives" that points to God? How does it tell us about God's greatness?

To express the idea that God is greater than all the words we have, this prayer uses a word-picture — "Even if our mouths were filled...." Another word-picture could be — "Even if our hands were filled with pen and ink like the _____." Can you make up a word-picture that begins — "Even if ______"?

We proclaim God our Ruler.

הַמֶּלֶךְ
יוֹשֵׁב עַל כִּסֵּא רָם וְנִשָּׂא.
שׁוֹכֵן עַד, מָרוֹם וְקָדוֹשׁ שְׁמוֹ. וְכָתוּב: רַנְּנוּ צַדִּיקִים בַּיְיָ
לַיְשָׁרִים נָאוָה תְהִלָּה.

You are our majestic unchanging Ruler. It is written in Psalms that the righteous rejoice in feeling God's closeness. It is fitting that they praise You.

בְּפִי יְשָׁרִים תִּתְרוֹמָם
וּבְדִבְרֵי צַדִּיקִים תִּתְבָּרַךְ
וּבִלְשׁוֹן חֲסִידִים תִּתְקַדָּשׁ
וּבְקֶרֶב קְדוֹשִׁים תִּתְהַלָּל.

You are honored by the mouth of the upright.
You are blessed by the words of the righteous.
You are declared holy by the tongue of the faithful.
You are praised in the hearts of good and kind people.

וּבְמַקְהֲלוֹת רִבְבוֹת עַמְּךָ בֵּית יִשְׂרָאֵל בְּרִנָּה יִתְפָּאַר שִׁמְךָ
מַלְכֵּנוּ בְּכָל־דּוֹר וָדוֹר. שֶׁכֵּן חוֹבַת כָּל־הַיְצוּרִים לְפָנֶיךָ
יְיָ אֱלֹהֵינוּ וֵאלֹהֵי אֲבוֹתֵינוּ לְהוֹדוֹת לְהַלֵּל לְשַׁבֵּחַ לְפָאֵר
לְרוֹמֵם לְהַדֵּר לְבָרֵךְ לְעַלֵּה וּלְקַלֵּס עַל כָּל־דִּבְרֵי
שִׁירוֹת וְתִשְׁבְּחוֹת דָּוִד בֶּן־יִשַׁי עַבְדְּךָ מְשִׁיחֶךָ.

In every generation, your people Israel gathers to sing your praises, adding songs to those written by King David, your dedicated servant.

יִשְׁתַּבַּח שִׁמְךָ לָעַד, מַלְכֵּנוּ הָאֵל הַמֶּלֶךְ הַגָּדוֹל וְהַקָּדוֹשׁ
בַּשָּׁמַיִם וּבָאָרֶץ. כִּי לְךָ נָאֶה, יְיָ אֱלֹהֵינוּ וֵאלֹהֵי אֲבוֹתֵינוּ,
שִׁיר וּשְׁבָחָה הַלֵּל וְזִמְרָה עֹז וּמֶמְשָׁלָה נֶצַח גְּדֻלָּה וּגְבוּרָה
תְּהִלָּה וְתִפְאֶרֶת קְדֻשָּׁה וּמַלְכוּת בְּרָכוֹת וְהוֹדָאוֹת מֵעַתָּה
וְעַד עוֹלָם. בָּרוּךְ אַתָּה יְיָ אֵל מֶלֶךְ גָּדוֹל בַּתִּשְׁבָּחוֹת, אֵל
הַהוֹדָאוֹת אֲדוֹן הַנִּפְלָאוֹת הַבּוֹחֵר בְּשִׁירֵי זִמְרָה, מֶלֶךְ אֵל
חֵי הָעוֹלָמִים.

May You be praised forever with songs that tell of Your strength, glory and holiness. We look to You for blessing as we offer You thanksgiving. Praised are You, *Adonai* our Ruler and Do-er of Wonders, Who delights in our songs.

ḤATZI KADDISH

Short *Kaddish* חֲצִי קַדִּישׁ

Leader:

יִתְגַּדַּל וְיִתְקַדַּשׁ שְׁמֵהּ רַבָּא בְּעָלְמָא דִּי בְרָא כִרְעוּתֵהּ,
וְיַמְלִיךְ מַלְכוּתֵהּ בְּחַיֵּיכוֹן וּבְיוֹמֵיכוֹן וּבְחַיֵּי דְכָל־בֵּית
יִשְׂרָאֵל בַּעֲגָלָא וּבִזְמַן קָרִיב, וְאִמְרוּ אָמֵן.

Congregation and Leader answer:

יְהֵא שְׁמֵהּ רַבָּא מְבָרַךְ לְעָלַם וּלְעָלְמֵי עָלְמַיָּא.

Y'hai shmai rabbah m'varaḥ l'olam u'l'olmei almay'ya.

Leader:

יִתְבָּרַךְ וְיִשְׁתַּבַּח וְיִתְפָּאַר וְיִתְרוֹמַם וְיִתְנַשֵּׂא וְיִתְהַדַּר
וְיִתְעַלֶּה וְיִתְהַלַּל שְׁמֵהּ דְּקֻדְשָׁא

Congregation and Leader answer:

בְּרִיךְ הוּא.

B'riḥ hu.

Leader:

לְעֵלָּא לְעֵלָּא מִכָּל־בִּרְכָתָא וְשִׁירָתָא תֻּשְׁבְּחָתָא וְנֶחֱמָתָא
דַּאֲמִירָן בְּעָלְמָא, וְאִמְרוּ אָמֵן.

About the *Kaddish*

The *Kaddish* is a prayer that glorifies and praises God. It expresses our hope that God's rule will occur in our lifetime. In the *Kaddish* we declare that God is greater than all the words we use in praise of God.

The *Kaddish* is used like punctuation at each prayer service. You might say that the *Ḥatzi Kaddish* is like a comma and the *Kaddish Shalem* is like a period. We say the *Ḥatzi* (half or short) *Kaddish* when we finish parts of the service, (e.g., before *barḥu* and before *Musaf*). We say the *Kaddish Shalem* (full) when we finish a main part of the service, *Shaḥarit* and *Musaf.*

Kaddish is also recited by mourners and those observing a *Yahrzeit* (the anniversary of the death of a close relative). This *Kaddish,* like the others, does not at all refer to the dead. It is a way for the living to show their love of God, despite their loss. By standing up and offering this prayer, they also honor the loved one who has died.

THE *SHEMA* AND ITS BLESSINGS:

We rise.

Leader:

בָּרְכוּ אֶת־יְיָ הַמְבֹרָךְ.

Let us praise.

Congregation then Leader:

בָּרוּךְ יְיָ הַמְבֹרָךְ לְעוֹלָם וָעֶד.

Praised are You, *Adonai,* the Source of all blessings, forever and ever.

Baruḥ Adonai ham'voraḥ l'olam va'ed.

We are seated.

בָּרוּךְ אַתָּה יְיָ אֱלֹהֵינוּ מֶלֶךְ הָעוֹלָם, יוֹצֵר אוֹר וּבוֹרֵא
חֹשֶׁךְ עוֹשֶׂה שָׁלוֹם וּבוֹרֵא אֶת־הַכֹּל.

Praised are You, *Adonai,* Source of all blessing, Who forms light and darkness, Who makes peace and creates all things.

Baruḥ atah Adonai, Eloheinu Meleḥ ha'olam, yotzer or u'vorei ḥosheḥ, oseh shalom u'vorei et hakol.

On weekdays only we say:

הַמֵּאִיר לָאָרֶץ וְלַדָּרִים עָלֶיהָ בְּרַחֲמִים וּבְטוּבוֹ מְחַדֵּשׁ
בְּכָל־יוֹם תָּמִיד מַעֲשֵׂה בְרֵאשִׁית. מָה רַבּוּ מַעֲשֶׂיךָ יְיָ,
כֻּלָּם בְּחָכְמָה עָשִׂיתָ, מָלְאָה הָאָרֶץ קִנְיָנֶךָ.

In Your mercy, You give light to the earth and all its inhabitants. In Your goodness, You renew each day the work of creation. You are firm like a rock and protecting like a shield. We have depended on You since the world began and have praised You from the beginning of time. Now, today, view us with kindness.

Imagine waking up one morning to total darkness. It would be rather scary for we count on the sun for light, warmth and vegetation. Although we count on sunlight, we should not take it for granted. Each day, we must be grateful for its appearance.

What else is a regular part of our lives that we should not take for granted?

On *Shabbat* we say this.

הַכֹּל יוֹדְוּךָ וְהַכֹּל יְשַׁבְּחְוּךָ, וְהַכֹּל יֹאמְרוּ אֵין קָדוֹשׁ כַּייָ.
הַכֹּל יְרוֹמְמְוּךָ סֶּלָה יוֹצֵר הַכֹּל, הָאֵל הַפּוֹתֵחַ בְּכָל־יוֹם
דַּלְתוֹת שַׁעֲרֵי מִזְרָח וּבוֹקֵעַ חַלּוֹנֵי רָקִיעַ, מוֹצִיא חַמָּה
מִמְּקוֹמָהּ וּלְבָנָה מִמְּכוֹן שִׁבְתָּהּ, וּמֵאִיר לָעוֹלָם כֻּלּוֹ וּלְיוֹשְׁבָיו
שֶׁבָּרָא בְּמִדַּת רַחֲמִים. הַמֵּאִיר לָאָרֶץ וְלַדָּרִים עָלֶיהָ
בְּרַחֲמִים וּבְטוּבוֹ מְחַדֵּשׁ בְּכָל־יוֹם תָּמִיד מַעֲשֵׂה בְרֵאשִׁית.

AN INTERPRETATION OF *EL ADON*

God, the Creator of all,
is praised by every soul.
God's greatness and essence
enter the world, as wisdom
announces the Holy Presence.

Your praises we laud
for we are so awed
by sun, moon, and stars
that we view from afar,
created by You skillfully,
with energy and beauty.

Full of splendor they shine,
doing what is assigned
to them by their Maker.
They rejoice so proud,
singing praises aloud
of the Holy One, the Creator.

אֵל אָדוֹן עַל כָּל־הַמַּעֲשִׂים, בָּרוּךְ וּמְבֹרָךְ בְּפִי כָּל־נְשָׁמָה.
גָּדְלוֹ וְטוּבוֹ מָלֵא עוֹלָם, דַּעַת וּתְבוּנָה סוֹבְבִים אוֹתוֹ.
הַמִּתְגָּאֶה עַל חַיּוֹת הַקֹּדֶשׁ, וְנֶהְדָּר בְּכָבוֹד עַל הַמֶּרְכָּבָה.
זְכוּת וּמִישׁוֹר לִפְנֵי כִסְאוֹ, חֶסֶד וְרַחֲמִים לִפְנֵי כְבוֹדוֹ.
טוֹבִים מְאוֹרוֹת שֶׁבָּרָא אֱלֹהֵינוּ, יְצָרָם בְּדַעַת בְּבִינָה וּבְהַשְׂכֵּל.
כֹּחַ וּגְבוּרָה נָתַן בָּהֶם, לִהְיוֹת מוֹשְׁלִים בְּקֶרֶב תֵּבֵל.
מְלֵאִים זִיו וּמְפִיקִים נֹגַהּ, נָאֶה זִיוָם בְּכָל־הָעוֹלָם.
שְׂמֵחִים בְּצֵאתָם וְשָׂשִׂים בְּבוֹאָם, עוֹשִׂים בְּאֵימָה רְצוֹן קוֹנָם.
פְּאֵר וְכָבוֹד נוֹתְנִים לִשְׁמוֹ, צָהֳלָה וְרִנָּה לְזֵכֶר מַלְכוּתוֹ.
קָרָא לַשֶּׁמֶשׁ וַיִּזְרַח אוֹר, רָאָה וְהִתְקִין צוּרַת הַלְּבָנָה.
שֶׁבַח נוֹתְנִים לוֹ כָּל־צְבָא מָרוֹם, תִּפְאֶרֶת וּגְדֻלָּה שְׂרָפִים
וְאוֹפַנִּים וְחַיּוֹת הַקֹּדֶשׁ.

We continue here on both *Shabbat* and weekdays.

"Just as I create worlds so do you."

This teaches us that one way we are like God is that we can be creative.

A Thought on God's Ways

God requires us to struggle for justice
and to work for freedom.
God asks us to end poverty
and to increase peace.
God invites us to become partners
in the work of creation.
May what we create make the world better and more beautiful.

הַמְחַדֵּשׁ בְּטוּבוֹ בְּכָל־יוֹם תָּמִיד מַעֲשֵׂה בְרֵאשִׁית, כָּאָמוּר:
לְעֹשֵׂה אוֹרִים גְּדֹלִים, כִּי לְעוֹלָם חַסְדּוֹ. אוֹר חָדָשׁ עַל צִיּוֹן
תָּאִיר וְנִזְכֶּה כֻלָּנוּ מְהֵרָה לְאוֹרוֹ. בָּרוּךְ אַתָּה יְיָ יוֹצֵר הַמְּאוֹרוֹת.

God, Who continues to create, cause a new light to shine on Zion. May this light help us to see a path to You. Praised are You, Creator of lights.

Or ḥadash al tziyon ta'ir,
v'nizkeh ḥulanu m'heirah l'oro.
Baruḥ atah Adonai, yotzer ha'me'orot.

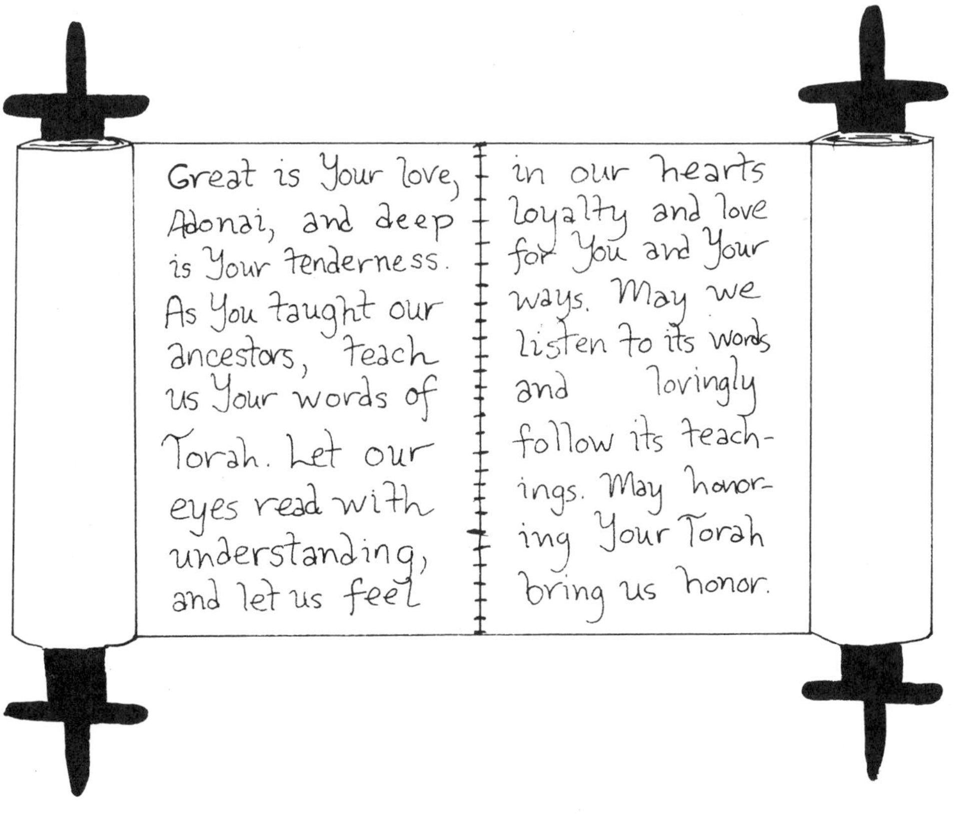

Great is Your love, Adonai, and deep is Your tenderness. As You taught our ancestors, teach us Your words of Torah. Let our eyes read with understanding, and let us feel
in our hearts loyalty and love for You and Your ways. May we listen to its words and lovingly follow its teachings. May honoring Your Torah bring us honor.

When we recite the verse *"v'havi'einu,"* we gather the four corners of our *tallit* and hold them while we say the passages of the *Shema.*

אַהֲבָה רַבָּה אֲהַבְתָּנוּ יְיָ אֱלֹהֵינוּ, חֶמְלָה גְדוֹלָה וִיתֵרָה
חָמַלְתָּ עָלֵינוּ. אָבִינוּ מַלְכֵּנוּ, בַּעֲבוּר אֲבוֹתֵינוּ שֶׁבָּטְחוּ בְךָ
וַתְּלַמְּדֵם חֻקֵּי חַיִּים כֵּן תְּחָנֵּנוּ וּתְלַמְּדֵנוּ. אָבִינוּ הָאָב
הָרַחֲמָן, הַמְרַחֵם, רַחֵם עָלֵינוּ וְתֵן בְּלִבֵּנוּ לְהָבִין
וּלְהַשְׂכִּיל לִשְׁמֹעַ לִלְמֹד וּלְלַמֵּד לִשְׁמֹר וְלַעֲשׂוֹת וּלְקַיֵּם
אֶת־כָּל־דִּבְרֵי תַלְמוּד תּוֹרָתֶךָ בְּאַהֲבָה. וְהָאֵר עֵינֵינוּ
בְּתוֹרָתֶךָ וְדַבֵּק לִבֵּנוּ בְּמִצְוֹתֶיךָ וְיַחֵד לְבָבֵנוּ לְאַהֲבָה
וּלְיִרְאָה שְׁמֶךָ וְלֹא נֵבוֹשׁ לְעוֹלָם וָעֶד. כִּי בְשֵׁם קָדְשְׁךָ
הַגָּדוֹל וְהַנּוֹרָא בָּטָחְנוּ, נָגִילָה וְנִשְׂמְחָה בִּישׁוּעָתֶךָ.

Safely gather our people from the four corners of the earth and bring us back to our ancient homeland. Draw us close to You so we can feel united as we proclaim Your oneness. Praised are You, *Adonai,* Who has lovingly chosen the people, Israel.

וַהֲבִיאֵנוּ לְשָׁלוֹם מֵאַרְבַּע כַּנְפוֹת הָאָרֶץ וְתוֹלִיכֵנוּ
קוֹמְמִיּוּת לְאַרְצֵנוּ כִּי אֵל פּוֹעֵל יְשׁוּעוֹת אָתָּה, וּבָנוּ
בָחַרְתָּ מִכָּל־עַם וְלָשׁוֹן וְקֵרַבְתָּנוּ לְשִׁמְךָ הַגָּדוֹל סֶלָה
בֶּאֱמֶת לְהוֹדוֹת לְךָ וּלְיַחֶדְךָ בְּאַהֲבָה. בָּרוּךְ אַתָּה יְיָ
הַבּוֹחֵר בְּעַמּוֹ יִשְׂרָאֵל בְּאַהֲבָה.

Avrum was interviewed between the ages of 9 and 13 by Robert Coles, a professor at Harvard University. Avrum grew up in Brookline, Mass., where he attended a Synagogue School at a Conservative congregation. These are his words:

"When I pray, I ask God to help me. I think I'm trying to find out what is the 'best,' by asking Him.... I hear Him; I hear Him saying that we should obey the Commandments and live good lives. I hear Him saying that one day He will bring all of us [Jews] back together. He made a pact with us, and He will help us — but we have to show Him we are deserving, we are ready.... God's voice is in you when you are making choices — it turns you towards the right direction. It's not only our decisions that count; it's His decision — to teach us the right way to be."

On Saying the *Shema* on *Yom Kippur*

After reciting the *Shema* on *Yom Kippur*, we respond aloud by saying, "Blessed is the name of Your glorious reign forever and ever." This is the only time of the year when we say this aloud. Some think it's because we were once prohibited by an emperor or king to declare God as our ruler. And so, we whispered our response very quietly. But when the people gathered on *Yom Kippur*, they found the courage to shout out this verse.

Some think that since we live in a country where we are free to worship God in our own way, we should always shout out this response. Others believe that by saying it aloud only once a year, we remember times when we were not free. Saying it on *Yom Kippur* then becomes very special. What do you think?

שְׁמַע יִשְׂרָאֵל יְהוָה אֱלֹהֵינוּ יְהוָה | אֶחָד׃

Shema Yisrael, Adonai Eloheinu, Adonai eḥad.

On *Rosh haShanah* we say the following in a whisper:
On *Yom Kippur* we say the following aloud:

בָּרוּךְ שֵׁם כְּבוֹד מַלְכוּתוֹ לְעוֹלָם וָעֶד.

Baruḥ shem k'vod malḥuto l'olam va'ed.

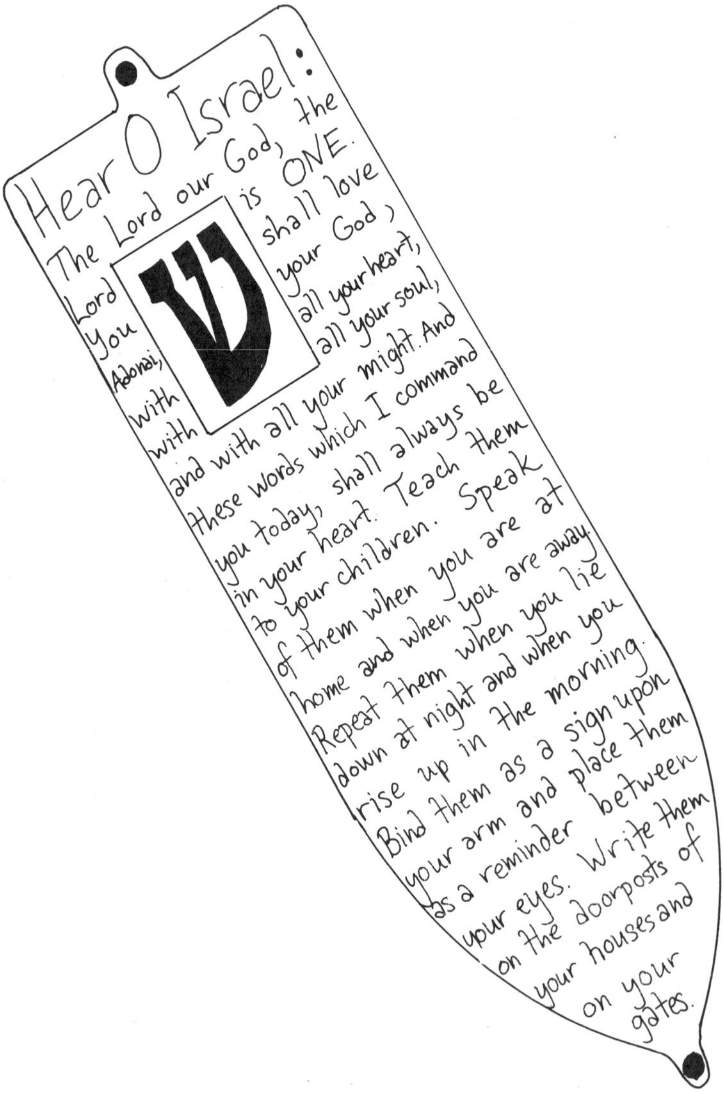

וְאָהַבְתָּ אֵת יְהוָה אֱלֹהֶיךָ בְּכָל־לְבָבְךָ וּבְכָל־נַפְשְׁךָ
וּבְכָל־מְאֹדֶךָ: וְהָיוּ הַדְּבָרִים הָאֵלֶּה אֲשֶׁר אָנֹכִי מְצַוְּךָ
הַיּוֹם עַל־לְבָבֶךָ: וְשִׁנַּנְתָּם לְבָנֶיךָ וְדִבַּרְתָּ בָּם בְּשִׁבְתְּךָ
בְּבֵיתֶךָ וּבְלֶכְתְּךָ בַדֶּרֶךְ וּבְשָׁכְבְּךָ וּבְקוּמֶךָ: וּקְשַׁרְתָּם
לְאוֹת עַל־יָדֶךָ וְהָיוּ לְטֹטָפֹת בֵּין עֵינֶיךָ: וּכְתַבְתָּם
עַל־מְזֻזוֹת בֵּיתֶךָ וּבִשְׁעָרֶיךָ:

How do you think parents can best get their messages across to their children?

If you were teaching a younger child about God, what would you say?

Once a student asked a rabbi, "What is the best way to love God?" The wise teacher replied, "The best way to love God is to love those God created."

A Thought on Oneness

Oneness is not sameness. Rainbows of colors delight us. Mountains and valleys challenge us. Different ideas stretch our minds. We are all on this planet together. We must find ways to come together and live in peace. We must find ways of sharing the earth's resources and enjoying its beauty. Oneness celebrates and unites differences. Oneness is the connection of people, God and nature.

וְהָיָה אִם־שָׁמֹעַ תִּשְׁמְעוּ אֶל־מִצְוֹתַי אֲשֶׁר אָנֹכִי מְצַוֶּה אֶתְכֶם
הַיּוֹם לְאַהֲבָה אֶת־יְהוָה אֱלֹהֵיכֶם וּלְעָבְדוֹ בְּכָל־לְבַבְכֶם
וּבְכָל־נַפְשְׁכֶם: וְנָתַתִּי מְטַר־אַרְצְכֶם בְּעִתּוֹ יוֹרֶה וּמַלְקוֹשׁ

וְאָסַפְתָּ דְגָנֶךָ וְתִירֹשְׁךָ וְיִצְהָרֶךָ: וְנָתַתִּי עֵשֶׂב בְּשָׂדְךָ לִבְהֶמְתֶּךָ
וְאָכַלְתָּ וְשָׂבָעְתָּ: הִשָּׁמְרוּ לָכֶם פֶּן־יִפְתֶּה לְבַבְכֶם וְסַרְתֶּם
וַעֲבַדְתֶּם אֱלֹהִים אֲחֵרִים וְהִשְׁתַּחֲוִיתֶם לָהֶם: וְחָרָה אַף־יְהוָה
בָּכֶם וְעָצַר אֶת־הַשָּׁמַיִם וְלֹא־יִהְיֶה מָטָר וְהָאֲדָמָה לֹא תִתֵּן
אֶת־יְבוּלָהּ וַאֲבַדְתֶּם מְהֵרָה מֵעַל הָאָרֶץ הַטֹּבָה אֲשֶׁר יְהוָה נֹתֵן
לָכֶם: וְשַׂמְתֶּם אֶת־דְּבָרַי אֵלֶּה עַל־לְבַבְכֶם וְעַל־נַפְשְׁכֶם
וּקְשַׁרְתֶּם אֹתָם לְאוֹת עַל־יֶדְכֶם וְהָיוּ לְטוֹטָפֹת בֵּין עֵינֵיכֶם:
וְלִמַּדְתֶּם אֹתָם אֶת־בְּנֵיכֶם לְדַבֵּר בָּם בְּשִׁבְתְּךָ בְּבֵיתֶךָ
וּבְלֶכְתְּךָ בַדֶּרֶךְ וּבְשָׁכְבְּךָ וּבְקוּמֶךָ: וּכְתַבְתָּם עַל־מְזוּזוֹת בֵּיתֶךָ
וּבִשְׁעָרֶיךָ: לְמַעַן יִרְבּוּ יְמֵיכֶם וִימֵי בְנֵיכֶם עַל הָאֲדָמָה אֲשֶׁר
נִשְׁבַּע יְהוָה לַאֲבֹתֵיכֶם לָתֵת לָהֶם כִּימֵי הַשָּׁמַיִם עַל־הָאָרֶץ:

If you sincerely follow My commandments, then I will favor your land with rain at the proper season. Then you will have a full harvest of grain, wine and oil and there will be grass in the fields for your cattle. You will eat and be satisfied. But if you turn from God's ways, there will be no rain and the earth will not bring forth its produce. In the end, you will even disappear from the good land which *Adonai* has given you.

In Biblical times, rain and good harvests were very important to the ancient Israelites. Today we might think how our observing the commandments can help make the world a better place for all. If we work at it, we can contribute to the elimination of hunger and poverty. If we waste resources, the world becomes worse. If we do good and act kindly, the world becomes a better place to live. Doing *mitzvot,* sacred deeds, can make us and the world better. A better world is our reward for doing *mitzvot*.

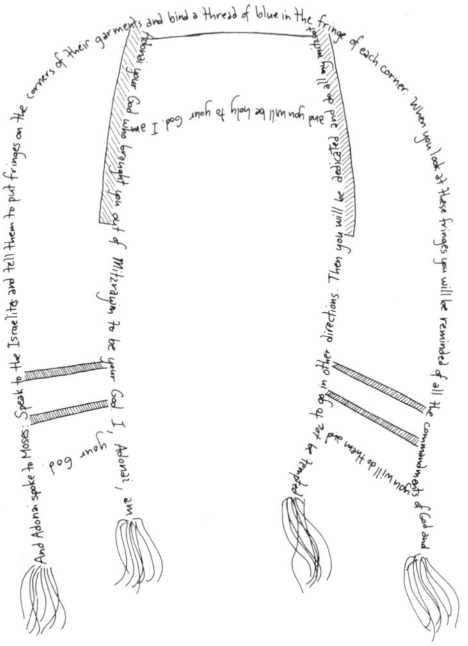

When we recite the *Vay'yomer* prayer, it is customary to kiss the *tzizit*, fringes, each time we mention them.

וַיֹּ֤אמֶר יְהֹוָה֙ אֶל־מֹשֶׁ֣ה לֵּאמֹֽר: דַּבֵּ֞ר אֶל־בְּנֵ֤י יִשְׂרָאֵל֙ וְאָמַרְתָּ֣
אֲלֵהֶ֔ם וְעָשׂ֨וּ לָהֶ֥ם צִיצִ֛ת עַל־כַּנְפֵ֥י בִגְדֵיהֶ֖ם לְדֹרֹתָ֑ם וְנָֽתְנ֛וּ
עַל־צִיצִ֥ת הַכָּנָ֖ף פְּתִ֥יל תְּכֵֽלֶת: וְהָיָ֣ה לָכֶם֮ לְצִיצִת֒ וּרְאִיתֶ֣ם
אֹת֗וֹ וּזְכַרְתֶּם֙ אֶת־כָּל־מִצְוֺ֣ת יְהֹוָ֔ה וַעֲשִׂיתֶ֖ם אֹתָ֑ם וְלֹֽא תָת֜וּרוּ
אַחֲרֵ֤י לְבַבְכֶם֙ וְאַחֲרֵ֣י עֵֽינֵיכֶ֔ם אֲשֶׁר־אַתֶּ֥ם זֹנִ֖ים אַחֲרֵיהֶֽם: לְמַ֣עַן
תִּזְכְּר֔וּ וַעֲשִׂיתֶ֖ם אֶת־כָּל־מִצְוֺתָ֑י וִהְיִיתֶ֥ם קְדֹשִׁ֖ים לֵֽאלֹֽהֵיכֶֽם:
אֲנִ֞י יְהֹוָ֣ה אֱלֹֽהֵיכֶ֗ם אֲשֶׁ֨ר הוֹצֵ֤אתִי אֶתְכֶם֙ מֵאֶ֣רֶץ מִצְרַ֔יִם לִֽהְי֥וֹת
לָכֶ֖ם לֵֽאלֹהִ֑ים אֲנִ֖י יְהֹוָ֥ה אֱלֹהֵיכֶֽם:

Leader says:

יְהֹוָ֥ה אֱלֹהֵיכֶ֖ם אֱמֶֽת.

And *Adonai* spoke to Moses: Speak to the Israelites and tell them to put fringes on the corners of their garments and bind a thread of blue in the fringe of each corner. When you look at these fringes you will be reminded of all the commandments of God and you will do them and not be tempted to go in other directions. Then you will be dedicated and do all my *mitzvot* and you will be holy to your God. I am *Adonai,* your God, who brought you out of *Mitzrayim* to be your God. I, *Adonai,* am your God.

When someone joins the police or a sports team, that person is given a uniform. The uniform not only tells us that the person is a member of that group; it also reminds the person that there is a job to do. The person must act in a certain way. So, too, with *tzizit.* They remind us that we belong to the Jewish people and should follow the *mitzvot* (commandments) of the Torah. What are some of the *mitzvot* that God wants us to do? How can doing *mitzvot* make us holy — closer to God?

At the shores of the Sea of Reeds,
    Moses and the Israelites joyfully proclaimed:
        "Who is like You, *Adonai,*
        among the mighty?
        Who is like You, *Adonai,*
        glorious in holiness,
        awesome in splendor,
        the Maker of miracles?"

The Israelites saw Your majesty when You split the waters and they crossed in safety. Then led by Moses and Miriam, they sang a song of rejoicing.

Together they cried out:

"ADONAI WILL RULE FOREVER."

Rock of Israel, arise to help Your people.
Blessed are You, Adonai, who helped the people Israel.

מִי־כָמְֽכָה בָּאֵלִם יְיָ,

מִי כָּמְֽכָה נֶאְדָּר בַּקֹּֽדֶשׁ,

נוֹרָא תְהִלֹּת, עֹֽשֵׂה פֶֽלֶא.

שִׁירָה חֲדָשָׁה שִׁבְּחוּ גְאוּלִים לְשִׁמְךָ עַל שְׂפַת הַיָּם. יַֽחַד
כֻּלָּם הוֹדוּ וְהִמְלִֽיכוּ וְאָמְֽרוּ:

יְיָ יִמְלֹךְ לְעֹלָם וָעֶד.

צוּר יִשְׂרָאֵל, קוּמָה בְּעֶזְרַת יִשְׂרָאֵל וּפְדֵה כִנְאֻמֶךָ יְהוּדָה וְיִשְׂרָאֵל.
גּוֹאֲלֵנוּ יְיָ צְבָאוֹת שְׁמוֹ קְדוֹשׁ יִשְׂרָאֵל. בָּרוּךְ אַתָּה יְיָ גָּאַל יִשְׂרָאֵל.

Naming Our Ancestory

By naming our ancestors in the first blessing of the *Amidah,* we identify ourselves to God. By reminding God from whom we came, we put our best foot forward to make a favorable impression.

By stating each ancestor separately, we show that each person must find God for himself or herself.

We also mention our ancestors because it makes us feel connected to them, even though they lived thousands of years ago. We feel we are like a link in a long chain — part of a big Jewish family.

DIRECTIONS FOR THE *AMIDAH:*

The *Amidah* means "the standing prayer" and we do, in fact, stand for the *Amidah.* As a sign of respect, we recite the *Amidah* with our feet together and at attention. It is also customary to bow when we say the opening blessing formula of the first blessing (*Baruḥ atah Adonai*) and its closing blessing formula. We bow again when we say *"modim anaḥnu laḥ"* and its closing blessing formula.

The version of the first blessing which speaks of our forefathers is found on page 29. The version which includes both the forefathers and mothers is found on page 31.

The *Amidah* for *Yom Kippur* begins on page 109 with the version of the first blessing which speaks of our forefathers. The version which includes both the forefathers and mothers is found on page 111.

THE *AMIDAH*
עֲמִידָה

We rise as the ark is opened.

Adonai, open my lips and my mouth shall praise You.

בָּרוּךְ אַתָּה יְיָ אֱלֹהֵינוּ וֵאלֹהֵי אֲבוֹתֵינוּ, אֱלֹהֵי אַבְרָהָם
אֱלֹהֵי יִצְחָק וֵאלֹהֵי יַעֲקֹב, הָאֵל הַגָּדוֹל הַגִּבּוֹר וְהַנּוֹרָא
אֵל עֶלְיוֹן גּוֹמֵל חֲסָדִים טוֹבִים וְקוֹנֵה הַכֹּל, וְזוֹכֵר חַסְדֵי
אָבוֹת וּמֵבִיא גוֹאֵל לִבְנֵי בְנֵיהֶם לְמַעַן שְׁמוֹ בְּאַהֲבָה.

זָכְרֵנוּ לְחַיִּים מֶלֶךְ חָפֵץ בַּחַיִּים,
וְכָתְבֵנוּ בְּסֵפֶר הַחַיִּים לְמַעַנְךָ אֱלֹהִים חַיִּים.

מֶלֶךְ עוֹזֵר וּמוֹשִׁיעַ וּמָגֵן. בָּרוּךְ אַתָּה יְיָ מָגֵן אַבְרָהָם.

אַתָּה גִּבּוֹר לְעוֹלָם אֲדֹנָי מְחַיֵּה מֵתִים אַתָּה רַב לְהוֹשִׁיעַ.
מְכַלְכֵּל חַיִּים בְּחֶסֶד מְחַיֵּה מֵתִים בְּרַחֲמִים רַבִּים, סוֹמֵךְ
נוֹפְלִים וְרוֹפֵא חוֹלִים וּמַתִּיר אֲסוּרִים וּמְקַיֵּם אֱמוּנָתוֹ
לִישֵׁנֵי עָפָר. מִי כָמוֹךָ בַּעַל גְּבוּרוֹת וּמִי דוֹמֶה לָּךְ, מֶלֶךְ
מֵמִית וּמְחַיֶּה וּמַצְמִיחַ יְשׁוּעָה.

מִי כָמוֹךָ אַב הָרַחֲמִים, זוֹכֵר יְצוּרָיו לְחַיִּים בְּרַחֲמִים.

וְנֶאֱמָן אַתָּה לְהַחֲיוֹת מֵתִים. בָּרוּךְ אַתָּה יְיָ מְחַיֵּה הַמֵּתִים.

Zoḥreinu l'ḥayim Meleḥ ḥafetz b'ḥayim,
v'ḥotveinu b'sefer haḥayim, l'ma'anḥa Elohim ḥayim.

Blessed are You, *Adonai,* our God and God of our ancestors,
God of Abraham, Isaac and Jacob.
Supreme God Who responds with kindness,
You remember the good deeds of our ancestors and
lovingly bring help to us.

On this day, we ask You for mercy.
Remember us for life, God Who delights in life.

Blessed are You, *Adonai,* Who protects Abraham.

You are the Source of life Who grants us healing and strength.

There is none as great and powerful as You.

We who are Your creation, *Adonai,* ask to be remembered for life.

Blessed are You, Source of life.

Continue on page 33.

THE *AMIDAH*

עֲמִידָה

We rise as the ark is opened.

Adonai, open my lips and my mouth shall praise You.

בָּרוּךְ אַתָּה יְיָ אֱלֹהֵינוּ וֵאלֹהֵי אֲבוֹתֵינוּ, אֱלֹהֵי אַבְרָהָם
אֱלֹהֵי יִצְחָק וֵאלֹהֵי יַעֲקֹב, אֱלֹהֵי שָׂרָה אֱלֹהֵי רִבְקָה
אֱלֹהֵי רָחֵל וֵאלֹהֵי לֵאָה, הָאֵל הַגָּדוֹל הַגִּבּוֹר וְהַנּוֹרָא אֵל
עֶלְיוֹן גּוֹמֵל חֲסָדִים טוֹבִים וְקוֹנֵה הַכֹּל, וְזוֹכֵר חַסְדֵי
אָבוֹת וּמֵבִיא גוֹאֵל לִבְנֵי בְנֵיהֶם לְמַעַן שְׁמוֹ בְּאַהֲבָה.

זָכְרֵנוּ לְחַיִּים מֶלֶךְ חָפֵץ בַּחַיִּים,
וְכָתְבֵנוּ בְּסֵפֶר הַחַיִּים לְמַעַנְךָ אֱלֹהִים חַיִּים.

מֶלֶךְ עוֹזֵר וּפוֹקֵד וּמוֹשִׁיעַ וּמָגֵן. בָּרוּךְ אַתָּה יְיָ מָגֵן
אַבְרָהָם וּפוֹקֵד שָׂרָה.

אַתָּה גִּבּוֹר לְעוֹלָם אֲדֹנָי מְחַיֵּה מֵתִים אַתָּה רַב לְהוֹשִׁיעַ.
מְכַלְכֵּל חַיִּים בְּחֶסֶד מְחַיֵּה מֵתִים בְּרַחֲמִים רַבִּים, סוֹמֵךְ
נוֹפְלִים וְרוֹפֵא חוֹלִים וּמַתִּיר אֲסוּרִים וּמְקַיֵּם אֱמוּנָתוֹ
לִישֵׁנֵי עָפָר. מִי כָמוֹךָ בַּעַל גְּבוּרוֹת וּמִי דּוֹמֶה לָּךְ, מֶלֶךְ
מֵמִית וּמְחַיֶּה וּמַצְמִיחַ יְשׁוּעָה.

מִי כָמוֹךָ אַב הָרַחֲמִים, זוֹכֵר יְצוּרָיו לְחַיִּים בְּרַחֲמִים.

וְנֶאֱמָן אַתָּה לְהַחֲיוֹת מֵתִים. בָּרוּךְ אַתָּה יְיָ מְחַיֵּה הַמֵּתִים.

Zoḥreinu l'ḥayim Meleḥ ḥafetz b'ḥayim,
v'ḥotveinu b'sefer haḥayim, l'ma'anḥa Elohim ḥayim.

Blessed are You, *Adonai,* our God and God of our ancestors,
God of Abraham, Isaac and Jacob,
God of Sarah, Rebecca, Leah and Rachel.
Supreme God Who responds with kindness,
You remember the good deeds of our ancestors and
lovingly bring help to us.

On this day, we ask You for mercy.
Remember us for life, God Who delights in life.

Blessed are You, *Adonai,* Who protects Abraham and
remembers Sarah.

You are the Source of life Who grants us healing and strength.

There is none as great and powerful as You.

We who are Your creation, *Adonai,* ask to be remembered for life.

Blessed are You, Source of life.

We recite the *Kedushah* which proclaims God's holiness.
(The congregation chants the indented lines aloud.)

נְקַדֵּשׁ אֶת־שִׁמְךָ בָּעוֹלָם כְּשֵׁם שֶׁמַּקְדִּישִׁים אוֹתוֹ בִּשְׁמֵי מָרוֹם כַּכָּתוּב עַל יַד נְבִיאֶךָ, וְקָרָא זֶה אֶל זֶה וְאָמַר:

קָדוֹשׁ קָדוֹשׁ יְיָ צְבָאוֹת, מְלֹא כָל־הָאָרֶץ כְּבוֹדוֹ.

אָז בְּקוֹל רַעַשׁ גָּדוֹל, אַדִּיר וְחָזָק, מַשְׁמִיעִים קוֹל, מִתְנַשְּׂאִים לְעֻמַּת שְׂרָפִים, לְעֻמָּתָם בָּרוּךְ יֹאמֵרוּ:

בָּרוּךְ כְּבוֹד יְיָ מִמְּקוֹמוֹ.

מִמְּקוֹמְךָ מַלְכֵּנוּ תוֹפִיעַ וְתִמְלֹךְ עָלֵינוּ כִּי מְחַכִּים אֲנַחְנוּ לָךְ. מָתַי תִּמְלֹךְ בְּצִיּוֹן. בְּקָרוֹב בְּיָמֵינוּ לְעוֹלָם וָעֶד תִּשְׁכֹּן. תִּתְגַּדַּל וְתִתְקַדַּשׁ בְּתוֹךְ יְרוּשָׁלַיִם עִירְךָ לְדוֹר וָדוֹר וּלְנֵצַח נְצָחִים. וְעֵינֵינוּ תִרְאֶינָה מַלְכוּתֶךָ כַּדָּבָר הָאָמוּר בְּשִׁירֵי עֻזֶּךָ עַל יְדֵי דָוִד מְשִׁיחַ צִדְקֶךָ:

יִמְלֹךְ יְיָ לְעוֹלָם אֱלֹהַיִךְ צִיּוֹן לְדֹר וָדֹר, הַלְלוּיָהּ.

לְדוֹר וָדוֹר נַגִּיד גָּדְלֶךָ, וּלְנֵצַח נְצָחִים קְדֻשָּׁתְךָ נַקְדִּישׁ, וְשִׁבְחֲךָ אֱלֹהֵינוּ מִפִּינוּ לֹא יָמוּשׁ לְעוֹלָם וָעֶד כִּי אֵל מֶלֶךְ גָּדוֹל וְקָדוֹשׁ אָתָּה.

We will declare God's holiness here on earth as we imagine heavenly angels do above:

Holy, holy, holy — the whole world is filled with God's glory.

In every generation we will speak of God's greatness and forever declare God's holiness.

Often the word *"kadosh"* is translated as "holy." We could also use the words "special" or "set apart." When we speak of God as *"kadosh,"* we mean that God is different from all else. We believe that we, too, can be made *"kadosh"* by following God's ways. Our tradition teaches that each of us can be *"kadosh,"* not just our leaders or a chosen few.

Let all creatures feel awe in Your presence and join together to follow Your will.

וּבְכֵן תֵּן פַּחְדְּךָ יְיָ אֱלֹהֵינוּ עַל כָּל־מַעֲשֶׂיךָ וְאֵימָתְךָ עַל
כָּל־מַה־שֶּׁבָּרָאתָ, וְיִירָאוּךָ כָּל־הַמַּעֲשִׂים וְיִשְׁתַּחֲווּ לְפָנֶיךָ
כָּל־הַבְּרוּאִים, וְיֵעָשׂוּ כֻלָּם אֲגֻדָּה אַחַת לַעֲשׂוֹת רְצוֹנְךָ
בְּלֵבָב שָׁלֵם.

Grant honor to Your people and glory to all who have faith in You. Give hope to those who seek You, and confidence to those who trust in You. Grant joy to Israel and gladness to Jerusalem. Answer our prayers to bring a time when we all share our blessings with each other.

וּבְכֵן תֵּן כָּבוֹד יְיָ לְעַמֶּךָ תְּהִלָּה לִירֵאֶיךָ וְתִקְוָה
לְדוֹרְשֶׁיךָ וּפִתְחוֹן פֶּה לַמְיַחֲלִים לָךְ, שִׂמְחָה לְאַרְצֶךָ
וְשָׂשׂוֹן לְעִירֶךָ וּצְמִיחַת קֶרֶן לְדָוִד עַבְדֶּךָ וַעֲרִיכַת נֵר
לְבֶן־יִשַׁי מְשִׁיחֶךָ בִּמְהֵרָה בְיָמֵינוּ.

When You remove cruel governments and wickedness from the world, then the righteous will be glad and the faithful ones will celebrate in song.

וּבְכֵן צַדִּיקִים יִרְאוּ וְיִשְׂמָחוּ וִישָׁרִים יַעֲלֹזוּ וַחֲסִידִים
בְּרִנָּה יָגִילוּ, וְעוֹלָתָה תִּקְפָּץ־פִּיהָ וְכָל־הָרִשְׁעָה כֻּלָּהּ
כְּעָשָׁן תִּכְלֶה כִּי תַעֲבִיר מֶמְשֶׁלֶת זָדוֹן מִן הָאָרֶץ.

בָּרוּךְ אַתָּה יְיָ הַמֶּלֶךְ הַקָּדוֹשׁ.

Blessed are You, *Adonai,* the holy Ruler.

The prayers above were written by Rabbi Yoḥanan ben Nuri during a terrible period of Roman oppression. The evil he wanted to see vanish was the cruel rule of Rome. What evil in our world today do you wish would disappear?

אַתָּה בְחַרְתָּנוּ מִכָּל־הָעַמִּים, אָהַבְתָּ אוֹתָנוּ וְרָצִיתָ בָּנוּ
וְרוֹמַמְתָּנוּ מִכָּל־הַלְּשׁוֹנוֹת וְקִדַּשְׁתָּנוּ בְּמִצְוֹתֶיךָ וְקֵרַבְתָּנוּ
מַלְכֵּנוּ לַעֲבוֹדָתֶךָ וְשִׁמְךָ הַגָּדוֹל וְהַקָּדוֹשׁ עָלֵינוּ קָרָאתָ.

וַתִּתֶּן־לָנוּ יְיָ אֱלֹהֵינוּ בְּאַהֲבָה אֶת־יוֹם (הַשַּׁבָּת הַזֶּה
וְאֶת־יוֹם) הַזִּכָּרוֹן הַזֶּה, יוֹם (זִכְרוֹן) תְּרוּעָה (בְּאַהֲבָה)
מִקְרָא קֹדֶשׁ, זֵכֶר לִיצִיאַת מִצְרָיִם.

You have called us to Your service through the *mitzvot* and chosen us to celebrate special, holy days.

Our God, and God of our ancestors, make our lives holy — special — through Your *mitzvot* and let Your Torah guide us. Blessed are You, *Adonai,* Ruler of the whole earth Who makes holy [the *Shabbat* and] the Jewish people and the Day of Remembering.

אֱלֹהֵינוּ וֵאלֹהֵי אֲבוֹתֵינוּ, (רְצֵה בִמְנוּחָתֵנוּ) קַדְּשֵׁנוּ בְּמִצְוֹתֶיךָ
וְתֵן חֶלְקֵנוּ בְּתוֹרָתֶךָ, שַׂבְּעֵנוּ מִטּוּבֶךָ וְשַׂמְּחֵנוּ בִּישׁוּעָתֶךָ
(וְהַנְחִילֵנוּ יְיָ אֱלֹהֵינוּ בְּאַהֲבָה וּבְרָצוֹן שַׁבַּת קָדְשֶׁךָ וְיָנוּחוּ בָהּ
יִשְׂרָאֵל מְקַדְּשֵׁי שְׁמֶךָ) וְטַהֵר לִבֵּנוּ לְעָבְדְּךָ בֶּאֱמֶת, כִּי אַתָּה
אֱלֹהִים אֱמֶת וּדְבָרְךָ אֱמֶת וְקַיָּם לָעַד. בָּרוּךְ אַתָּה יְיָ מֶלֶךְ
עַל כָּל־הָאָרֶץ מְקַדֵּשׁ (הַשַּׁבָּת וְ)יִשְׂרָאֵל וְיוֹם הַזִּכָּרוֹן.

רְצֵה יְיָ אֱלֹהֵינוּ בְּעַמְּךָ יִשְׂרָאֵל וּבִתְפִלָּתָם וְהָשֵׁב
אֶת־הָעֲבוֹדָה לִדְבִיר בֵּיתֶךָ וּתְפִלָּתָם בְּאַהֲבָה תְקַבֵּל בְּרָצוֹן
וּתְהִי לְרָצוֹן תָּמִיד עֲבוֹדַת יִשְׂרָאֵל עַמֶּךָ. וְתֶחֱזֶינָה עֵינֵינוּ
בְּשׁוּבְךָ לְצִיּוֹן בְּרַחֲמִים. בָּרוּךְ אַתָּה יְיָ הַמַּחֲזִיר שְׁכִינָתוֹ לְצִיּוֹן.

Accept in love the prayers of Your people. Praised are You, *Adonai,* Who seeks closeness to us. May we feel Your closeness in Zion.

מוֹדִים אֲנַחְנוּ לָךְ שָׁאַתָּה הוּא יְיָ אֱלֹהֵינוּ וֵאלֹהֵי אֲבוֹתֵינוּ לְעוֹלָם
וָעֶד, צוּר חַיֵּינוּ מָגֵן יִשְׁעֵנוּ אַתָּה הוּא. לְדוֹר וָדוֹר נוֹדֶה לְּךָ
וּנְסַפֵּר תְּהִלָּתֶךָ עַל חַיֵּינוּ הַמְּסוּרִים בְּיָדֶךָ וְעַל נִשְׁמוֹתֵינוּ
הַפְּקוּדוֹת לָךְ וְעַל נִסֶּיךָ שֶׁבְּכָל־יוֹם עִמָּנוּ וְעַל נִפְלְאוֹתֶיךָ
וְטוֹבוֹתֶיךָ שֶׁבְּכָל־עֵת עֶרֶב וָבֹקֶר וְצָהֳרָיִם. הַטּוֹב כִּי לֹא כָלוּ
רַחֲמֶיךָ וְהַמְרַחֵם כִּי לֹא תַמּוּ חֲסָדֶיךָ מֵעוֹלָם קִוִּינוּ לָךְ.
וְעַל כֻּלָּם יִתְבָּרַךְ וְיִתְרוֹמַם שִׁמְךָ מַלְכֵּנוּ תָּמִיד לְעוֹלָם וָעֶד.

וּכְתֹב לְחַיִּים טוֹבִים כָּל־בְּנֵי בְרִיתֶךָ.

וְכֹל הַחַיִּים יוֹדוּךָ סֶּלָה וִיהַלְלוּ אֶת־שִׁמְךָ בֶּאֱמֶת הָאֵל יְשׁוּעָתֵנוּ
וְעֶזְרָתֵנוּ סֶלָה. בָּרוּךְ אַתָּה יְיָ הַטּוֹב שִׁמְךָ וּלְךָ נָאֶה לְהוֹדוֹת.

How grateful we are to You, God of our ancestors, the Eternal One. You are the source of our strength just as You have been the protecting shield of each generation.

We thank You for our lives which are in Your hand and our souls which are in Your care. We thank You for Your miracles which surround us all the time and the wondrous acts of Your kindness that we experience each morning, noon and night.

You are the source of never-ending lovingkindness. You are our hope forever.

May we all look forward to a good year of life.

Blessed are You, *Adonai,* Who deserves our praise.

THE PRIESTLY BLESSING

אֱלֹהֵינוּ וֵאלֹהֵי אֲבוֹתֵינוּ, בָּרְכֵנוּ בַבְּרָכָה הַמְשֻׁלֶּשֶׁת בַּתּוֹרָה הַכְּתוּבָה עַל יְדֵי מֹשֶׁה עַבְדֶּךָ, הָאֲמוּרָה מִפִּי אַהֲרֹן וּבָנָיו כֹּהֲנִים עַם קְדוֹשֶׁךָ, כָּאָמוּר:

Leader:	Congregation answers:
יְבָרֶכְךָ יְיָ וְיִשְׁמְרֶךָ.	כֵּן יְהִי רָצוֹן.
יָאֵר יְיָ פָּנָיו אֵלֶיךָ וִיחֻנֶּךָּ.	כֵּן יְהִי רָצוֹן.
יִשָּׂא יְיָ פָּנָיו אֵלֶיךָ וְיָשֵׂם לְךָ שָׁלוֹם.	כֵּן יְהִי רָצוֹן.

God of our ancestors, bless us with the threefold blessing recited by the priests of old:

May *Adonai* bless and protect you;

May *Adonai* shine upon you with graciousness;

May *Adonai* look upon you with favor and grant you peace.

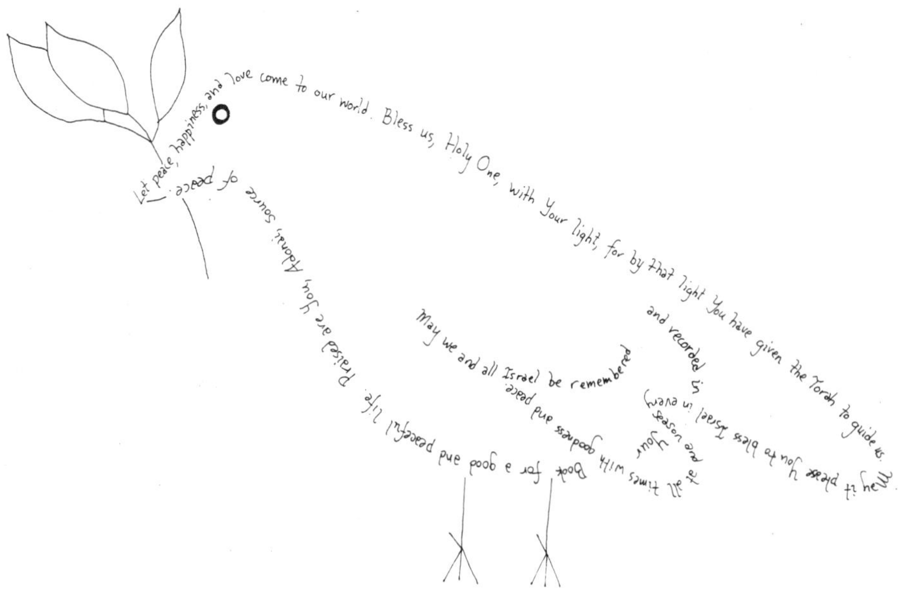

שִׂים שָׁלוֹם בָּעוֹלָם, טוֹבָה וּבְרָכָה חֵן וָחֶסֶד וְרַחֲמִים עָלֵינוּ
וְעַל כָּל־יִשְׂרָאֵל עַמֶּךָ. בָּרְכֵנוּ אָבִינוּ כֻּלָּנוּ כְּאֶחָד בְּאוֹר
פָּנֶיךָ, כִּי בְאוֹר פָּנֶיךָ נָתַתָּ לָּנוּ יְיָ אֱלֹהֵינוּ תּוֹרַת חַיִּים וְאַהֲבַת
חֶסֶד וּצְדָקָה וּבְרָכָה וְרַחֲמִים וְחַיִּים וְשָׁלוֹם. וְטוֹב בְּעֵינֶיךָ
לְבָרֵךְ אֶת־עַמְּךָ יִשְׂרָאֵל בְּכָל־עֵת וּבְכָל־שָׁעָה בִּשְׁלוֹמֶךָ.

בְּסֵפֶר חַיִּים בְּרָכָה וְשָׁלוֹם וּפַרְנָסָה טוֹבָה נִזָּכֵר וְנִכָּתֵב
לְפָנֶיךָ אֲנַחְנוּ וְכָל־עַמְּךָ בֵּית יִשְׂרָאֵל לְחַיִּים טוֹבִים וּלְשָׁלוֹם.

בָּרוּךְ אַתָּה יְיָ עוֹשֵׂה הַשָּׁלוֹם.

Let peace, happiness and love come to our world, to us and to all the Jewish people. Bless us all, Holy One, with Your light, for by that light You have given the Torah to guide us. May it please You to bless the Jewish people in every season and at all times with goodness and peace.

May we and all the Jewish people be remembered and recorded in Your book for a good and peaceful life.

Praised are You, *Adonai,* Source of peace.

B'seifer ḥayim b'raḥah v'shalom ufarnasah tovah, nizaḥer v'nikatev l'faneḥa, anaḥnu v'ḥol amḥa beit Yisrael, l'ḥayim tovim ul'shalom.

At the end of the *Amidah* it is customary for those who wish to do so to add their own personal prayers. You may do this by using words or just being silent and trying to feel God's presence and the holiness of the day.

The Field of Sisterly Love

King Solomon was considered the wisest man on earth. Yet, he was baffled by one problem — where to build the holy Temple? This question troubled him so much that he could not sleep. One night, as he tossed and turned on his royal bed, he heard a voice deep inside telling him to go to Mount Moriah in Jerusalem.

There Solomon found a field owned by two sisters. They each lived in a house at opposite ends of the field. One sister lived alone while the other lived with her husband and four children. Together they tilled and tended this field and divided its harvest equally.

That night, King Solomon was not the only one who could not sleep. These two sisters both stayed awake worrying.

The first sister thought to herself, "I'm a lucky woman. I have a family who will take care of me in my old age. My sister is alone. I must bring her extra wheat so she can store it for the future."

The second sister said to herself, "I live alone and don't really need so much wheat. My sister should have a larger share for her big family."

And so, the two sisters rushed to their granaries, filled their arms with bundles of wheat and dashed across the field to the other's storage bin. In the dim light of the moon, with their wheat piled high in their arms, they did not notice each other or Solomon. But the king quietly observed them.

The next morning, the sisters were each astonished to find that when they looked in their granary they had the same amount of wheat as before. "This is indeed a puzzle for King Solomon, the Wise!" they both thought to themselves.

For several nights, the sisters continued to exchange the wheat. Each morning, they would find that their own supply was not any less. Finally, they bumped into each other in the middle of the field. Realizing what had been happening, the two sisters laughed and laughed as they hugged each other.

The puzzle about the wheat sheaves was solved and so was Solomon's problem about where to build the holy Temple. He now knew that he would build it on this "field of sisterly love." And so he did.

It is said that the prayer, *Avinu Malkeinu,* had its beginning when once Rabbi Akiva opened the ark to ask God to send rain to the dry land.

In this prayer, we talk to God in the same way we talk to a loving parent. We feel that our lives are special because God cares about us and everything we do — like a parent cares for a child.

God is not a person. God does not sit with a book and enter names into it. So what do you think it means when we ask God "to be recorded" for a good year in the Book of Life?

Omit on *Shabbat.*
We open the ark and rise:

אָבִינוּ מַלְכֵּנוּ, אֵין לָנוּ מֶלֶךְ אֶלָּא אָתָּה.
אָבִינוּ מַלְכֵּנוּ, עֲשֵׂה עִמָּנוּ לְמַעַן שְׁמֶךָ.
אָבִינוּ מַלְכֵּנוּ, חַדֵּשׁ עָלֵינוּ שָׁנָה טוֹבָה.

אָבִינוּ מַלְכֵּנוּ, בַּטֵּל מֵעָלֵינוּ כָּל־גְּזֵרוֹת קָשׁוֹת.
אָבִינוּ מַלְכֵּנוּ, בַּטֵּל מַחְשְׁבוֹת שׂוֹנְאֵינוּ.

אָבִינוּ מַלְכֵּנוּ, מְחֵה וְהַעֲבֵר פְּשָׁעֵינוּ וְחַטֹּאתֵינוּ מִנֶּגֶד עֵינֶיךָ.

אָבִינוּ מַלְכֵּנוּ, הַחֲזִירֵנוּ בִּתְשׁוּבָה שְׁלֵמָה לְפָנֶיךָ.

אָבִינוּ מַלְכֵּנוּ, שְׁלַח רְפוּאָה שְׁלֵמָה לְחוֹלֵי עַמֶּךָ.

אָבִינוּ מַלְכֵּנוּ, כָּתְבֵנוּ בְּסֵפֶר חַיִּים טוֹבִים.
אָבִינוּ מַלְכֵּנוּ, כָּתְבֵנוּ בְּסֵפֶר גְּאֻלָּה וִישׁוּעָה.
אָבִינוּ מַלְכֵּנוּ, כָּתְבֵנוּ בְּסֵפֶר סְלִיחָה וּמְחִילָה.

אָבִינוּ מַלְכֵּנוּ, חָנֵּנוּ וַעֲנֵנוּ, כִּי אֵין בָּנוּ מַעֲשִׂים,
עֲשֵׂה עִמָּנוּ צְדָקָה וָחֶסֶד וְהוֹשִׁיעֵנוּ.

Avinu Malkeinu
You Who are our only God, grant us a good New Year.

Avinu Malkeinu
Rid us of oppressors and let there be no more war and destruction.

Avinu Malkeinu
Forgive and pardon our sins.

Avinu Malkeinu
Help us to turn to You.

Avinu Malkeinu
Heal the sick and remember those in need.

Avinu Malkeinu
Write us in the Book of Happiness.

Avinu Malkeinu
Write us in the Book of Forgiveness.

Avinu Malkeinu
Show us mercy and lovingkindness.

Avinu Malkeinu
Do not turn us away unanswered.

Avinu Malkeinu, ḥoneinu va'aneinu, ki ein banu ma'asim;
aseh imanu tzedakah vaḥesed v'hoshi'einu.

KADDISH SHALEM

Full *Kaddish* קַדִּישׁ שָׁלֵם

Leader:

יִתְגַּדַּל וְיִתְקַדַּשׁ שְׁמֵהּ רַבָּא בְּעָלְמָא דִּי בְרָא כִרְעוּתֵהּ,
וְיַמְלִיךְ מַלְכוּתֵהּ בְּחַיֵּיכוֹן וּבְיוֹמֵיכוֹן וּבְחַיֵּי דְכָל־בֵּית
יִשְׂרָאֵל בַּעֲגָלָא וּבִזְמַן קָרִיב, וְאִמְרוּ אָמֵן.

Congregation and Leader answer:

יְהֵא שְׁמֵהּ רַבָּא מְבָרַךְ לְעָלַם וּלְעָלְמֵי עָלְמַיָּא.

Y'hai shmai rabbah m'varaḥ l'olam u'l'olmei almay'ya.

Leader:

יִתְבָּרַךְ וְיִשְׁתַּבַּח וְיִתְפָּאַר וְיִתְרוֹמַם וְיִתְנַשֵּׂא וְיִתְהַדַּר
וְיִתְעַלֶּה וְיִתְהַלַּל שְׁמֵהּ דְּקֻדְשָׁא

Congregation and Leader answer:

בְּרִיךְ הוּא.

B'riḥ hu.

Leader:

לְעֵלָּא לְעֵלָּא מִכָּל־בִּרְכָתָא וְשִׁירָתָא תֻּשְׁבְּחָתָא וְנֶחֱמָתָא
דַּאֲמִירָן בְּעָלְמָא, וְאִמְרוּ אָמֵן.

תִּתְקַבֵּל צְלוֹתְהוֹן וּבָעוּתְהוֹן דְּכָל־יִשְׂרָאֵל קֳדָם אֲבוּהוֹן
דִּי בִשְׁמַיָּא, וְאִמְרוּ אָמֵן.

יְהֵא שְׁלָמָא רַבָּא מִן שְׁמַיָּא וְחַיִּים עָלֵינוּ וְעַל כָּל־יִשְׂרָאֵל,
וְאִמְרוּ אָמֵן.

עוֹשֶׂה שָׁלוֹם בִּמְרוֹמָיו הוּא יַעֲשֶׂה שָׁלוֹם עָלֵינוּ וְעַל
כָּל־יִשְׂרָאֵל, וְאִמְרוּ אָמֵן.

Ein ka'moḥa va'Elohim Adonai
v'ein k'ma'aseḥa.

אֵין כָּמֽוֹךָ בָאֱלֹהִים אֲדֹנָי
וְאֵין כְּמַעֲשֶׂיךָ.

Malḥut'ḥa malḥut kol olamim,
umem'shalt'ḥa b'ḥol dor va'dor.

מַלְכוּתְךָ מַלְכוּת כָּל־עֹלָמִים
וּמֶמְשַׁלְתְּךָ בְּכָל־דּוֹר וָדֹר.

Adonai Meleḥ, Adonai malaḥ,
Adonai yimloḥ l'olam va'ed.

יְיָ מֶֽלֶךְ, יְיָ מָלָךְ,
יְיָ יִמְלֹךְ לְעֹלָם וָעֶד.

Adonai oz l'amo yiten,
Adonai y'vareḥ et amo va'shalom.

יְיָ עֹז לְעַמּוֹ יִתֵּן,
יְיָ יְבָרֵךְ אֶת־עַמּוֹ בַשָּׁלוֹם.

We rise.

The ark is opened.

Vay'hi binso'a ha'aron,

וַיְהִי בִּנְסֹֽעַ הָאָרֹן

vay'yomer Mosheh:

וַיֹּֽאמֶר מֹשֶׁה:

Kuma Adonai v'yafutzu oyveḥa,

קוּמָה יְיָ וְיָפֻֽצוּ אֹיְבֶֽיךָ

v'yanusu m'saneḥa mipaneḥa.

וְיָנֻֽסוּ מְשַׂנְאֶֽיךָ מִפָּנֶֽיךָ.

Ki mitziyon teitzei Torah,

כִּי מִצִּיּוֹן תֵּצֵא תוֹרָה

u'd'var Adonai mirushalayim.

וּדְבַר יְיָ מִירוּשָׁלָֽיִם.

Baruḥ shenatan Torah l'amo

בָּרוּךְ שֶׁנָּתַן תּוֹרָה לְעַמּוֹ

Yisrael bik'dushato.

יִשְׂרָאֵל בִּקְדֻשָּׁתוֹ.

Torah shall come out of Zion and the word of God from Jerusalem

Blessed is the One Who gave the Torah to the people of Israel.

We omit on *Shabbat*.

יְיָ יְיָ אֵל רַחוּם וְחַנּוּן, אֶרֶךְ אַפַּיִם וְרַב חֶסֶד וֶאֱמֶת
נֹצֵר חֶסֶד לָאֲלָפִים נֹשֵׂא עָוֹן וָפֶשַׁע וְחַטָּאָה, וְנַקֵּה.

וַאֲנִי תְפִלָּתִי לְךָ יְיָ עֵת רָצוֹן, אֱלֹהִים בְּרָב־חַסְדֶּךָ, עֲנֵנִי
בֶּאֱמֶת יִשְׁעֶךָ.

Adonai, Adonai, merciful and patient God,
You remember our kind acts for a thousand generations.
You accept our shortcomings and pardon our sins.

May the words I say today be acceptable to You, *Adonai*.
Show me kindness and answer the prayers of my heart.

Adonai, Adonai, El raḥum v'ḥanun,
ereḥ apayim v'rav ḥesed ve'emet.
Notzer ḥesed la'alafim,
nosei avon vafesha v'ḥata'ah v'nakeh.

Va'ani t'filati l'ḥa Adonai et ratzon.
Elohim b'rov ḥasdeḥa aneini be'emet yish'eḥa.

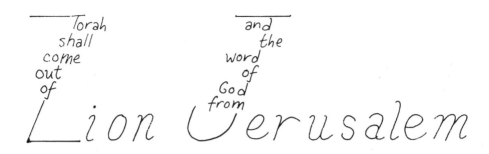

The Torah is taken and held.
Leader and then congregation say:

שְׁמַע יִשְׂרָאֵל יְיָ אֱלֹהֵינוּ יְיָ אֶחָד.

Hear, O Israel: The Lord our God, the Lord is One.

Shema Yisrael Adonai Eloheinu Adonai eḥad.

Leader and then congregation say:

אֶחָד אֱלֹהֵינוּ גָּדוֹל אֲדוֹנֵינוּ קָדוֹשׁ וְנוֹרָא שְׁמוֹ.

Our God is One, Great and Holy.

Eḥad Eloheinu, gadol Adoneinu, kadosh v'nora sh'mo.

Leader bows and says:

גַּדְּלוּ לַייָ אִתִּי, וּנְרוֹמְמָה שְׁמוֹ יַחְדָּו.

Join me in proclaiming God's greatness.
Together, let us praise God.

As the Torah is carried around the congregation,
we kiss the Torah and all sing:

לְךָ יְיָ הַגְּדֻלָּה וְהַגְּבוּרָה וְהַתִּפְאֶרֶת וְהַנֵּצַח וְהַהוֹד, כִּי כֹל
בַּשָּׁמַיִם וּבָאָרֶץ, לְךָ יְיָ הַמַּמְלָכָה וְהַמִּתְנַשֵּׂא לְכֹל לְרֹאשׁ.

רוֹמְמוּ יְיָ אֱלֹהֵינוּ וְהִשְׁתַּחֲווּ לַהֲדֹם רַגְלָיו, קָדוֹשׁ הוּא.
רוֹמְמוּ יְיָ אֱלֹהֵינוּ וְהִשְׁתַּחֲווּ לְהַר קָדְשׁוֹ, כִּי קָדוֹשׁ יְיָ אֱלֹהֵינוּ.

Yours, *Adonai,* is the greatness, power and splendor.
Yours is the triumph and the majesty.
For all in heaven and on earth is Yours.
You rule over all.

Praise *Adonai,* the Holy One. Worship at God's holy mountain,
for there is none like *Adonai,* our God.

L'ḥa Adonai hag'dulah v'hag'vurah v'hatiferet v'hanetzaḥ v'hahod.
Ki ḥol bashamayim u'va'aretz,
L'ḥa Adonai hamamlaḥa v'hamitnasei l'ḥol l'rosh.
Romemu Adonai Eloheinu v'hishtaḥavu lahadom raglav, kadosh hu.
Romemu Adonai Eloheinu v'hishtaḥavu l'har kod'sho,
Ki kadosh Adonai Eloheinu.

Here are some additional Torah songs for everyone to sing:

Yisrael v'orayta v'kudsha	יִשְׂרָאֵל וְאוֹרַיְתָא וְקוּדְשָׁא
briḥ hu ḥad hu	בְּרִיךְ הוּא חַד הוּא
Torah orah halleluyah.	תּוֹרָה אוֹרָה הַלְלוּיָה.

* * *

V'ha'er eineinu b'Torateḥa	וְהָאֵר עֵינֵינוּ בְּתוֹרָתֶךָ
v'dabeik libeinu b'mitzvoteḥa	וְדַבֵּק לִבֵּנוּ בְּמִצְוֹתֶיךָ
v'yaḥed l'vaveinu l'ahavah	וְיַחֵד לְבָבֵנוּ לְאַהֲבָה
u'l'yir'ah et sh'meḥa	וּלְיִרְאָה אֶת שְׁמֶךָ
v'lo neivosh l'olam va'ed.	וְלֹא נֵבוֹשׁ לְעוֹלָם וָעֶד.
Ki v'shem kodsh'ḥa hagadol	כִּי בְשֵׁם קָדְשְׁךָ הַגָּדוֹל
v'hanora bataḥnu	וְהַנּוֹרָא בָּטָחְנוּ
nagilah v'nis'm'ḥah bishu'ateḥa.	נָגִילָה וְנִשְׂמְחָה בִּישׁוּעָתֶךָ.

* * *

Torah tzivah lanu Mosheh	תּוֹרָה צִוָּה לָנוּ מֹשֶׁה
morashah k'hilat Ya'akov.	מוֹרָשָׁה קְהִלַּת יַעֲקֹב.

Congregants are honored by being called up to the *bimah* (platform) to bless the Torah before and after each selection. This is called an *aliyah* (meaning "going up").

If *Rosh haShanah* is on a weekday, there are five selections from the Torah that are read aloud. If *Rosh haShanah* is on a *Shabbat,* seven selections are read.

Because each section for an *aliyah* should contain at least three verses, we have selected a few more than twenty-one for the Torah reading of the first day of *Rosh haShanah* which can fall on *Shabbat.*

At a children's service, if there is a small group or if only one selection is to be read, an alternative is to have a group *aliyah.* Then the blessings before and after the Torah reading are recited together.

If you are going to read less than five/seven sections, we recommend that you choose:

First day: *Sh'lishi* and *Revi'i* (vs. 10-18)

Second day: *Sh'lishi-Ḥamishi* (vs. 9-19)

TORAH BLESSINGS

The one(s) being honored say(s):

בָּרְכוּ אֶת־יְיָ הַמְבֹרָךְ.

Praise *Adonai,* Source of all blessing.

The congregation answers:

בָּרוּךְ יְיָ הַמְבֹרָךְ לְעוֹלָם וָעֶד.

Praise *Adonai,* Source of all blessing, forever and ever.

The one(s) being honored repeat(s) the above line and continue(s):

בָּרוּךְ אַתָּה יְיָ אֱלֹהֵינוּ מֶלֶךְ הָעוֹלָם אֲשֶׁר בָּחַר בָּנוּ
מִכָּל־הָעַמִּים וְנָתַן לָנוּ אֶת־תּוֹרָתוֹ. בָּרוּךְ אַתָּה יְיָ נוֹתֵן הַתּוֹרָה.

Praised are You, *Adonai,* Ruler of the universe, Who has chosen us with the gift of the Torah. Praised are You, *Adonai,* Giver of the Torah.

After the Torah is read, the one(s) being honored say(s):

בָּרוּךְ אַתָּה יְיָ אֱלֹהֵינוּ מֶלֶךְ הָעוֹלָם אֲשֶׁר נָתַן לָנוּ תּוֹרַת
אֱמֶת וְחַיֵּי עוֹלָם נָטַע בְּתוֹכֵנוּ. בָּרוּךְ אַתָּה יְיָ נוֹתֵן הַתּוֹרָה.

Praised are You, *Adonai,* Ruler of the universe, Who has given us the Torah of truth, a guide forever. Praised are You, *Adonai,* Giver of the Torah.

TORAH READING
FIRST DAY OF *ROSH HASHANAH*

Genesis 21:1-34

God kept the promise to Sarah and she gave birth to a son. Abraham named him Isaac, meaning laughter. This was because Sarah had laughed when she learned that she and Abraham would have a child in their old age.

As Isaac grew up, Sarah demanded that Abraham send away Ishmael, the son he had with Hagar. Trying to understand Sarah's behavior, the Rabbis explained that Sarah was afraid that Ishmael would have a bad influence on Isaac. Abraham was bothered by Sarah's demand and did not know what to do.

But God told him to follow Sarah's advice, for Isaac would be the one to continue the covenant between God and Israel. Abraham must not be troubled about Ishmael. His destiny would be to become the father of another great nation.

So in the morning, Abraham gave Hagar some bread and a container of water and sent her and Ishmael away. She then wandered about in the wilderness of Beer-Sheba. When there was no more water left, Hagar moved away from her son, because she did not want to see him die. Alone and afraid, she burst into tears.

God heard the cry of Ishmael. At the same time, an angel reassured Hagar. Then God opened Hagar's eyes and she saw a well of water from which she let Ishmael drink. As promised, God was with Ishmael as he grew into an adult. He became a bowman in the wilderness of Paran.

In this story, God remembers and keeps promises to Abraham, Sarah and Hagar. This is why we read it on *Rosh haShanah*, the "Day of Remembering." Can you tell what each promise was?

Abraham had a difficult choice to make. Do you think he did the right thing?

Why does God seem to respond more directly to the voice of the boy than the tears of Hagar?

Why did God need to open Hagar's eyes to see the well? Why didn't she see it herself?

Although they led separate lives, Isaac and Ishmael later reunited to bury their father, Abraham. We, the Jewish people, are the descendants of Abraham and Isaac. The Arabs are said to be the descendants of Ishmael. Today, how can the descendants of Isaac and Ishmael get together to make peace?

TORAH READING FOR THE FIRST DAY OF *ROSH HASHANAH*

Genesis 21:1-21

בְּרֵאשִׁית כא

Kohen

וַיהוָה פָּקַד אֶת־שָׂרָה כַּאֲשֶׁר אָמָר וַיַּעַשׂ יְהוָה לְשָׂרָה
כַּאֲשֶׁר דִּבֵּר׃ וַתַּהַר וַתֵּלֶד שָׂרָה לְאַבְרָהָם בֵּן לִזְקֻנָיו
לַמּוֹעֵד אֲשֶׁר־דִּבֶּר אֹתוֹ אֱלֹהִים׃ וַיִּקְרָא אַבְרָהָם
אֶת־שֶׁם־בְּנוֹ הַנּוֹלַד־לוֹ אֲשֶׁר־יָלְדָה־לּוֹ שָׂרָה יִצְחָק׃

Levi

וַיָּמָל אַבְרָהָם אֶת־יִצְחָק בְּנוֹ בֶּן־שְׁמֹנַת יָמִים כַּאֲשֶׁר צִוָּה
אֹתוֹ אֱלֹהִים׃ וְאַבְרָהָם בֶּן־מְאַת שָׁנָה בְּהִוָּלֶד לוֹ אֵת
יִצְחָק בְּנוֹ׃ וַתֹּאמֶר שָׂרָה צְחֹק עָשָׂה לִי אֱלֹהִים
כָּל־הַשֹּׁמֵעַ יִצְחַק־לִי׃ On Shabbat: Shlishi וַתֹּאמֶר מִי
מִלֵּל לְאַבְרָהָם הֵינִיקָה בָנִים שָׂרָה כִּי־יָלַדְתִּי בֵן
לִזְקֻנָיו׃ וַיִּגְדַּל הַיֶּלֶד וַיִּגָּמַל וַיַּעַשׂ אַבְרָהָם מִשְׁתֶּה גָדוֹל
בְּיוֹם הִגָּמֵל אֶת־יִצְחָק׃ וַתֵּרֶא שָׂרָה אֶת־בֶּן־הָגָר הַמִּצְרִית
אֲשֶׁר־יָלְדָה לְאַבְרָהָם מְצַחֵק׃

Shlishi

On Shabbat: R'vi'i

וַתֹּאמֶר לְאַבְרָהָם גָּרֵשׁ הָאָמָה הַזֹּאת וְאֶת־בְּנָהּ כִּי לֹא
יִירַשׁ בֶּן־הָאָמָה הַזֹּאת עִם־בְּנִי עִם־יִצְחָק׃ וַיֵּרַע הַדָּבָר
מְאֹד בְּעֵינֵי אַבְרָהָם עַל אוֹדֹת בְּנוֹ׃ וַיֹּאמֶר אֱלֹהִים

אֶל־אַבְרָהָ֗ם אַל־יֵרַ֤ע בְּעֵינֶ֙יךָ֙ עַל־הַנַּ֣עַר וְעַל־אֲמָתֶ֔ךָ כֹּל֩
אֲשֶׁ֨ר תֹּאמַ֥ר אֵלֶ֛יךָ שָׂרָ֖ה שְׁמַ֣ע בְּקֹלָ֑הּ כִּ֣י בְיִצְחָ֔ק יִקָּרֵ֥א
לְךָ֖ זָֽרַע׃ On Shabbat: Ḥamishi וְגַ֥ם אֶת־בֶּן־הָאָמָ֖ה לְג֣וֹי
אֲשִׂימֶ֑נּוּ כִּ֥י זַרְעֲךָ֖ הֽוּא׃ וַיַּשְׁכֵּ֣ם אַבְרָהָ֣ם ׀ בַּבֹּ֡קֶר
וַיִּֽקַּֽח־לֶ֩חֶם֩ וְחֵ֨מַת מַ֜יִם וַיִּתֵּ֣ן אֶל־הָ֠גָר שָׂ֧ם עַל־שִׁכְמָ֛הּ
וְאֶת־הַיֶּ֖לֶד וַֽיְשַׁלְּחֶ֑הָ וַתֵּ֣לֶךְ וַתֵּ֔תַע בְּמִדְבַּ֖ר בְּאֵ֥ר שָֽׁבַע׃
וַיִּכְל֥וּ הַמַּ֖יִם מִן־הַחֵ֑מֶת וַתַּשְׁלֵ֣ךְ אֶת־הַיֶּ֔לֶד תַּ֖חַת אַחַ֥ד
הַשִּׂיחִֽם׃

R'vi'i

On Shabbat: Shishi

וַתֵּלֶךְ֩ וַתֵּ֨שֶׁב לָ֜הּ מִנֶּ֗גֶד הַרְחֵק֙ כִּמְטַחֲוֵ֣י קֶ֔שֶׁת כִּ֣י אָֽמְרָ֔ה
אַל־אֶרְאֶ֖ה בְּמ֣וֹת הַיָּ֑לֶד וַתֵּ֣שֶׁב מִנֶּ֔גֶד וַתִּשָּׂ֥א אֶת־קֹלָ֖הּ
וַתֵּֽבְךְּ׃ וַיִּשְׁמַ֣ע אֱלֹהִים֮ אֶת־ק֣וֹל הַנַּ֒עַר֒ וַיִּקְרָא֩ מַלְאַ֨ךְ
אֱלֹהִ֤ים ׀ אֶל־הָגָר֙ מִן־הַשָּׁמַ֔יִם וַיֹּ֥אמֶר לָ֖הּ מַה־לָּ֣ךְ הָגָ֑ר
אַל־תִּ֣ירְאִ֔י כִּֽי־שָׁמַ֧ע אֱלֹהִ֛ים אֶל־ק֥וֹל הַנַּ֖עַר בַּאֲשֶׁ֥ר
הוּא־שָֽׁם׃ ק֚וּמִי שְׂאִ֣י אֶת־הַנַּ֔עַר וְהַחֲזִ֥יקִי אֶת־יָדֵ֖ךְ בּ֑וֹ
כִּֽי־לְג֥וֹי גָּד֖וֹל אֲשִׂימֶֽנּוּ׃

Ḥamishi

On Shabbat: Sh'vi'i

וַיִּפְקַ֤ח אֱלֹהִים֙ אֶת־עֵינֶ֔יהָ וַתֵּ֖רֶא בְּאֵ֣ר מָ֑יִם וַתֵּ֜לֶךְ וַתְּמַלֵּ֤א
אֶת־הַחֵ֙מֶת֙ מַ֔יִם וַתַּ֖שְׁקְ אֶת־הַנָּֽעַר׃ וַיְהִ֧י אֱלֹהִ֛ים אֶת־הַנַּ֖עַר
וַיִּגְדָּ֑ל וַיֵּ֙שֶׁב֙ בַּמִּדְבָּ֔ר וַיְהִ֖י רֹבֶ֥ה קַשָּֽׁת׃ וַיֵּ֖שֶׁב בְּמִדְבַּ֣ר
פָּארָ֑ן וַתִּֽקַּֽח־ל֥וֹ אִמּ֛וֹ אִשָּׁ֖ה מֵאֶ֥רֶץ מִצְרָֽיִם׃

TORAH READING
SECOND DAY OF *ROSH HASHANAH*

Genesis 22:1-24

After some time, God tested Abraham, saying, "Take your son, your favorite one, your beloved Isaac and go to the land of Moriah and offer him there as a sacrifice on a mountain which I will show you."

So early next morning, Abraham saddled his donkey and took two of his young servants with him and his son, Isaac. Then he cut the wood for the offering and set out for the place where God had told him.

On the third day, Abraham saw this place in the distance. He then said to his servants: "Stay here with the donkey while we go there. The boy and I will worship and we will then return to you." Abraham took the wood and placed it on Isaac for him to carry. He himself took the firestone and the knife. The two walked off together. Then Isaac asked Abraham where the sheep for the offering was. Abraham replied that God would provide the sheep. And the two continued on together.

When they arrived at the designated place, Abraham made all the preparations for the sacrifice. He bound Isaac and placed him on the altar. As he picked up the knife, he heard a voice calling him: "Abraham! Abraham!" and he answered, "Here I am." And the voice said, "Do not raise your hand against the boy, for now I know how deep your faith is in me." When Abraham looked up, he saw a ram caught in a thicket by the horns. He took it and sacrificed the ram instead of Isaac.

The voice again spoke to Abraham and said, "Because of what you were prepared to do, you have my promise that I will bless you. I will make your descendants as numerous as the stars in the heavens and as the sand on the seashore. Your children will become a blessing."

To think about ...

In the story of the *Akeidah* (The Binding of Isaac), there are many action words, but no words to describe feelings. Try to retell the story, adding how you imagine each character felt.

Sometimes, the Torah gives us a clue as to how someone is feeling. For example, in Genesis 22:3 it says, "So early next morning, Abraham saddled his donkey and took with him two of his servants and his son Isaac. He split the wood for the burnt offering, and he set out for the place of which God had told him."

Abraham seems to be doing things out of order. Even though in the first verse he answered God with a firm *"Hineini"* ("Here I am"), perhaps he is troubled and his actions show mixed feelings deep inside.

Can you find other clues as to how Abraham and Isaac are feeling?

Why do you think Abraham did not tell his wife Sarah what he was planning to do?

In your opinion, would Sarah have agreed to sacrifice Isaac? How would she have answered God?

When we read this Torah portion, it seems that Isaac understands what is going to happen. If so, is his faith equal to or greater than Abraham's?

When the story of the binding of Isaac is told, Isaac is often pictured as a boy. However, many believe he was really a young man at the time. Does this surprise you? What difference does it make?

The *Akeidah* is usually seen as God's way of testing Abraham. Another way to look at the story is to see it as Abraham's way to test God, to see if God would really demand this sacrifice.

During the time of the matriarchs and patriarchs, there were other nations that actually sacrificed children to their gods. Many think this story was meant to teach us that God does not want such sacrifices.

TORAH READING FOR THE SECOND DAY OF *ROSH HASHANAH*

Genesis 22:1-19

בְּרֵאשִׁית כב

Kohen

וַיְהִ֗י אַחַר֙ הַדְּבָרִ֣ים הָאֵ֔לֶּה וְהָ֣אֱלֹהִ֔ים נִסָּ֖ה אֶת־אַבְרָהָ֑ם
וַיֹּ֣אמֶר אֵלָ֔יו אַבְרָהָ֖ם וַיֹּ֥אמֶר הִנֵּֽנִי׃ וַיֹּ֡אמֶר קַח־נָ֠א אֶת־בִּנְךָ֙
אֶת־יְחִֽידְךָ֤ אֲשֶׁר־אָהַ֙בְתָּ֙ אֶת־יִצְחָ֔ק וְלֶךְ־לְךָ֔ אֶל־אֶ֖רֶץ
הַמֹּרִיָּ֑ה וְהַעֲלֵ֤הוּ שָׁם֙ לְעֹלָ֔ה עַ֚ל אַחַ֣ד הֶֽהָרִ֔ים אֲשֶׁ֖ר אֹמַ֥ר
אֵלֶֽיךָ׃ וַיַּשְׁכֵּ֨ם אַבְרָהָ֜ם בַּבֹּ֗קֶר וַֽיַּחֲבֹשׁ֙ אֶת־חֲמֹר֔וֹ וַיִּקַּ֞ח
אֶת־שְׁנֵ֤י נְעָרָיו֙ אִתּ֔וֹ וְאֵ֖ת יִצְחָ֣ק בְּנ֑וֹ וַיְבַקַּע֙ עֲצֵ֣י עֹלָ֔ה
וַיָּ֣קָם וַיֵּ֔לֶךְ אֶל־הַמָּק֖וֹם אֲשֶׁר־אָֽמַר־ל֥וֹ הָאֱלֹהִֽים׃

Levi

בַּיּ֣וֹם הַשְּׁלִישִׁ֗י וַיִּשָּׂ֨א אַבְרָהָ֧ם אֶת־עֵינָ֛יו וַיַּ֥רְא אֶת־הַמָּק֖וֹם
מֵרָחֹֽק׃ וַיֹּ֨אמֶר אַבְרָהָ֜ם אֶל־נְעָרָ֗יו שְׁבוּ־לָכֶ֥ם פֹּה֙
עִֽם־הַחֲמ֔וֹר וַאֲנִ֣י וְהַנַּ֔עַר נֵלְכָ֖ה עַד־כֹּ֑ה וְנִֽשְׁתַּחֲוֶ֖ה וְנָשׁ֥וּבָה
אֲלֵיכֶֽם׃ וַיִּקַּ֨ח אַבְרָהָ֜ם אֶת־עֲצֵ֣י הָעֹלָ֗ה וַיָּ֙שֶׂם֙ עַל־יִצְחָ֣ק
בְּנ֔וֹ וַיִּקַּ֣ח בְּיָד֔וֹ אֶת־הָאֵ֖שׁ וְאֶת־הַמַּאֲכֶ֑לֶת וַיֵּלְכ֥וּ שְׁנֵיהֶ֖ם
יַחְדָּֽו׃ וַיֹּ֨אמֶר יִצְחָ֜ק אֶל־אַבְרָהָ֤ם אָבִיו֙ וַיֹּ֣אמֶר אָבִ֔י וַיֹּ֖אמֶר
הִנֶּ֣נִּֽי בְנִ֑י וַיֹּ֗אמֶר הִנֵּ֤ה הָאֵשׁ֙ וְהָ֣עֵצִ֔ים וְאַיֵּ֥ה הַשֶּׂ֖ה לְעֹלָֽה׃
וַיֹּ֙אמֶר֙ אַבְרָהָ֔ם אֱלֹהִ֞ים יִרְאֶה־לּ֥וֹ הַשֶּׂ֛ה לְעֹלָ֖ה בְּנִ֑י וַיֵּלְכ֥וּ
שְׁנֵיהֶ֖ם יַחְדָּֽו׃

Shlishi

וַיָּבֹ֗אוּ אֶֽל־הַמָּקוֹם֮ אֲשֶׁ֣ר אָֽמַר־ל֣וֹ הָֽאֱלֹהִים֒ וַיִּ֨בֶן שָׁ֤ם
אַבְרָהָם֙ אֶת־הַמִּזְבֵּ֔חַ וַֽיַּעֲרֹ֖ךְ אֶת־הָֽעֵצִ֑ים וַֽיַּעֲקֹד֙
אֶת־יִצְחָ֣ק בְּנ֔וֹ וַיָּ֤שֶׂם אֹתוֹ֙ עַל־הַמִּזְבֵּ֔חַ מִמַּ֖עַל לָֽעֵצִֽים׃
וַיִּשְׁלַ֤ח אַבְרָהָם֙ אֶת־יָד֔וֹ וַיִּקַּ֖ח אֶת־הַֽמַּֽאֲכֶ֑לֶת לִשְׁחֹ֖ט
אֶת־בְּנֽוֹ׃ וַיִּקְרָ֨א אֵלָ֜יו מַלְאַ֤ךְ יְהוָה֙ מִן־הַשָּׁמַ֔יִם וַיֹּ֖אמֶר
אַבְרָהָ֣ם ׀ אַבְרָהָ֑ם וַיֹּ֖אמֶר הִנֵּֽנִי׃

R'vi'i

וַיֹּ֗אמֶר אַל־תִּשְׁלַ֤ח יָֽדְךָ֙ אֶל־הַנַּ֔עַר וְאַל־תַּ֥עַשׂ ל֖וֹ מְא֑וּמָה
כִּ֣י ׀ עַתָּ֣ה יָדַ֗עְתִּי כִּֽי־יְרֵ֤א אֱלֹהִים֙ אַ֔תָּה וְלֹ֥א חָשַׂ֛כְתָּ
אֶת־בִּנְךָ֥ אֶת־יְחִֽידְךָ֖ מִמֶּֽנִּי׃ וַיִּשָּׂ֨א אַבְרָהָ֜ם אֶת־עֵינָ֗יו וַיַּרְא֙
וְהִנֵּה־אַ֔יִל אַחַ֕ר נֶֽאֱחַ֥ז בַּסְּבַ֖ךְ בְּקַרְנָ֑יו וַיֵּ֤לֶךְ אַבְרָהָם֙
וַיִּקַּ֣ח אֶת־הָאַ֔יִל וַיַּֽעֲלֵ֥הוּ לְעֹלָ֖ה תַּ֣חַת בְּנֽוֹ׃ וַיִּקְרָ֧א
אַבְרָהָ֛ם שֵֽׁם־הַמָּק֥וֹם הַה֖וּא יְהוָ֣ה ׀ יִרְאֶ֑ה אֲשֶׁר֙ יֵֽאָמֵ֣ר
הַיּ֔וֹם בְּהַ֥ר יְהוָ֖ה יֵֽרָאֶֽה׃

Ḥamishi

וַיִּקְרָ֛א מַלְאַ֥ךְ יְהוָ֖ה אֶל־אַבְרָהָ֑ם שֵׁנִ֖ית מִן־הַשָּׁמָֽיִם׃
וַיֹּ֕אמֶר בִּ֥י נִשְׁבַּ֖עְתִּי נְאֻם־יְהוָ֑ה כִּ֗י יַ֚עַן אֲשֶׁ֤ר עָשִׂ֨יתָ֙
אֶת־הַדָּבָ֣ר הַזֶּ֔ה וְלֹ֥א חָשַׂ֖כְתָּ אֶת־בִּנְךָ֥ אֶת־יְחִידֶֽךָ׃
כִּֽי־בָרֵ֣ךְ אֲבָרֶכְךָ֗ וְהַרְבָּ֨ה אַרְבֶּ֤ה אֶֽת־זַרְעֲךָ֙ כְּכֽוֹכְבֵ֣י
הַשָּׁמַ֔יִם וְכַח֕וֹל אֲשֶׁ֖ר עַל־שְׂפַ֣ת הַיָּ֑ם וְיִרַ֣שׁ זַרְעֲךָ֔ אֵ֖ת
שַׁ֥עַר אֹֽיְבָֽיו׃ וְהִתְבָּֽרֲכ֣וּ בְזַרְעֲךָ֔ כֹּ֖ל גּוֹיֵ֣י הָאָ֑רֶץ עֵ֕קֶב
אֲשֶׁ֥ר שָׁמַ֖עְתָּ בְּקֹלִֽי׃ וַיָּ֤שָׁב אַבְרָהָם֙ אֶל־נְעָרָ֔יו וַיָּקֻ֜מוּ
וַיֵּֽלְכ֥וּ יַחְדָּ֖ו אֶל־בְּאֵ֣ר שָׁ֑בַע וַיֵּ֥שֶׁב אַבְרָהָ֖ם בִּבְאֵ֥ר שָֽׁבַע׃

We stand as the Torah is raised and we say:

וְזֹאת הַתּוֹרָה אֲשֶׁר שָׂם מֹשֶׁה לִפְנֵי בְּנֵי יִשְׂרָאֵל עַל פִּי יְיָ
בְּיַד מֹשֶׁה.

This is the Torah of God, given through Moses who presented it to the people of Israel.

V'zot haTorah asher sam Mosheh lifnei b'nei Yisrael al pi Adonai b'yad Mosheh.

MAFTIR

On *Rosh haShanah,* in adult congregations, we read from a second scroll. The reading comes from the fourth of the Five Books of the Torah, Numbers (29:1-6). It includes the following:

"... on the first day of the month, you shall observe a holy occasion. You shall do no work and shall observe it as a day of the sounding of the horn."

HAFTARAH
FIRST DAY OF *ROSH HASHANAH*

I Samuel 1:1-2:10

There was a man named Elkanah from the hill country of Ephraim who had two wives. One was named Ḥanah and the other, Peninah. Peninah had children but Ḥanah did not. Although her husband loved her dearly, Ḥanah was still sad that she was childless. Peninah teased Ḥanah about this to purposely upset her.

Once when the family was visiting Shiloh to worship and make a sacrifice, Ḥanah wept bitterly and prayed. She took a vow that if God would remember her and give her a child, she would dedicate this child to God.

Eli, the priest, saw her lips moving but did not hear Ḥanah utter a sound. She was praying silently from her heart. Thinking she was drunk, Eli scolded Ḥanah. When she explained herself, Eli understood and blessed her.

God remembered Ḥanah and she had a son. She called him *Shmu-el* (Samuel), meaning "I asked him of God (and God heard)." When he was old enough, Ḥanah remembered her promise and brought her son to Eli, the priest. He grew up at Shiloh, serving God. This pleased Ḥanah so much, that she sang a song of praise: "My heart rejoices in *Adonai*... Who shields those who are faithful and Who puts an end to the wicked.... We can not succeed without God's help."

To think about ...

According to the Rabbis, it was on *Rosh haShanah* that God remembered the prayer of Ḥanah for a child. In this story both God and Ḥanah remember their promises to each other.

Has someone ever made a promise to you that they did not keep? How did you feel about this? Did anyone ever go to great lengths to keep a promise to you? How did this make you feel?

Ḥanah teaches us that we can show our appreciation to God for the gift of life in good ways. What are some things we can do to express our thanks to God?

HAFTARAH
SECOND DAY OF *ROSH HASHANAH*

Jeremiah 31:1-19

Adonai has spoken: A voice is heard in Ramah. It is Mother Rachel weeping for her children who are scattered and gone. "Do not weep anymore, Rachel. Your children will return from living in enemy lands. There is hope for your future."

"Is not Ephraim my favorite child? I still cherish his memory and my heart reaches out to him. I will surely have compassion on him," says *Adonai*.

To think about ...

Rachel is the fourth mother mentioned on *Rosh haShanah*. Why do you think we read about mothers in the Torah and *Haftarah* on *Rosh haShanah*?

When the *Haftarah* refers to Rachel's children, it does not mean just her sons Joseph and Benjamin but rather the entire people of Israel.

This *Haftarah* teaches that there is hope for the future of the Jewish people. How does this connect to the Torah portion?

The prophet Jeremiah teaches us that God and the Jewish people must make up, just like a parent and child who have grown apart or who have had an argument.

Think about a time you had a disagreement with someone close to you. Was it hard making up? How did you do it? How did you feel afterward?

Blessings before the *Haftarah*

בָּרוּךְ אַתָּה יְיָ אֱלֹהֵינוּ מֶלֶךְ הָעוֹלָם אֲשֶׁר בָּחַר בִּנְבִיאִים
טוֹבִים וְרָצָה בְדִבְרֵיהֶם הַנֶּאֱמָרִים בֶּאֱמֶת. בָּרוּךְ אַתָּה יְיָ
הַבּוֹחֵר בַּתּוֹרָה וּבְמֹשֶׁה עַבְדּוֹ וּבְיִשְׂרָאֵל עַמּוֹ וּבִנְבִיאֵי
הָאֱמֶת וָצֶדֶק.

FROM THE *HAFTARAH* FOR THE FIRST DAY

I Samuel 1: 1-8

שמואל א: א-ח

וַיְהִי֩ אִ֨ישׁ אֶחָ֜ד מִן־הָרָמָתַ֛יִם צוֹפִ֖ים מֵהַ֣ר אֶפְרָ֑יִם וּשְׁמ֡וֹ אֶ֠לְקָנָה
בֶּן־יְרֹחָ֧ם בֶּן־אֱלִיה֛וּא בֶּן־תֹּ֥חוּ בֶן־צ֖וּף אֶפְרָתִֽי׃ וְלוֹ֙ שְׁתֵּ֣י נָשִׁ֔ים שֵׁ֤ם
אַחַת֙ חַנָּ֔ה וְשֵׁ֥ם הַשֵּׁנִ֖ית פְּנִנָּ֑ה וַיְהִ֤י לִפְנִנָּה֙ יְלָדִ֔ים וּלְחַנָּ֖ה אֵ֥ין יְלָדִֽים׃
וְעָלָה֩ הָאִ֨ישׁ הַה֤וּא מֵֽעִירוֹ֙ מִיָּמִ֣ים ׀ יָמִ֔ימָה לְהִשְׁתַּחֲוֺ֧ת וְלִזְבֹּ֛חַ לַיהוָ֥ה
צְבָא֖וֹת בְּשִׁלֹ֑ה וְשָׁ֞ם שְׁנֵ֣י בְנֵֽי־עֵלִ֗י חָפְנִי֙ וּפִ֣נְחָ֔ס כֹּהֲנִ֖ים לַיהוָֽה׃ וַיְהִ֣י
הַיּ֔וֹם וַיִּזְבַּ֖ח אֶלְקָנָ֑ה וְנָתַ֞ן לִפְנִנָּ֣ה אִשְׁתּ֗וֹ וּֽלְכָל־בָּנֶ֛יהָ וּבְנוֹתֶ֖יהָ מָנֽוֹת׃
וּלְחַנָּ֕ה יִתֵּ֛ן מָנָ֥ה אַחַ֖ת אַפָּ֑יִם כִּ֤י אֶת־חַנָּה֙ אָהֵ֔ב וַֽיהוָ֖ה סָגַ֥ר רַחְמָֽהּ׃
וְכִעֲסַ֤תָּה צָֽרָתָהּ֙ גַּם־כַּ֔עַס בַּעֲב֖וּר הַרְּעִמָ֑הּ כִּֽי־סָגַ֥ר יְהוָ֖ה בְּעַ֥ד רַחְמָֽהּ׃
וְכֵ֨ן יַעֲשֶׂ֜ה שָׁנָ֣ה בְשָׁנָ֗ה מִדֵּ֤י עֲלֹתָהּ֙ בְּבֵ֣ית יְהוָ֔ה כֵּ֖ן תַּכְעִסֶ֑נָּה וַתִּבְכֶּ֖ה
וְלֹ֥א תֹאכַֽל׃ וַיֹּ֨אמֶר לָ֜הּ אֶלְקָנָ֣ה אִישָׁ֗הּ חַנָּה֙ לָ֣מֶה תִבְכִּ֗י וְלָ֙מֶה֙ לֹ֣א
תֹֽאכְלִ֔י וְלָ֖מֶה יֵרַ֣ע לְבָבֵ֑ךְ הֲל֤וֹא אָֽנֹכִי֙ ט֣וֹב לָ֔ךְ מֵעֲשָׂרָ֖ה בָּנִֽים׃

FROM THE *HAFTARAH* FOR THE SECOND DAY

Jeremiah 31: 1-5

ירמיה לא: א-ה

כֹּ֚ה אָמַ֣ר יְהוָ֔ה מָצָ֥א חֵן֙ בַּמִּדְבָּ֔ר עַ֖ם שְׂרִ֣ידֵי חָ֑רֶב הָל֖וֹךְ לְהַרְגִּיע֥וֹ
יִשְׂרָאֵֽל׃ מֵֽרָח֔וֹק יְהוָ֖ה נִרְאָ֣ה לִ֑י וְאַהֲבַ֤ת עוֹלָם֙ אֲהַבְתִּ֔יךְ עַל־כֵּ֖ן
מְשַׁכְתִּ֥יךְ חָֽסֶד׃ ע֣וֹד אֶבְנֵ֤ךְ וְנִבְנֵית֙ בְּתוּלַ֣ת יִשְׂרָאֵ֔ל ע֚וֹד תַּעְדִּ֣י תֻפַּ֔יִךְ
וְיָצָ֖את בִּמְח֥וֹל מְשַׂחֲקִֽים׃ ע֚וֹד תִּטְּעִ֣י כְרָמִ֔ים בְּהָרֵ֖י שֹׁמְר֑וֹן נָטְע֥וּ
נֹטְעִ֖ים וְחִלֵּֽלוּ׃ כִּ֣י יֶשׁ־י֔וֹם קָרְא֥וּ נֹצְרִ֖ים בְּהַ֣ר אֶפְרָ֑יִם ק֚וּמוּ וְנַעֲלֶ֣ה
צִיּ֔וֹן אֶל־יְהוָ֖ה אֱלֹהֵֽינוּ׃

Blessings after the *Haftarah*

בָּרוּךְ אַתָּה יְיָ אֱלֹהֵינוּ מֶלֶךְ הָעוֹלָם, צוּר כָּל־הָעוֹלָמִים,
צַדִּיק בְּכָל־הַדּוֹרוֹת, הָאֵל הַנֶּאֱמָן הָאוֹמֵר וְעוֹשֶׂה הַמְדַבֵּר
וּמְקַיֵּם, שֶׁכָּל־דְּבָרָיו אֱמֶת וָצֶדֶק. נֶאֱמָן אַתָּה הוּא יְיָ
אֱלֹהֵינוּ וְנֶאֱמָנִים דְּבָרֶיךָ, וְדָבָר אֶחָד מִדְּבָרֶיךָ אָחוֹר לֹא
יָשׁוּב רֵיקָם, כִּי אֵל מֶלֶךְ נֶאֱמָן וְרַחֲמָן אָתָּה. בָּרוּךְ אַתָּה
יְיָ הָאֵל הַנֶּאֱמָן בְּכָל־דְּבָרָיו.

רַחֵם עַל צִיּוֹן כִּי הִיא בֵּית חַיֵּינוּ. וְלַעֲלוּבַת נֶפֶשׁ תּוֹשִׁיעַ
בִּמְהֵרָה בְיָמֵינוּ. בָּרוּךְ אַתָּה יְיָ מְשַׂמֵּחַ צִיּוֹן בְּבָנֶיהָ.

שַׂמְּחֵנוּ יְיָ אֱלֹהֵינוּ בְּאֵלִיָּהוּ הַנָּבִיא עַבְדֶּךָ וּבְמַלְכוּת בֵּית דָּוִד
מְשִׁיחֶךָ. בִּמְהֵרָה יָבוֹא וְיָגֵל לִבֵּנוּ, עַל כִּסְאוֹ לֹא יֵשֶׁב זָר
וְלֹא יִנְחֲלוּ עוֹד אֲחֵרִים אֶת־כְּבוֹדוֹ, כִּי בְשֵׁם קָדְשְׁךָ נִשְׁבַּעְתָּ
לּוֹ שֶׁלֹּא יִכְבֶּה נֵרוֹ לְעוֹלָם וָעֶד. בָּרוּךְ אַתָּה יְיָ מָגֵן דָּוִד.

עַל הַתּוֹרָה וְעַל הָעֲבוֹדָה וְעַל הַנְּבִיאִים (וְעַל יוֹם הַשַּׁבָּת
הַזֶּה) וְעַל יוֹם הַזִּכָּרוֹן הַזֶּה שֶׁנָּתַתָּ לָּנוּ יְיָ אֱלֹהֵינוּ (לִקְדֻשָּׁה
וְלִמְנוּחָה) לְכָבוֹד וּלְתִפְאָרֶת. עַל הַכֹּל יְיָ אֱלֹהֵינוּ אֲנַחְנוּ
מוֹדִים לָךְ, וּמְבָרְכִים אוֹתָךְ. יִתְבָּרַךְ שִׁמְךָ בְּפִי כָּל־חַי תָּמִיד
לְעוֹלָם וָעֶד. וּדְבָרְךָ אֱמֶת וְקַיָּם לָעַד. בָּרוּךְ אַתָּה יְיָ מֶלֶךְ
עַל כָּל־הָאָרֶץ מְקַדֵּשׁ (הַשַּׁבָּת וְ)יִשְׂרָאֵל וְיוֹם הַזִּכָּרוֹן.

THE SOUNDING OF THE *SHOFAR*

(omitted on *Shabbat*)

Where Was Rabbi David?

Rabbi David of Lelov was the *shofar* blower at the synagogue of the great Rabbi Jacob Isaac, who was known as the Seer of Lublin. But on one *Rosh haShanah*, when it was time to blow the *shofar,* Rabbi David was nowhere to be found. The Seer of Lublin sent one of the students to find him. After searching and searching, he found Rabbi David in the marketplace feeding the horses. When the student scolded Rabbi David for being late, he replied, "I know that all the Jewish wagon drivers are in the synagogue today and I was worried that they may have forgotten to feed their horses. It is a *mitzvah* to prevent cruelty to animals." They both returned to the synagogue and Rabbi David blew the *shofar.* Then the Seer of Lublin remarked, "Today Rabbi David did a holy deed."

Thoughts on the Sounding of the *Shofar*

When the *shofar* sounds, we hear the voices of our ancestors reminding us to be loyal to our people.

When the *shofar* sounds, we hear a voice deep inside us urging us to improve.

When the *shofar* sounds, we hear the voice of God.

*

Wake up! cries the *shofar* and we are sad. We remember our wrongdoing this past year.

Wake up! cries the *shofar* and we are glad. There's time to change; we need not fear.

*

Teshuvah: turn
change our ways.
Torah: learn
all of our days.

***T**eshuvah* means we can turn ourselves around. If, for example, we have been teasing a younger brother or sister, we can decide to stop doing that. We can even go further and vow to do something especially nice for him or her. *Teshuvah* can also mean going off in a new direction. You could decide to shovel off an elderly neighbor's walk or make a casserole for the homeless. You could organize a recycling project at school or arrange a youth group car wash to raise funds for the Jewish blind. Can you think of other positive actions you can take to make you a better you?

THE *SHOFAR* SERVICE

(omitted on *Shabbat*)

The *shofar* blower recites the following two blessings before blowing the *shofar*. The congregation responds: *"Amen."*

בָּרוּךְ אַתָּה יְיָ אֱלֹהֵינוּ מֶלֶךְ הָעוֹלָם אֲשֶׁר קִדְּשָׁנוּ בְּמִצְוֹתָיו וְצִוָּנוּ לִשְׁמֹעַ קוֹל שׁוֹפָר.

Congregation: אָמֵן

Blessed are You, *Adonai,* Ruler of the Universe, Who has made us holy through the *mitzvot* and commanded us to hear the sound of the *shofar*.

בָּרוּךְ אַתָּה יְיָ אֱלֹהֵינוּ מֶלֶךְ הָעוֹלָם שֶׁהֶחֱיָנוּ וְקִיְּמָנוּ וְהִגִּיעָנוּ לַזְּמַן הַזֶּה.

Congregation: אָמֵן

Blessed are You, *Adonai,* Ruler of the Universe, Who has granted us life and health and has enabled us to reach this special day.

תְּקִיעָה שְׁבָרִים תְּרוּעָה תְּקִיעָה
תְּקִיעָה שְׁבָרִים תְּרוּעָה תְּקִיעָה
תְּקִיעָה שְׁבָרִים תְּרוּעָה תְּקִיעָה

תְּקִיעָה שְׁבָרִים תְּקִיעָה
תְּקִיעָה שְׁבָרִים תְּקִיעָה
תְּקִיעָה שְׁבָרִים תְּקִיעָה

תְּקִיעָה תְּרוּעָה תְּקִיעָה
תְּקִיעָה תְּרוּעָה תְּקִיעָה
תְּקִיעָה תְּרוּעָה תְּקִיעָה גְדוֹלָה

אַשְׁרֵי הָעָם יוֹדְעֵי תְרוּעָה, יְיָ בְּאוֹר פָּנֶיךָ יְהַלֵּכוּן.

Happy are those who experience the *shofar* blowing.

Happy are those who dwell in Your house, for they will continually praise You. Happy is the people whose God is *Adonai*.

אַשְׁרֵי יוֹשְׁבֵי בֵיתֶךָ, עוֹד יְהַלְלוּךָ סֶּלָה.
אַשְׁרֵי הָעָם שֶׁכָּכָה לּוֹ, אַשְׁרֵי הָעָם שֶׁיְיָ אֱלֹהָיו.

תְּהִלָּה לְדָוִד.

אֲרוֹמִמְךָ אֱלוֹהַי הַמֶּלֶךְ וַאֲבָרְכָה שִׁמְךָ לְעוֹלָם וָעֶד.
בְּכָל־יוֹם אֲבָרְכֶךָּ וַאֲהַלְלָה שִׁמְךָ לְעוֹלָם וָעֶד.
גָּדוֹל יְיָ וּמְהֻלָּל מְאֹד וְלִגְדֻלָּתוֹ אֵין חֵקֶר.
דּוֹר לְדוֹר יְשַׁבַּח מַעֲשֶׂיךָ וּגְבוּרֹתֶיךָ יַגִּידוּ.
הֲדַר כְּבוֹד הוֹדֶךָ וְדִבְרֵי נִפְלְאֹתֶיךָ אָשִׂיחָה.
וֶעֱזוּז נוֹרְאֹתֶיךָ יֹאמֵרוּ וּגְדוּלָּתְךָ אֲסַפְּרֶנָּה.
זֵכֶר רַב טוּבְךָ יַבִּיעוּ וְצִדְקָתְךָ יְרַנֵּנוּ.
חַנּוּן וְרַחוּם יְיָ, אֶרֶךְ אַפַּיִם וּגְדָל־חָסֶד.
טוֹב יְיָ לַכֹּל וְרַחֲמָיו עַל כָּל־מַעֲשָׂיו.
יוֹדוּךָ יְיָ כָּל־מַעֲשֶׂיךָ וַחֲסִידֶיךָ יְבָרְכוּכָה.
כְּבוֹד מַלְכוּתְךָ יֹאמֵרוּ וּגְבוּרָתְךָ יְדַבֵּרוּ.
לְהוֹדִיעַ לִבְנֵי הָאָדָם גְּבוּרֹתָיו וּכְבוֹד הֲדַר מַלְכוּתוֹ.
מַלְכוּתְךָ מַלְכוּת כָּל־עֹלָמִים וּמֶמְשַׁלְתְּךָ בְּכָל־דּוֹר וָדֹר.

סוֹמֵךְ יְיָ לְכָל־הַנֹּפְלִים וְזוֹקֵף לְכָל־הַכְּפוּפִים.
עֵינֵי כֹל אֵלֶיךָ יְשַׂבֵּרוּ וְאַתָּה נוֹתֵן לָהֶם אֶת־אָכְלָם בְּעִתּוֹ.
פּוֹתֵחַ אֶת־יָדֶךָ וּמַשְׂבִּיעַ לְכָל־חַי רָצוֹן.
צַדִּיק יְיָ בְּכָל־דְּרָכָיו וְחָסִיד בְּכָל־מַעֲשָׂיו.
קָרוֹב יְיָ לְכָל־קֹרְאָיו, לְכֹל אֲשֶׁר יִקְרָאֻהוּ בֶאֱמֶת.
רְצוֹן יְרֵאָיו יַעֲשֶׂה וְאֶת־שַׁוְעָתָם יִשְׁמַע וְיוֹשִׁיעֵם.
שׁוֹמֵר יְיָ אֶת־כָּל־אֹהֲבָיו וְאֵת כָּל־הָרְשָׁעִים יַשְׁמִיד.
תְּהִלַּת יְיָ יְדַבֶּר־פִּי וִיבָרֵךְ כָּל־בָּשָׂר שֵׁם קָדְשׁוֹ לְעוֹלָם וָעֶד.
וַאֲנַחְנוּ נְבָרֵךְ יָהּ מֵעַתָּה וְעַד עוֹלָם. הַלְלוּיָהּ.

A Prayersong of David (selections)

I glorify You, my God, my Ruler, and I will praise Your name forever.

God is to be praised though there are not adequate words to describe God's greatness.

One generation tells the next about Your acts.

They speak of Your wonders and Your majesty.

They tell of Your goodness and sing about Your love for us.

Adonai is close to all who pray with a sincere heart.

We shall praise *Adonai,* now and always, Halleluyah!

Everyone stands as the Torah is lifted up and returned to the ark.
As the Torah is carried around the congregation, the leader sings:

יְהַלְלוּ אֶת־שֵׁם יְיָ כִּי נִשְׂגָּב שְׁמוֹ לְבַדּוֹ.

The congregation sings:

הוֹדוֹ עַל אֶרֶץ וְשָׁמָיִם. וַיָּרֶם קֶרֶן לְעַמּוֹ
תְּהִלָּה לְכָל־חֲסִידָיו, לִבְנֵי יִשְׂרָאֵל עַם קְרֹבוֹ. הַלְלוּיָהּ.

Hodo al eretz v'shamayim. Va'yarem keren l'amo,
t'hilah l'ḥol ḥasidav, livnei Yisrael am k'rovo, haleluyah.

We sing this only on *Shabbat:*

מִזְמוֹר לְדָוִד. הָבוּ לַייָ בְּנֵי אֵלִים, הָבוּ לַייָ כָּבוֹד וָעֹז.
הָבוּ לַייָ כְּבוֹד שְׁמוֹ, הִשְׁתַּחֲווּ לַייָ בְּהַדְרַת קֹדֶשׁ.
קוֹל יְיָ עַל הַמָּיִם, אֵל הַכָּבוֹד הִרְעִים, יְיָ עַל מַיִם רַבִּים.
קוֹל יְיָ בַּכֹּחַ, קוֹל יְיָ בֶּהָדָר.
קוֹל יְיָ שֹׁבֵר אֲרָזִים, וַיְשַׁבֵּר יְיָ אֶת־אַרְזֵי הַלְּבָנוֹן.
וַיַּרְקִידֵם כְּמוֹ עֵגֶל, לְבָנוֹן וְשִׂרְיוֹן כְּמוֹ בֶן־רְאֵמִים.
יְיָ עֹז לְעַמּוֹ יִתֵּן, יְיָ יְבָרֵךְ אֶת־עַמּוֹ בַשָּׁלוֹם.

We sing this on weekdays.

לְדָוִד מִזְמוֹר. לַייָ הָאָרֶץ וּמְלוֹאָהּ, תֵּבֵל וְיֹשְׁבֵי בָהּ. כִּי
הוּא עַל יַמִּים יְסָדָהּ, וְעַל נְהָרוֹת יְכוֹנְנֶהָ. מִי יַעֲלֶה בְהַר
יְיָ, וּמִי יָקוּם בִּמְקוֹם קָדְשׁוֹ. נְקִי כַפַּיִם וּבַר לֵבָב,
אֲשֶׁר לֹא נָשָׂא לַשָּׁוְא נַפְשִׁי, וְלֹא נִשְׁבַּע לְמִרְמָה.

The Torah is placed in the ark.

וּבְנֻחֹה יֹאמַר: שׁוּבָה יְיָ, רִבְבוֹת אַלְפֵי יִשְׂרָאֵל. קוּמָה יְיָ
לִמְנוּחָתֶךָ, אַתָּה וַאֲרוֹן עֻזֶּךָ. כֹּהֲנֶיךָ יִלְבְּשׁוּ־צֶדֶק,
וַחֲסִידֶיךָ יְרַנֵּנוּ. בַּעֲבוּר דָּוִד עַבְדֶּךָ, אַל תָּשֵׁב פְּנֵי
מְשִׁיחֶךָ. כִּי לֶקַח טוֹב נָתַתִּי לָכֶם, תּוֹרָתִי אַל תַּעֲזֹבוּ.

עֵץ חַיִּים הִיא לַמַּחֲזִיקִים בָּהּ, וְתֹמְכֶיהָ מְאֻשָּׁר.
דְּרָכֶיהָ דַרְכֵי־נֹעַם, וְכָל־נְתִיבֹתֶיהָ שָׁלוֹם.
הֲשִׁיבֵנוּ יְיָ אֵלֶיךָ וְנָשׁוּבָה, חַדֵּשׁ יָמֵינוּ כְּקֶדֶם.

The Torah is a tree of life to those who live by its teachings.
Its ways are ways of pleasantness and its paths are paths of peace.
Guide us back to You, *Adonai*.
Renew our glory as in days of old.

Eitz ḥayim hi lamaḥazikim bah,
V'tomḥeha m'ushar.
D'raḥeha darḥei no'am v'ḥol n'tivoteha shalom.
Hashiveinu Adonai eileḥa v'nashuvah,
ḥadesh yameinu k'kedem.

ḤATZI KADDISH

Short *Kaddish* חֲצִי קַדִּישׁ

Leader:

יִתְגַּדַּל וְיִתְקַדַּשׁ שְׁמֵהּ רַבָּא בְּעָלְמָא דִּי בְרָא כִרְעוּתֵהּ,
וְיַמְלִיךְ מַלְכוּתֵהּ בְּחַיֵּיכוֹן וּבְיוֹמֵיכוֹן וּבְחַיֵּי דְכָל־בֵּית
יִשְׂרָאֵל בַּעֲגָלָא וּבִזְמַן קָרִיב, וְאִמְרוּ אָמֵן.

Congregation and Leader answer:

יְהֵא שְׁמֵהּ רַבָּא מְבָרַךְ לְעָלַם וּלְעָלְמֵי עָלְמַיָּא.

Y'hai shmai rabbah m'varaḥ l'olam u'l'olmei almay'ya.

Leader:

יִתְבָּרַךְ וְיִשְׁתַּבַּח וְיִתְפָּאַר וְיִתְרוֹמַם וְיִתְנַשֵּׂא וְיִתְהַדַּר
וְיִתְעַלֶּה וְיִתְהַלַּל שְׁמֵהּ דְּקֻדְשָׁא

Congregation and Leader answer:

בְּרִיךְ הוּא.

Briḥ hu.

Leader:

לְעֵלָּא לְעֵלָּא מִכָּל־בִּרְכָתָא וְשִׁירָתָא תֻּשְׁבְּחָתָא וְנֶחֱמָתָא
דַּאֲמִירָן בְּעָלְמָא, וְאִמְרוּ אָמֵן.

The version of the first blessing which speaks of our forefathers is found on page 70. The version which includes both the forefathers and mothers is found on page 72.

THE *AMIDAH*
עֲמִידָה

(We rise as the ark is opened.)

Adonai, open my lips and my mouth shall praise You.

בָּרוּךְ אַתָּה יְיָ אֱלֹהֵינוּ וֵאלֹהֵי אֲבוֹתֵינוּ, אֱלֹהֵי אַבְרָהָם אֱלֹהֵי יִצְחָק וֵאלֹהֵי יַעֲקֹב, הָאֵל הַגָּדוֹל הַגִּבּוֹר וְהַנּוֹרָא אֵל עֶלְיוֹן גּוֹמֵל חֲסָדִים טוֹבִים וְקוֹנֵה הַכֹּל, וְזוֹכֵר חַסְדֵי אָבוֹת וּמֵבִיא גוֹאֵל לִבְנֵי בְנֵיהֶם לְמַעַן שְׁמוֹ בְּאַהֲבָה.

זָכְרֵנוּ לְחַיִּים מֶלֶךְ חָפֵץ בַּחַיִּים,
וְכָתְבֵנוּ בְּסֵפֶר הַחַיִּים לְמַעַנְךָ אֱלֹהִים חַיִּים.

מֶלֶךְ עוֹזֵר וּמוֹשִׁיעַ וּמָגֵן. בָּרוּךְ אַתָּה יְיָ מָגֵן אַבְרָהָם.

אַתָּה גִּבּוֹר לְעוֹלָם אֲדֹנָי מְחַיֵּה מֵתִים אַתָּה רַב לְהוֹשִׁיעַ. מְכַלְכֵּל חַיִּים בְּחֶסֶד מְחַיֵּה מֵתִים בְּרַחֲמִים רַבִּים, סוֹמֵךְ נוֹפְלִים וְרוֹפֵא חוֹלִים וּמַתִּיר אֲסוּרִים וּמְקַיֵּם אֱמוּנָתוֹ לִישֵׁנֵי עָפָר. מִי כָמוֹךָ בַּעַל גְּבוּרוֹת וּמִי דוֹמֶה לָּךְ, מֶלֶךְ מֵמִית וּמְחַיֶּה וּמַצְמִיחַ יְשׁוּעָה.

מִי כָמוֹךָ אַב הָרַחֲמִים, זוֹכֵר יְצוּרָיו לְחַיִּים בְּרַחֲמִים.

וְנֶאֱמָן אַתָּה לְהַחֲיוֹת מֵתִים. בָּרוּךְ אַתָּה יְיָ מְחַיֵּה הַמֵּתִים.

Zoḥrenu l'ḥayim Meleḥ ḥafetz b'ḥayim,
v'ḥotveinu b'sefer haḥayim, l'ma'anḥa Elohim ḥayim.

Blessed are You, *Adonai,* our God and God of our ancestors,
God of Abraham, Isaac and Jacob.
Supreme God Who responds with kindness,
You remember the good deeds of our ancestors and
lovingly bring help to us.

On this day, we ask You for mercy.
Remember us for life, God Who delights in life.

Blessed are You, *Adonai,* Who protects Abraham.

You are the Source of life Who grants us healing and strength.

There is none as great and powerful as You.

We who are Your creation, *Adonai,* ask to be remembered for life.

Blessed are You, Source of life.

Continue on page 74.

THE *AMIDAH*
עֲמִידָה

(We rise as the ark is opened.)

Adonai, open my lips and my mouth shall praise You.

בָּרוּךְ אַתָּה יְיָ אֱלֹהֵינוּ וֵאלֹהֵי אֲבוֹתֵינוּ, אֱלֹהֵי אַבְרָהָם
אֱלֹהֵי יִצְחָק וֵאלֹהֵי יַעֲקֹב, אֱלֹהֵי שָׂרָה אֱלֹהֵי רִבְקָה
אֱלֹהֵי רָחֵל וֵאלֹהֵי לֵאָה, הָאֵל הַגָּדוֹל הַגִּבּוֹר וְהַנּוֹרָא אֵל
עֶלְיוֹן גּוֹמֵל חֲסָדִים טוֹבִים וְקוֹנֵה הַכֹּל, וְזוֹכֵר חַסְדֵי
אָבוֹת וּמֵבִיא גּוֹאֵל לִבְנֵי בְנֵיהֶם לְמַעַן שְׁמוֹ בְּאַהֲבָה.

זָכְרֵנוּ לְחַיִּים מֶלֶךְ חָפֵץ בַּחַיִּים,
וְכָתְבֵנוּ בְּסֵפֶר הַחַיִּים לְמַעַנְךָ אֱלֹהִים חַיִּים.

מֶלֶךְ עוֹזֵר וּפֹקֵד וּמוֹשִׁיעַ וּמָגֵן. בָּרוּךְ אַתָּה יְיָ מָגֵן
אַבְרָהָם וּפֹקֵד שָׂרָה.

אַתָּה גִּבּוֹר לְעוֹלָם אֲדֹנָי מְחַיֵּה מֵתִים אַתָּה רַב לְהוֹשִׁיעַ.
מְכַלְכֵּל חַיִּים בְּחֶסֶד מְחַיֵּה מֵתִים בְּרַחֲמִים רַבִּים, סוֹמֵךְ
נוֹפְלִים וְרוֹפֵא חוֹלִים וּמַתִּיר אֲסוּרִים וּמְקַיֵּם אֱמוּנָתוֹ
לִישֵׁנֵי עָפָר. מִי כָמוֹךָ בַּעַל גְּבוּרוֹת וּמִי דּוֹמֶה לָּךְ, מֶלֶךְ
מֵמִית וּמְחַיֶּה וּמַצְמִיחַ יְשׁוּעָה.

מִי כָמוֹךָ אַב הָרַחֲמִים, זוֹכֵר יְצוּרָיו לְחַיִּים בְּרַחֲמִים.

וְנֶאֱמָן אַתָּה לְהַחֲיוֹת מֵתִים. בָּרוּךְ אַתָּה יְיָ מְחַיֵּה הַמֵּתִים.

Zoḥrenu l'ḥayim Meleḥ ḥafetz b'ḥayim,
v'ḥotveinu b'sefer haḥayim, l'ma'anḥa Elohim ḥayim.

Blessed are You, *Adonai,* our God and God of our ancestors,
God of Abraham, Isaac and Jacob,
God of Sarah, Rebecca, Leah and Rachel.
Supreme God Who responds with kindness,
You remember the good deeds of our ancestors and
lovingly bring help to us.

On this day, we ask You for mercy.
Remember us for life, God Who delights in life.

Blessed are You, *Adonai,* Who protects Abraham and
remembers Sarah.

You are the Source of life Who grants us healing and strength.

There is none as great and powerful as You.

We who are Your creation, *Adonai,* ask to be remembered for life.

Blessed are You, Source of life.

וּנְתַנֶּה תֹּקֶף קְדֻשַּׁת הַיּוֹם כִּי הוּא נוֹרָא וְאָיֹם. וּבוֹ תִּנַּשֵּׂא
מַלְכוּתֶךָ וְיִכּוֹן בְּחֶסֶד כִּסְאֶךָ וְתֵשֵׁב עָלָיו בֶּאֱמֶת. אֱמֶת כִּי
אַתָּה הוּא דַיָּן וּמוֹכִיחַ וְיוֹדֵעַ וָעֵד, וְכוֹתֵב וְחוֹתֵם וְסוֹפֵר
וּמוֹנֶה, וְתִזְכֹּר כָּל־הַנִּשְׁכָּחוֹת, וְתִפְתַּח אֶת־סֵפֶר הַזִּכְרוֹנוֹת,
וּמֵאֵלָיו יִקָּרֵא וְחוֹתַם יַד כָּל־אָדָם בּוֹ.

וּבְשׁוֹפָר גָּדוֹל יִתָּקַע וְקוֹל דְּמָמָה דַקָּה יִשָּׁמַע. וּמַלְאָכִים
יֵחָפֵזוּן וְחִיל וּרְעָדָה יֹאחֵזוּן וְיֹאמְרוּ הִנֵּה יוֹם הַדִּין.
לִפְקֹד עַל צְבָא מָרוֹם בַּדִּין כִּי לֹא יִזְכּוּ בְעֵינֶיךָ בַּדִּין,
וְכָל־בָּאֵי עוֹלָם יַעַבְרוּן לְפָנֶיךָ כִּבְנֵי מָרוֹן. כְּבַקָּרַת
רוֹעֶה עֶדְרוֹ מַעֲבִיר צֹאנוֹ תַּחַת שִׁבְטוֹ, כֵּן תַּעֲבִיר וְתִסְפֹּר
וְתִמְנֶה וְתִפְקֹד נֶפֶשׁ כָּל־חָי, וְתַחְתֹּךְ קִצְבָה לְכָל־בְּרִיָּה
וְתִכְתֹּב אֶת־גְּזַר דִּינָם.

Let us declare the greatness of this day of holiness! It is a day that acknowledges You, God, as our Judge. Today we pass before You like sheep. Each is precious to You and none goes unnoticed.

Help us to look into our hearts to judge ourselves. Give us the strength and courage to improve in the coming year.

We know, too, that our days on earth are precious. Only You can predict our future. But only we can decide how to live our lives.

בְּרֹאשׁ הַשָּׁנָה יִכָּתֵבוּן וּבְיוֹם צוֹם כִּפּוּר יֵחָתֵמוּן.

B'rosh hashanah yikateivun,
U'vyom tzom kippur yeiḥateimun.

Through prayer, charitable deeds and turning to God for forgiveness, we can make our lives better. May You soften our judgment, God, for You are the God of life.

וּתְשׁוּבָה וּתְפִלָּה וּצְדָקָה
מַעֲבִירִין אֶת־רֹעַ הַגְּזֵרָה.

Teshuvah, tefillah and *tzedakah* can change our lives.

U'teshuvah u'tefillah u'tzedakah ma'avirin et ro'a ha'g'zerah.

The prayer *"U'netaneh Tokef"* which means "We will declare the greatness of this day of holiness," was composed in the Middle Ages by Rabbi Amnon who was tortured for refusing to convert to Christianity.

What Does *Tzedakah* Mean?

Tzedakah not only means "giving money to charity"; *tzedakah* means giving with sensitivity to those who need, and giving because sharing is the just and proper way for us to behave.

Thinking About Looking Ahead

In a way, we are partners with God in determining what will happen to us.

Can we pray to God for a good grade on a math test? Not unless we study for the test! However, we can pray to God to give us the strength and the calmness needed to do our best on the test (after we have prepared for it).

If we don't do our homework one week, for example, it makes it harder for us to succeed the next week. If we get a bad test grade, it is not God's fault but ours. A lesson to learn is that our past affects our future. Can you give other examples of this?

On *Rosh haShanah*, we each have to write our own page in the Book of Life. If we do something terrible to ourselves (like take drugs), we may not live! If we decide to get plenty of exercise, eat good foods and get plenty of rest, we may be healthier. Think of other decisions that you can make to either harm your life or improve it.

"Who is a hero? — The one who conquers his or her evil impulse."

On *Rosh haShanah*, we begin to measure ourselves to see if we're the people we want to be. Each person must say, "How did I measure up?"

Rosh haShanah also teaches us that we can change. Think about someone you know who has changed for the better. In what way did he or she change or improve? How have you changed for the better?

God made us free to choose how we will grow up. What's scary about this? What's wonderful about this?

Our world is full of many possibilities. What are some new things you'd like to do in the coming year?

KEDUSHAH

The ark is closed. We recite the *Kedushah* while standing.
The congregation chants the indented lines.

עֲשֵׂה לְמַעַן שְׁמֶךָ וְקַדֵּשׁ אֶת־שִׁמְךָ עַל מַקְדִּישֵׁי שְׁמֶךָ, בַּעֲבוּר כְּבוֹד שִׁמְךָ הַנַּעֲרָץ וְהַנִּקְדָּשׁ כְּסוֹד שִׂיחַ שַׂרְפֵי־קֹדֶשׁ הַמַּקְדִּישִׁים שִׁמְךָ בַּקֹּדֶשׁ, דָּרֵי מַעְלָה עִם דָּרֵי מַטָּה כַּכָּתוּב עַל יַד נְבִיאֶךָ, וְקָרָא זֶה אֶל זֶה וְאָמַר:

קָדוֹשׁ קָדוֹשׁ קָדוֹשׁ יְיָ צְבָאוֹת, מְלֹא כָל־הָאָרֶץ כְּבוֹדוֹ.

כְּבוֹדוֹ מָלֵא עוֹלָם, מְשָׁרְתָיו שׁוֹאֲלִים זֶה לָזֶה אַיֵּה מְקוֹם כְּבוֹדוֹ, לְעֻמָּתָם בָּרוּךְ יֹאמֵרוּ:

בָּרוּךְ כְּבוֹד יְיָ מִמְּקוֹמוֹ.

מִמְּקוֹמוֹ הוּא יִפֶן בְּרַחֲמִים וְיָחֹן עַם הַמְיַחֲדִים שְׁמוֹ עֶרֶב וָבֹקֶר בְּכָל־יוֹם תָּמִיד פַּעֲמַיִם בְּאַהֲבָה שְׁמַע אוֹמְרִים:

שְׁמַע יִשְׂרָאֵל יְיָ אֱלֹהֵינוּ יְיָ אֶחָד.

הוּא אֱלֹהֵינוּ הוּא אָבִינוּ הוּא מַלְכֵּנוּ הוּא מוֹשִׁיעֵנוּ, וְהוּא יַשְׁמִיעֵנוּ בְּרַחֲמָיו שֵׁנִית לְעֵינֵי כָּל־חָי, לִהְיוֹת לָכֶם לֵאלֹהִים:

אֲנִי יְיָ אֱלֹהֵיכֶם.

אַדִּיר אַדִּירֵנוּ יְיָ אֲדוֹנֵינוּ, מָה אַדִּיר שִׁמְךָ בְּכָל־הָאָרֶץ. וְהָיָה יְיָ לְמֶלֶךְ עַל כָּל־הָאָרֶץ, בַּיּוֹם הַהוּא יִהְיֶה יְיָ אֶחָד וּשְׁמוֹ אֶחָד. וּבְדִבְרֵי קָדְשְׁךָ כָּתוּב לֵאמֹר:

יִמְלֹךְ יְיָ לְעוֹלָם אֱלֹהַיִךְ צִיּוֹן לְדֹר וָדֹר, הַלְלוּיָהּ.

לְדוֹר וָדוֹר נַגִּיד גָּדְלֶךָ, וּלְנֵצַח נְצָחִים קְדֻשָּׁתְךָ נַקְדִּישׁ.
וְשִׁבְחֲךָ אֱלֹהֵינוּ מִפִּינוּ לֹא יָמוּשׁ לְעוֹלָם וָעֶד כִּי אֵל מֶלֶךְ
גָּדוֹל וְקָדוֹשׁ אָתָּה.

We imagine heavenly angels, together with us on earth, singing the praises of God. They call to one another:

> Holy, holy, holy — the whole world is filled with God's glory.

And we, the Jewish people, declare:

> *Shema Yisrael* — Hear, O Israel: The Lord Our God, the Lord is One.

In every generation we will speak of God's greatness and forever declare God's holiness.

Leader says:	Congregation says:
וְכָל מַאֲמִינִים...	
שֶׁהוּא דַּיָּן אֱמֶת	הָאוֹחֵז בְּיָד מִדַּת מִשְׁפָּט
שֶׁהוּא זוֹכֵר הַבְּרִית	הָעֶלְיוֹן וְעֵינָיו עַל יְרֵאָיו
שֶׁהוּא נוֹצֵר חֶסֶד	הַנּוֹהֵג בְּחַסְדּוֹ עִם כָּל־דּוֹר
שֶׁהוּא טוֹב לַכֹּל	הַפּוֹתֵחַ לְדוֹפְקֵי פִּתְחוֹ בִּתְשׁוּבָה

Leader says:	Congregation says:
God....	We believe....
judges the earth.	in God's truth.
is good to the faithful.	in God's promises.
guides us with mercy.	in God's kindness.
waits for our returning.	in God's love.

In the above prayer, the author describes characteristics of God. Our tradition teaches us that we should follow in God's ways. This means, for example, that —

if God keeps promises, we, too, should keep promises;

if God is kind, we, too, should be kind.

Can you add to this list?

וּבְכֵן תֵּן פַּחְדְּךָ יְיָ אֱלֹהֵינוּ עַל כָּל־מַעֲשֶׂיךָ וְאֵימָתְךָ עַל־כָּל־מַה־שֶּׁבָּרָאתָ, וְיִירָאוּךָ כָּל־הַמַּעֲשִׂים וְיִשְׁתַּחֲווּ לְפָנֶיךָ כָּל־הַבְּרוּאִים, וְיֵעָשׂוּ כֻלָּם אֲגֻדָּה אַחַת לַעֲשׂוֹת רְצוֹנְךָ בְּלֵבָב שָׁלֵם.

וּבְכֵן תֵּן כָּבוֹד יְיָ לְעַמֶּךָ תְּהִלָּה לִירֵאֶיךָ וְתִקְוָה לְדוֹרְשֶׁיךָ וּפִתְחוֹן פֶּה לַמְיַחֲלִים לָךְ, שִׂמְחָה לְאַרְצֶךָ וְשָׂשׂוֹן לְעִירֶךָ וּצְמִיחַת קֶרֶן לְדָוִד עַבְדֶּךָ וַעֲרִיכַת נֵר לְבֶן־יִשַׁי מְשִׁיחֶךָ בִּמְהֵרָה בְיָמֵינוּ.

וּבְכֵן צַדִּיקִים יִרְאוּ וְיִשְׂמָחוּ וִישָׁרִים יַעֲלֹזוּ וַחֲסִידִים בְּרִנָּה יָגִילוּ, וְעוֹלָתָה תִּקְפָּץ־פִּיהָ וְכָל־הָרִשְׁעָה כֻּלָּהּ כְּעָשָׁן תִּכְלֶה כִּי תַעֲבִיר מֶמְשֶׁלֶת זָדוֹן מִן הָאָרֶץ.

בָּרוּךְ אַתָּה יְיָ הַמֶּלֶךְ הַקָּדוֹשׁ.

Let all creatures feel awe in Your presence and join together to follow Your will.

Grant honor to Your people and glory to all who have faith in You. Give hope to those who seek You, and confidence to those who trust in You. Grant joy to Israel and gladness to Jerusalem.

May the day come when all wickedness will end.

אַתָּה בְחַרְתָּנוּ מִכָּל־הָעַמִּים, אָהַבְתָּ אוֹתָנוּ וְרָצִיתָ בָּנוּ
וְרוֹמַמְתָּנוּ מִכָּל־הַלְּשׁוֹנוֹת וְקִדַּשְׁתָּנוּ בְּמִצְוֹתֶיךָ וְקֵרַבְתָּנוּ
מַלְכֵּנוּ לַעֲבוֹדָתֶךָ וְשִׁמְךָ הַגָּדוֹל וְהַקָּדוֹשׁ עָלֵינוּ קָרָאתָ.

וַתִּתֶּן־לָנוּ יְיָ אֱלֹהֵינוּ בְּאַהֲבָה אֶת־יוֹם (הַשַּׁבָּת הַזֶּה
וְאֶת־יוֹם) הַזִּכָּרוֹן הַזֶּה, (יוֹם זִכְרוֹן) תְּרוּעָה (בְּאַהֲבָה)
מִקְרָא קֹדֶשׁ זֵכֶר לִיצִיאַת מִצְרָיִם.

You have called us to Your service through the *mitzvot.*

Because You love us, You have given us [the *Shabbat* and] this Day of Remembering the sound of the *shofar.*

We say this only on *Shabbat.*

יִשְׂמְחוּ בְמַלְכוּתְךָ שׁוֹמְרֵי שַׁבָּת וְקוֹרְאֵי עֹנֶג. עַם מְקַדְּשֵׁי
שְׁבִיעִי כֻּלָּם יִשְׂבְּעוּ וְיִתְעַנְּגוּ מִטּוּבֶךָ. וְהַשְּׁבִיעִי רָצִיתָ בּוֹ
וְקִדַּשְׁתּוֹ, חֶמְדַּת יָמִים אוֹתוֹ קָרָאתָ זֵכֶר לְמַעֲשֵׂה בְרֵאשִׁית.

MALḤUYOT
GOD IS RULER

Some scholars tell us that autumn was the time when other people who lived in the Middle East had coronation festivals for their kings. *Rosh haShanah* became our yearly coronation festival for God.

In the days when the *maḥzor* was originally written, people could more easily picture God as a king because they lived under the rule of kings.

In traditional *maḥzorim,* God is referred to as King.

The *Aleinu* is the central prayer of the *Malḥuyot* (God is Ruler) Section of our *Rosh haShanah* prayers. It speaks of God as the Supreme Ruler of the universe. It was originally written for *Rosh haShanah* by the great talmudic rabbi, Rav, about 1600 years ago. It later became the concluding prayer for every Jewish service.

In this *maḥzor,* God is referred to as "Ruler" and not "King." Why do you think this was done?

Why is it better to have God instead of a person as our ruler?

The *Malḥuyot* section ends by declaring the oneness of God and the oneness of God's name. Yet, we think of God in many ways and use different names for God. For example, we call God the Source of Life, the All, and the One Who Is Everywhere. We also address God as our Rock and Shield, our Comforter and Helper. Although we each think of God in our own way and call God different names, God is One, the Force That Unifies All Life.

The *Aleinu* also expresses our hope for a time when all people, Jew and non-Jew, will live in a way that honors God. How do you picture a world in which everyone honors God?

A Thought on God, the Ruler

Malḥuyot teaches us that God cannot be the Supreme Ruler until we crown God. It is our actions in the world that make this happen.

We stand.

עָלֵינוּ לְשַׁבֵּחַ לַאֲדוֹן הַכֹּל, לָתֵת גְּדֻלָּה לְיוֹצֵר בְּרֵאשִׁית,
שֶׁלֹּא עָשָׂנוּ כְּגוֹיֵי הָאֲרָצוֹת וְלֹא שָׂמָנוּ כְּמִשְׁפְּחוֹת הָאֲדָמָה,
שֶׁלֹּא שָׂם חֶלְקֵנוּ כָּהֶם וְגוֹרָלֵנוּ כְּכָל־הֲמוֹנָם.

The leader (or all present) falls on his/her knees as did the High Priest in the days of the Temple.

וַאֲנַחְנוּ כּוֹרְעִים וּמִשְׁתַּחֲוִים וּמוֹדִים לִפְנֵי מֶלֶךְ מַלְכֵי
הַמְּלָכִים הַקָּדוֹשׁ בָּרוּךְ הוּא.

We are seated.

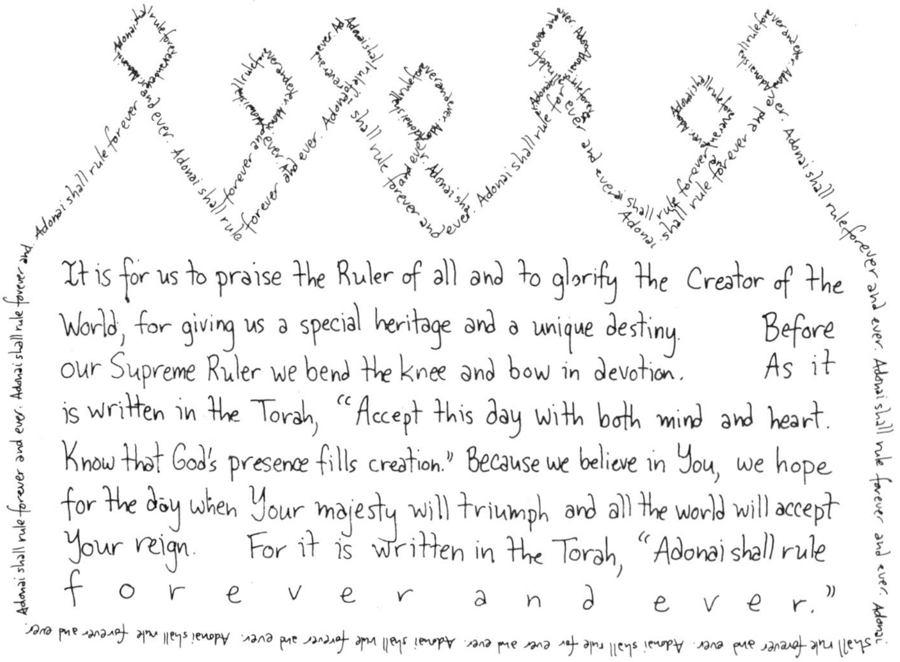
Adonai shall rule forever and ever.
It is for us to praise the Ruler of all and to glorify the Creator of the World, for giving us a special heritage and a unique destiny. Before our Supreme Ruler we bend the knee and bow in devotion. As it is written in the Torah, "Accept this day with both mind and heart. Know that God's presence fills creation." Because we believe in You, we hope for the day when Your majesty will triumph and all the world will accept Your reign. For it is written in the Torah, "Adonai shall rule forever and ever."

שֶׁהוּא נוֹטֶה שָׁמַיִם וְיוֹסֵד אָרֶץ וּמוֹשַׁב יְקָרוֹ בַּשָּׁמַיִם מִמַּעַל וּשְׁכִינַת עֻזּוֹ בְּגָבְהֵי מְרוֹמִים. הוּא אֱלֹהֵינוּ אֵין עוֹד. אֱמֶת מַלְכֵּנוּ אֶפֶס זוּלָתוֹ, כַּכָּתוּב בְּתוֹרָתוֹ: וְיָדַעְתָּ הַיּוֹם וַהֲשֵׁבֹתָ אֶל לְבָבֶךָ כִּי יְיָ הוּא הָאֱלֹהִים בַּשָּׁמַיִם מִמַּעַל וְעַל הָאָרֶץ מִתָּחַת, אֵין עוֹד.

כַּכָּתוּב בְּתוֹרָתֶךָ: יְיָ יִמְלֹךְ לְעֹלָם וָעֶד.
וְנֶאֱמַר: וְהָיָה יְיָ לְמֶלֶךְ עַל כָּל־הָאָרֶץ, בַּיּוֹם הַהוּא יִהְיֶה יְיָ אֶחָד וּשְׁמוֹ אֶחָד. וּבְתוֹרָתְךָ כָּתוּב לֵאמֹר: שְׁמַע יִשְׂרָאֵל יְיָ אֱלֹהֵינוּ יְיָ אֶחָד.

It is for us to praise the Ruler of all and to glorify the Creator of the world for giving us a special heritage and a unique destiny.

Before our Supreme Ruler we bend the knee and bow in devotion.

As it is written in the Torah, "Accept this day with both mind and heart. Know that God's presence fills all of creation."

Because we believe in You, we hope for the day when Your majesty will triumph and all the world will accept Your reign.

For it is written in the Torah, "*Adonai* shall rule for ever and ever" and "Hear, O Israel: The Lord our God, the Lord is One."

אֱלֹהֵינוּ וֵאלֹהֵי אֲבוֹתֵינוּ, מְלֹךְ עַל כָּל־הָעוֹלָם כֻּלּוֹ
בִּכְבוֹדֶךָ וְהִנָּשֵׂא עַל כָּל־הָאָרֶץ בִּיקָרֶךָ, וְהוֹפַע בַּהֲדַר גְּאוֹן
עֻזֶּךָ עַל כָּל־יוֹשְׁבֵי תֵבֵל אַרְצֶךָ. וְיֵדַע כָּל־פָּעוּל כִּי אַתָּה
פְעַלְתּוֹ וְיָבִין כָּל־יָצוּר כִּי אַתָּה יְצַרְתּוֹ, וְיֹאמַר כֹּל אֲשֶׁר
נְשָׁמָה בְאַפּוֹ: יְיָ אֱלֹהֵי יִשְׂרָאֵל מֶלֶךְ, וּמַלְכוּתוֹ בַּכֹּל מָשָׁלָה.
אֱלֹהֵינוּ וֵאלֹהֵי אֲבוֹתֵינוּ, (רְצֵה בִמְנוּחָתֵנוּ) קַדְּשֵׁנוּ בְּמִצְוֹתֶיךָ
וְתֵן חֶלְקֵנוּ בְּתוֹרָתֶךָ, שַׂבְּעֵנוּ מִטּוּבֶךָ וְשַׂמְּחֵנוּ בִּישׁוּעָתֶךָ,
(וְהַנְחִילֵנוּ יְיָ אֱלֹהֵינוּ בְּאַהֲבָה וּבְרָצוֹן שַׁבַּת קָדְשֶׁךָ וְיָנוּחוּ
בָהּ יִשְׂרָאֵל מְקַדְּשֵׁי שְׁמֶךָ) וְטַהֵר לִבֵּנוּ לְעָבְדְּךָ בֶּאֱמֶת, כִּי
אַתָּה אֱלֹהִים אֱמֶת וּדְבָרְךָ אֱמֶת וְקַיָּם לָעַד. בָּרוּךְ אַתָּה יְיָ
מֶלֶךְ עַל כָּל־הָאָרֶץ מְקַדֵּשׁ (הַשַּׁבָּת וְ)יִשְׂרָאֵל וְיוֹם הַזִּכָּרוֹן.

Our God and God of our ancestors, may every living form know that You have formed it. May every creature understand that You are Creator. May everything that breathes declare that You rule the world in glory.

Our God and God of our ancestors, [may our *Shabbat* rest be acceptable to You and] let Your *mitzvot* lead us to holy deeds and the study of Torah. Let us find happiness in Your blessings and joy in Your supporting power. Let our hearts be pure to serve You with sincerity, for You are a God of truth.

Blessed are You, *Adonai,* Ruler of the universe, who has made holy [the Sabbath,] the Jewish people and this Day of Remembering.

(The *shofar* is not sounded on *Shabbat*.)
We rise for the sounding of the *shofar*.

תְּקִיעָה שְׁבָרִים תְּרוּעָה תְּקִיעָה

תְּקִיעָה שְׁבָרִים תְּקִיעָה

תְּקִיעָה תְּרוּעָה תְּקִיעָה

הַיּוֹם הֲרַת עוֹלָם. הַיּוֹם יַעֲמִיד בַּמִּשְׁפָּט כָּל־יְצוּרֵי עוֹלָמִים אִם כְּבָנִים אִם כַּעֲבָדִים. אִם כְּבָנִים, רַחֲמֵנוּ כְּרַחֵם אָב עַל בָּנִים. וְאִם כַּעֲבָדִים, עֵינֵינוּ לְךָ תְלוּיוֹת עַד שֶׁתְּחָנֵּנוּ וְתוֹצִיא כָאוֹר מִשְׁפָּטֵנוּ, אָיֹם קָדוֹשׁ.

Today is the birthday of the world! Today all creation stands before You to be judged. If we are Your children, treat us with a parent's love. If we are Your servants, treat us with kindness, for You are the Holy One.

This is not said on *Shabbat*.

אֲרֶשֶׁת שְׂפָתֵינוּ יֶעֱרַב לְפָנֶיךָ, אֵל רָם וְנִשָּׂא, מֵבִין וּמַאֲזִין מַבִּיט וּמַקְשִׁיב לְקוֹל תְּקִיעָתֵנוּ, וּתְקַבֵּל בְּרַחֲמִים וּבְרָצוֹן סֵדֶר מַלְכֻיּוֹתֵינוּ.

We are seated.

ZIḤRONOT

GOD REMEMBERS

In the Torah, *Rosh haShanah* is called *Yom haZikaron*, the Day of Remembering.

We call *Rosh haShanah* the Day of Remembering because we pray that God will remember to write us in the Book of Life for a good year.

Imagine that you have just finished the school year or returned home from camp. What could you have done differently so your friends, teachers or counselors would have a better memory of you? What good memories will your friends, teachers or counselors have of you?

What do you want God to remember about you this past year?

These words, by a girl named Ilona, tell where and when she feels close to God.

> "When you go on a plane, you're nearer to God — because you can see the world, a lot of it, more than you see when you're on land, and you can realize how big the whole universe is, and people, they're not even visible. The cars are moving, and you know that people are in them, driving, but you can't see them. That's why you have to stop yourself (once in a while, at least) and say: Are you remembering God, and are you looking at the big picture, the way He does, or are you inside a car, and all you're thinking of is where you want to go, right away (and watch out, anyone else!)?"

Is there a place where you remember God the most and think of the "big picture"?

אֱלֹהֵינוּ וֵאלֹהֵי אֲבוֹתֵינוּ, זָכְרֵנוּ בְּזִכְרוֹן טוֹב לְפָנֶיךָ וּפָקְדֵנוּ בִּפְקֻדַּת יְשׁוּעָה וְרַחֲמִים מִשְּׁמֵי שְׁמֵי קֶדֶם. וּזְכָר־לָנוּ יְיָ אֱלֹהֵינוּ אֶת־הַבְּרִית וְאֶת־הַחֶסֶד וְאֶת־הַשְּׁבוּעָה אֲשֶׁר נִשְׁבַּעְתָּ לְאַבְרָהָם אָבִינוּ בְּהַר הַמּוֹרִיָּה. בָּרוּךְ אַתָּה יְיָ זוֹכֵר הַבְּרִית.

Our God and God of our ancestors, remember Your covenant with our people which began with Abraham and Sarah. Blessed are You, *Adonai,* Who remembers the covenant.

(The *shofar* is not sounded on *Shabbat*.)
We rise for the sounding of the *shofar*.

תְּקִיעָה שְׁבָרִים תְּרוּעָה תְּקִיעָה

תְּקִיעָה שְׁבָרִים תְּקִיעָה

תְּקִיעָה תְּרוּעָה תְּקִיעָה

SHOFAROT

The Drum

The Magid of Dubna told the following story to teach people the importance of understanding and not just hearing the *shofar*'s blasts:

Once a peasant came to town just when a fire had broken out. He was surprised to see a number of people blowing trumpets and beating drums and then others running out with axes, shovels and pails.

He asked a small child why a musical band was playing in the town square. The child replied, "The trumpeting and drum-beating is to put out the fire." The peasant quickly went into a nearby shop to purchase a drum to take back to his village.

A year later, a fire broke out in his village. The peasant announced that no one needed to fight the fire, for his drum would quench the flames.

As he beat his drum, the fire quickly spread. Seeing that their village would soon be destroyed, the townspeople started shouting: "You idiot! The drum is only meant as an alarm to alert us to danger. We then need to do something about the fire if we are to save ourselves and our village."

And so it is with the hearing of the *shofar*. The *shofar* can only alert us to the need for change. *Only we can change and improve ourselves.*

R*osh haShanah* is called *Yom T'ruah* — the Day of Sounding the *Shofar*.

The *shofar* was sounded at Mt. Sinai when the Israelites were given the Ten Commandments. It was blown in ancient times to announce the coming of the king or the appearance of the new moon. The *shofar* even called people together for special meetings and signaled armies to go to war. Today the *shofar* calls us to review our deeds and to turn to God. The *shofar* also calls us to stand together as Jews and to work hard to make a better world for all peoples.

Some think the *t'kiah* sounds like an alarm, the *sh'varim* sounds like wailing and the *t'ruah* like broken sobs. Listen and see if you agree.

Some say a *shofar* is curved in shape to show that we bow before God. Others say it is this way so we may bend our hearts towards God.

A *shofar* is usually made from a ram's horn because it reminds God that Abraham was willing to sacrifice his son. God stopped the sacrifice and a ram was substituted for Isaac. Therefore the *shofar* also shows God's mercy.

The *mitzvah* is to **hear** the *shofar*, not to blow it. This is fortunate because blowing the *shofar* is very difficult. Have you ever tried?

When we hear the *shofar*, it is easy to say, "I'll be better next year." But it is harder to work at just being a little better in day-to-day living. How can we keep the memory of the sound of the *shofar* with us?

"**W**here those who do *teshuvah* stand, the completely righteous cannot stand." The Sages teach that the one who does *teshuvah* is honored because that person had to work hard to change.

A Thought on Hearing the *Shofar*

The sounds of the *shofar* are like a secret language between us and God. Without using words, our prayers reach God Who knows what is in each of our hearts.

Our God and God of our ancestors, sound the great *shofar* for our freedom. Raise high the banner to gather the scattered and troubled of our people and unite Jews from around the world.

Lead us with joyful song to Zion, Your holy city, to Jerusalem, the site of Your ancient Temple, where our ancestors brought offerings to You as commanded by the Torah.

Blessed are You, *Adonai,* who hears with love the *shofar* sounded by the Jewish people.

אֱלֹהֵֽינוּ וֵאלֹהֵי אֲבוֹתֵֽינוּ, תְּקַע בְּשׁוֹפָר גָּדוֹל לְחֵרוּתֵֽנוּ,
וְשָׂא נֵס לְקַבֵּץ גָּלֻיּוֹתֵֽינוּ וְקָרֵב פְּזוּרֵֽינוּ מִבֵּין הַגּוֹיִם
וּנְפוּצוֹתֵֽינוּ כַּנֵּס מִיַּרְכְּתֵי־אָֽרֶץ. וַהֲבִיאֵֽנוּ לְצִיּוֹן עִירְךָ
בְּרִנָּה וְלִירוּשָׁלַֽיִם בֵּית מִקְדָּשְׁךָ בְּשִׂמְחַת עוֹלָם, שֶׁשָּׁם עָשׂוּ
אֲבוֹתֵֽינוּ לְפָנֶֽיךָ אֶת־עוֹלוֹתֵיהֶם וְאֶת־זִבְחֵי שַׁלְמֵיהֶם.

כִּי אַתָּה שׁוֹמֵֽעַ קוֹל שׁוֹפָר וּמַאֲזִין תְּרוּעָה וְאֵין דּֽוֹמֶה לָּךְ.
בָּרוּךְ אַתָּה יְיָ שׁוֹמֵֽעַ קוֹל תְּרוּעַת עַמּוֹ יִשְׂרָאֵל בְּרַחֲמִים.

(The *shofar* is not sounded on *Shabbat.*)
We rise for the sounding of the *shofar.*

תְּקִיעָה שְׁבָרִים תְּרוּעָה תְּקִיעָה

תְּקִיעָה שְׁבָרִים תְּקִיעָה

תְּקִיעָה תְּרוּעָה תְּקִיעָה

We are seated.

רְצֵה יְיָ אֱלֹהֵינוּ בְּעַמְּךָ יִשְׂרָאֵל וּבִתְפִלָּתָם וְהָשֵׁב
אֶת־הָעֲבוֹדָה לִדְבִיר בֵּיתֶךָ וּתְפִלָּתָם בְּאַהֲבָה תְקַבֵּל
בְּרָצוֹן וּתְהִי לְרָצוֹן תָּמִיד עֲבוֹדַת יִשְׂרָאֵל עַמֶּךָ. וְתֶחֱזֶינָה
עֵינֵינוּ בְּשׁוּבְךָ לְצִיּוֹן בְּרַחֲמִים. בָּרוּךְ אַתָּה יְיָ הַמַּחֲזִיר
שְׁכִינָתוֹ לְצִיּוֹן.

Accept the prayer of Your people and look on us with favor. May we witness the return of Your glory to Zion.

We thank You for our lives which are in Your care. You are the Source of never-ending lovingkindness.

מוֹדִים אֲנַחְנוּ לָךְ שָׁאַתָּה הוּא יְיָ אֱלֹהֵינוּ וֵאלֹהֵי אֲבוֹתֵינוּ
לְעוֹלָם וָעֶד, צוּר חַיֵּינוּ מָגֵן יִשְׁעֵנוּ אַתָּה הוּא. לְדוֹר וָדוֹר
נוֹדֶה לְּךָ וּנְסַפֵּר תְּהִלָּתֶךָ עַל חַיֵּינוּ הַמְּסוּרִים בְּיָדֶךָ וְעַל
נִשְׁמוֹתֵינוּ הַפְּקוּדוֹת לָךְ וְעַל נִסֶּיךָ שֶׁבְּכָל־יוֹם עִמָּנוּ וְעַל
נִפְלְאוֹתֶיךָ וְטוֹבוֹתֶיךָ שֶׁבְּכָל־עֵת עֶרֶב וָבֹקֶר וְצָהֳרָיִם. הַטּוֹב
כִּי לֹא כָלוּ רַחֲמֶיךָ וְהַמְרַחֵם כִּי לֹא תַמּוּ חֲסָדֶיךָ מֵעוֹלָם
קִוִּינוּ לָךְ.

וְעַל כֻּלָּם יִתְבָּרַךְ וְיִתְרוֹמַם שִׁמְךָ מַלְכֵּנוּ תָּמִיד לְעוֹלָם וָעֶד.

May we look forward to a good year of life.

וּכְתֹב לְחַיִּים טוֹבִים כָּל־בְּנֵי בְרִיתֶךָ.

Blessed are You, *Adonai,* Who deserves our praise.

וְכֹל הַחַיִּים יוֹדוּךָ סֶּלָה וִיהַלְלוּ אֶת־שִׁמְךָ בֶּאֱמֶת הָאֵל יְשׁוּעָתֵנוּ
וְעֶזְרָתֵנוּ סֶלָה. בָּרוּךְ אַתָּה יְיָ הַטּוֹב שִׁמְךָ וּלְךָ נָאֶה לְהוֹדוֹת.

The poem "Birdsong" was written in 1941 by a child in the Terezin concentration camp. We do not even know his or her name. We do know from the words of the poem that she or he saw beyond the misery and the cruelty of Terezin. The author of "Birdsong" inspires us to look for beauty in the world and appreciate how precious life is.

BIRDSONG

He doesn't know the world at all
Who stays in his nest and doesn't go out,
He doesn't know what birds know best
Nor what I want to sing about,
That the world is full of loveliness.

When dewdrops sparkle in the grass
And earth's aflood with morning light
A blackbird sings upon a bush
To greet the dawning after night
Then I know how fine it is to live.

Hey, try to open up your heart
To beauty; go to the woods someday
And weave a wreath of memory there
Then if the tears obscure your way
You'll know how wonderful it is to be alive.

אֱלֹהֵינוּ וֵאלֹהֵי אֲבוֹתֵינוּ, בָּרְכֵנוּ בַבְּרָכָה הַמְשֻׁלֶּשֶׁת בַּתּוֹרָה
הַכְּתוּבָה עַל יְדֵי מֹשֶׁה עַבְדֶּךָ, הָאֲמוּרָה מִפִּי אַהֲרֹן וּבָנָיו
כֹּהֲנִים עַם קְדוֹשֶׁךָ, כָּאָמוּר:

Leader:	Congregation answers:
יְבָרֶכְךָ יְיָ וְיִשְׁמְרֶךָ.	כֵּן יְהִי רָצוֹן.
יָאֵר יְיָ פָּנָיו אֵלֶיךָ וִיחֻנֶּךָּ.	כֵּן יְהִי רָצוֹן.
יִשָּׂא יְיָ פָּנָיו אֵלֶיךָ וְיָשֵׂם לְךָ שָׁלוֹם.	כֵּן יְהִי רָצוֹן.

God of our ancestors, bless us with the threefold blessing recited by the priests of old:

May *Adonai* bless and protect you;
May *Adonai* shine upon you with graciousness;
May *Adonai* look upon you with favor and grant you peace.

שִׂים שָׁלוֹם בָּעוֹלָם, טוֹבָה וּבְרָכָה חֵן וָחֶסֶד וְרַחֲמִים
עָלֵינוּ וְעַל כָּל־יִשְׂרָאֵל עַמֶּךָ. בָּרְכֵנוּ אָבִינוּ כֻּלָּנוּ כְּאֶחָד
בְּאוֹר פָּנֶיךָ, כִּי בְאוֹר פָּנֶיךָ נָתַתָּ לָּנוּ יְיָ אֱלֹהֵינוּ תּוֹרַת
חַיִּים וְאַהֲבַת חֶסֶד וּצְדָקָה וּבְרָכָה וְרַחֲמִים וְחַיִּים וְשָׁלוֹם.
וְטוֹב בְּעֵינֶיךָ לְבָרֵךְ אֶת־עַמְּךָ יִשְׂרָאֵל בְּכָל־עֵת
וּבְכָל־שָׁעָה בִּשְׁלוֹמֶךָ.

Let peace, prosperity, happiness, and lovingkindness come to our world, to us, and to all the Jewish people. Bless us all, Holy One, with Your light, for by that light You have given the Torah to guide us. May it please You to bless the Jewish people in every season and at all times with goodness and peace.

בְּסֵפֶר חַיִּים בְּרָכָה וְשָׁלוֹם וּפַרְנָסָה טוֹבָה נִזָּכֵר וְנִכָּתֵב
לְפָנֶיךָ אֲנַחְנוּ וְכָל־עַמְּךָ בֵּית יִשְׂרָאֵל לְחַיִּים טוֹבִים וּלְשָׁלוֹם.

May we and all the Jewish people be remembered and recorded in Your book for a good and peaceful life.

Praised are You, *Adonai,* Source of peace.

B'seifer ḥayim b'raḥah v'shalom ufarnasah tovah, nizaḥer v'nikatev l'faneḥa, anaḥnu v'ḥol amḥa beit Yisrael, l'ḥayim tovim ul'shalom.

Grant peace, happiness and blessing to the world.
Bless us all with Your light which teaches us Torah and leads us to

PEACE

The ark is opened and we rise.

הַיּוֹם תְּאַמְּצֵנוּ. אָמֵן.

הַיּוֹם תְּבָרְכֵנוּ. אָמֵן.

הַיּוֹם תְּגַדְּלֵנוּ. אָמֵן.

הַיּוֹם תִּדְרְשֵׁנוּ לְטוֹבָה. אָמֵן.

הַיּוֹם תִּכְתְּבֵנוּ לְחַיִּים טוֹבִים. אָמֵן.

On This Day

give us strength.
bless us.
help us grow.
write us in Your Book of Life.
accept our prayers.

AMEN

Hayom t'amtzeinu. *Amen.*
Hayom t'varḥeinu. *Amen.*
Hayom t'gadleinu. *Amen.*
Hayom tidr'sheinu l'tovah. *Amen.*
Hayom tiḥt'veinu l'ḥayim tovim. *Amen.*

The ark is closed and we are seated.

בָּרוּךְ אַתָּה יְיָ עוֹשֵׂה הַשָּׁלוֹם.

Praised are You, *Adonai,* Source of peace.

1
On this day
strengthen us.
bless us.
bring us joy.
remember us for good.
hear our cries.
answer our prayers.
judge us kindly.
show Your love.

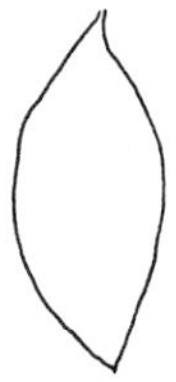

Today is the birthday of the world! Today all creation stands before You to be judged. If we are Your children, treat us with a parent's love. If we are Your servants, treat us with kindness. For You are the Holy One.

הַיּוֹם הֲרַת עוֹלָם. הַיּוֹם יַעֲמִיד בַּמִּשְׁפָּט כָּל־יְצוּרֵי
עוֹלָמִים אִם כְּבָנִים אִם כַּעֲבָדִים. אִם כְּבָנִים, רַחֲמֵנוּ
כְּרַחֵם אָב עַל בָּנִים. וְאִם כַּעֲבָדִים, עֵינֵינוּ לְךָ תְלוּיוֹת
עַד שֶׁתְּחָנֵּנוּ וְתוֹצִיא כָאוֹר מִשְׁפָּטֵנוּ, אָיֹם קָדוֹשׁ.

Some Thoughts About *Rosh haShanah*

***R**osh haShanah* marks the birthday of the world. In what ways do we celebrate *Rosh haShanah* like a birthday party? How is it different?

How is *Rosh haShanah* unlike the secular New Year celebration? Is there anything similar about the way we observe these two new years?

According to a Jewish tradition, the world began with the new moon on *Rosh haShanah*. The first day of creation began at sunset, as it says in the Torah, "...there was evening and there was morning on the first day." This is why on the Jewish calendar, every new day begins at sunset.

"...**A**nd on the first day of *Tishrei* is a *rosh* (head) *hashanah* for years." One teaching is that *Tishrei* is not just the beginning of a new calendar but the "head and nerve center, setting the pace for the entire year." Because it is a month of beginnings, each thought and each act is then that much more important.

The Jewish calendar is full of days to remember and festivals to celebrate. Each holiday is seen as a meeting point with God. What do we do with God on this holiday that is different from what we do on other holidays?

אֵין כֵּאלֹהֵינוּ, אֵין כַּאדוֹנֵינוּ, אֵין כְּמַלְכֵּנוּ, אֵין כְּמוֹשִׁיעֵנוּ.

מִי כֵאלֹהֵינוּ, מִי כַאדוֹנֵינוּ, מִי כְמַלְכֵּנוּ, מִי כְמוֹשִׁיעֵנוּ.

נוֹדֶה לֵאלֹהֵינוּ, נוֹדֶה לַאדוֹנֵינוּ, נוֹדֶה לְמַלְכֵּנוּ, נוֹדֶה לְמוֹשִׁיעֵנוּ.

בָּרוּךְ אֱלֹהֵינוּ, בָּרוּךְ אֲדוֹנֵינוּ, בָּרוּךְ מַלְכֵּנוּ, בָּרוּךְ מוֹשִׁיעֵנוּ.

אַתָּה הוּא אֱלֹהֵינוּ, אַתָּה הוּא אֲדוֹנֵינוּ, אַתָּה הוּא מַלְכֵּנוּ,
אַתָּה הוּא מוֹשִׁיעֵנוּ.

None compares to You
Our God
Our Lord
Ruler
and Deliverer.

Let us praise You for You are
Our God
Our Lord
Ruler
and Deliverer.

Ein keloheinu, Ein kadoneinu, Ein k'malkeinu, Ein k'moshi'einu.

Mi keiloheinu, Mi kadoneinu, Mi k'malkeinu, Mi k'moshi'einu.

Nodeh leloheinu, Nodeh ladoneinu, Nodeh l'malkeinu,
Nodeh l'moshi'einu.

Baruḥ Eloheinu, Baruḥ Adoneinu. Baruḥ Malkeinu, Baruḥ Moshi'einu.

Atah hu Eloheinu, Atah hu Adoneinu, Atah hu Malkeinu,
Atah hu Moshi'einu.

In the *Aleinu* prayer, we acknowledge that God is the Source of creation as well as order and unity in the world.

We rise.

עָלֵֽינוּ לְשַׁבֵּֽחַ לַאֲדוֹן הַכֹּל, לָתֵת גְּדֻלָּה לְיוֹצֵר בְּרֵאשִׁית,
שֶׁלֹּא עָשָֽׂנוּ כְּגוֹיֵי הָאֲרָצוֹת וְלֹא שָׂמָֽנוּ כְּמִשְׁפְּחוֹת הָאֲדָמָה,
שֶׁלֹּא שָׂם חֶלְקֵֽנוּ כָּהֶם וְגוֹרָלֵֽנוּ כְּכָל־הֲמוֹנָם. וַאֲנַֽחְנוּ
כּוֹרְעִים וּמִשְׁתַּחֲוִים וּמוֹדִים לִפְנֵי מֶֽלֶךְ מַלְכֵי הַמְּלָכִים
הַקָּדוֹשׁ בָּרוּךְ הוּא, שֶׁהוּא נוֹטֶה שָׁמַֽיִם וְיוֹסֵד אָֽרֶץ וּמוֹשַׁב
יְקָרוֹ בַּשָּׁמַֽיִם מִמַּֽעַל וּשְׁכִינַת עֻזּוֹ בְּגָבְהֵי מְרוֹמִים. הוּא
אֱלֹהֵֽינוּ אֵין עוֹד. אֱמֶת מַלְכֵּֽנוּ אֶֽפֶס זוּלָתוֹ, כַּכָּתוּב
בְּתוֹרָתוֹ: וְיָדַעְתָּ הַיּוֹם וַהֲשֵׁבֹתָ אֶל לְבָבֶֽךָ כִּי יְיָ הוּא
הָאֱלֹהִים בַּשָּׁמַֽיִם מִמַּֽעַל וְעַל הָאָֽרֶץ מִתָּֽחַת, אֵין עוֹד.

Aleinu l'shabei'aḥ la'adon hakol,
latet g'dulah l'yotzer b'reishit.
Shelo asanu k'goyei ha'aratzot,
v'lo samanu k'mishp'ḥot ha'adamah.
Shelo sam ḥelkeinu kahem,
v'goraleinu k'ḥol hamonam.

Va'anaḥnu korim umishtaḥavim umodim,
lifnei Meleḥ malḥei ham'laḥim,
hakadosh baruḥ hu.

It is for us to praise the Ruler of all and to glorify the Creator of the world for giving us a special heritage and a unique destiny.

Before our Supreme Ruler we bend the knee and bow in devotion.

As it is written in the Torah, "Accept this day with both mind and heart. Know that God's presence fills creation."

Because we believe in You, we hope for the day when Your majesty will triumph and all will work to mend the world and live according to Your ways. For it is written in the Torah, "*Adonai* shall rule for ever and ever."

עַל כֵּן נְקַוֶּה לְּךָ יְיָ אֱלֹהֵינוּ לִרְאוֹת מְהֵרָה בְּתִפְאֶרֶת
עֻזֶּךָ, לְהַעֲבִיר גִּלּוּלִים מִן הָאָרֶץ וְהָאֱלִילִים כָּרוֹת
יִכָּרֵתוּן, לְתַקֵּן עוֹלָם בְּמַלְכוּת שַׁדַּי וְכָל־בְּנֵי בָשָׂר יִקְרְאוּ
בִשְׁמֶךָ, לְהַפְנוֹת אֵלֶיךָ כָּל־רִשְׁעֵי־אָרֶץ. יַכִּירוּ וְיֵדְעוּ
כָּל־יוֹשְׁבֵי תֵבֵל כִּי לְךָ תִּכְרַע כָּל־בֶּרֶךְ תִּשָּׁבַע כָּל־לָשׁוֹן.
לְפָנֶיךָ יְיָ אֱלֹהֵינוּ יִכְרְעוּ וְיִפֹּלוּ וְלִכְבוֹד שִׁמְךָ יְקָר יִתֵּנוּ,
וִיקַבְּלוּ כֻלָּם אֶת־עֹל מַלְכוּתֶךָ וְתִמְלֹךְ עֲלֵיהֶם מְהֵרָה
לְעוֹלָם וָעֶד, כִּי הַמַּלְכוּת שֶׁלְּךָ הִיא וּלְעוֹלְמֵי עַד תִּמְלֹךְ
בְּכָבוֹד, כַּכָּתוּב בְּתוֹרָתֶךָ: יְיָ יִמְלֹךְ לְעֹלָם וָעֶד.
וְנֶאֱמַר: וְהָיָה יְיָ לְמֶלֶךְ עַל כָּל־הָאָרֶץ, בַּיּוֹם הַהוּא יִהְיֶה
יְיָ אֶחָד וּשְׁמוֹ אֶחָד.

"We must learn to live together as brothers or we will perish together like fools." (Martin Luther King)

V'ne'emar, v'hayah Adonai l'Meleḥ al kol ha'aretz.
Bayom hahu yih'yeh Adonai eḥad ush'mo eḥad.

MOURNER'S *KADDISH*

Mourners and those observing a memorial day rise and say:

יִתְגַּדַּל וְיִתְקַדַּשׁ שְׁמֵהּ רַבָּא בְּעָלְמָא דִּי בְרָא כִרְעוּתֵהּ,
וְיַמְלִיךְ מַלְכוּתֵהּ בְּחַיֵּיכוֹן וּבְיוֹמֵיכוֹן וּבְחַיֵּי דְכָל־בֵּית
יִשְׂרָאֵל בַּעֲגָלָא וּבִזְמַן קָרִיב, וְאִמְרוּ אָמֵן.

The congregation says together with the mourners:

יְהֵא שְׁמֵהּ רַבָּא מְבָרַךְ לְעָלַם וּלְעָלְמֵי עָלְמַיָּא.

Y'hai shmai rabbah m'varaḥ l'olam u'l'olmei almay'ya.

Mourners continue:

יִתְבָּרַךְ וְיִשְׁתַּבַּח וְיִתְפָּאַר וְיִתְרוֹמַם וְיִתְנַשֵּׂא וְיִתְהַדַּר
וְיִתְעַלֶּה וְיִתְהַלַּל שְׁמֵהּ דְּקֻדְשָׁא

Congregation together with mourners:

בְּרִיךְ הוּא.

B'riḥ hu.

לְעֵלָּא לְעֵלָּא מִכָּל־בִּרְכָתָא וְשִׁירָתָא תֻּשְׁבְּחָתָא וְנֶחֱמָתָא
דַּאֲמִירָן בְּעָלְמָא, וְאִמְרוּ אָמֵן.

יְהֵא שְׁלָמָא רַבָּא מִן שְׁמַיָּא וְחַיִּים עָלֵינוּ וְעַל כָּל־יִשְׂרָאֵל,
וְאִמְרוּ אָמֵן.

עוֹשֶׂה שָׁלוֹם בִּמְרוֹמָיו הוּא יַעֲשֶׂה שָׁלוֹם עָלֵינוּ וְעַל
כָּל־יִשְׂרָאֵל, וְאִמְרוּ אָמֵן.

The Traveler

Due to a terrible storm, a merchant ship had been blown off course. It would be days before it could safely dock. The cook sadly reported to the captain that their food supplies were almost gone. The captain then announced that he would ask a wealthy merchant on board to help, for he knew that the merchant was carrying crates of dried dates and figs as well as olives from the Holy Land. Surely he would sell them some supplies for a reasonable price.

The captain was shocked and disappointed when his request was denied. "Why should I give you some of my fruit," growled the merchant, "when I can get a higher price when we dock?" With a heavy heart, the captain went to tell the cook that the hungry people on board would not be fed.

The cook surprised the captain by announcing that he wanted a chance to change the merchant's mind. "Meet me at that miser's cabin in five minutes," he declared.

When the captain arrived, the cook knocked at the merchant's cabin door. "What is it? Why are you bothering me? I told you I won't share any of my supplies!" the merchant grumbled.

"Please come with us," said the cook. "There is something we must show you in the ship's hold." Thinking there could be a problem with the goods that he stored there, the merchant agreed to follow them. When they arrived, the cook took a borer from behind a box and began to make a hole in the ship's hold. The merchant began screaming in alarm, "What are you doing? You are acting crazy!"

"It's no concern of yours," said the cook, "I'm just making a hole under my spot in the boat. I'd rather die now than starve before we reach our destination."

"But your hole will flood the boat and soon we'll all die," cried the merchant.

"I don't care about you," stated the cook, "I only care about my own needs." With that remark, he continued his drilling.

At last the merchant understood. "I see what you're trying to teach me. We're all travelers on the same boat. What each of us does affects us all. Here are my crates, there's plenty of food to share. We can all reach port together safe and sound."

אֲדוֹן עוֹלָם אֲשֶׁר מָלַךְ בְּטֶרֶם כָּל־יְצִיר נִבְרָא.
לְעֵת נַעֲשָׂה בְחֶפְצוֹ כֹּל אֲזַי מֶלֶךְ שְׁמוֹ נִקְרָא.
וְאַחֲרֵי כִּכְלוֹת הַכֹּל לְבַדּוֹ יִמְלֹךְ נוֹרָא.
וְהוּא הָיָה וְהוּא הֹוֶה וְהוּא יִהְיֶה בְּתִפְאָרָה.
וְהוּא אֶחָד וְאֵין שֵׁנִי לְהַמְשִׁיל לוֹ לְהַחְבִּירָה.
בְּלִי רֵאשִׁית בְּלִי תַכְלִית וְלוֹ הָעֹז וְהַמִּשְׂרָה.
וְהוּא אֵלִי וְחַי גּוֹאֲלִי וְצוּר חֶבְלִי בְּעֵת צָרָה.
וְהוּא נִסִּי וּמָנוֹס לִי מְנָת כּוֹסִי בְּיוֹם אֶקְרָא.
בְּיָדוֹ אַפְקִיד רוּחִי בְּעֵת אִישַׁן וְאָעִירָה.
וְעִם רוּחִי גְּוִיָּתִי יְיָ לִי וְלֹא אִירָא.

God ruled before the world came to be
and will rule at the end of time.
Our days and nights are in God's care.
Because we trust in God, we have no fear.

לְשָׁנָה טוֹבָה תִּכָּתֵבוּ.

May you be recorded for a good new year!

A Thought — Ten Days For Changing

Rosh haShanah begins the Ten Days of *Teshuvah* (which means "returning"). Between *Rosh haShanah* and *Yom Kippur*, we try to get back on the right track. One way we do this is to pray to God to forgive us for our wrongdoings. God, however, cannot forgive us for the bad things we've done to family and friends. We need to say we're sorry to them directly and ask their forgiveness. We must also promise not to hurt or wrong them again.

Between now and *Yom Kippur* think about to whom you want to say you are sorry and what you want to say. Then do it! You and they will then feel good inside.

May this year bring you everything good!

Thoughts on *Teshuvah*

On *Yom Kippur*, we acknowledge that we have not been able to fully turn from our bad ways. We turn to God for mercy and ask for a clean slate so that we can begin again. This is called doing *teshuvah*.

***T**eshuvah* means returning to the right path. It means not just a change of heart but a change of actions as well.

There are four steps to doing *teshuvah:*

- admit that what was done was wrong.
- feel sorry about it.
- ask forgiveness.
- promise not to do it again.

How can you know if you are sincere in your *teshuvah?* The answer is that if you have the opportunity to do the same thing, you will not do it again. Can you think of a time you did something wrong but did not do it again when you had the chance?

The Holy One said, "My hands reach out to all who ask for forgiveness. If one comes towards Me, I will go towards that person."

יום כפור

YOM KIPPUR
SERVICE

BEFORE *YOM KIPPUR*

Kol Nidrei is the evening service with which *Yom Kippur* begins. It takes its name from the opening prayer of the service. The last meal before the fast must be eaten well before sunset so that we can get to synagogue on time. To avoid headaches during the fast, it is recommended that alcohol and caffeine beverages not be part of this meal and that carbohydrates be plentiful to make the fast easier.

Before going to synagogue, *Yahrzeit* (memorial) candles are lit for deceased relatives. Then, holiday candles are lit with the following blessings:

בָּרוּךְ אַתָּה יְיָ אֱלֹהֵינוּ מֶלֶךְ הָעוֹלָם אֲשֶׁר קִדְּשָׁנוּ
בְּמִצְוֹתָיו וְצִוָּנוּ לְהַדְלִיק נֵר שֶׁל (שַׁבָּת וְשֶׁל) יוֹם הַכִּפּוּרִים.

Baruḥ atah Adonai Eloheinu Meleḥ ha'olam asher kid'deshanu b'mitzvotav v'tzivanu l'hadlik ner shel (Shabbat v'shel) Yom haKippurim.

We praise You, *Adonai* our God, Ruler of the Universe, Who makes us holy by Your *mitzvot* and commands us to light the [Sabbath and] *Yom Kippur* lights.

בָּרוּךְ אַתָּה יְיָ אֱלֹהֵינוּ מֶלֶךְ הָעוֹלָם שֶׁהֶחֱיָנוּ וְקִיְּמָנוּ
וְהִגִּיעָנוּ לַזְּמַן הַזֶּה.

Baruḥ atah Adonai Eloheinu Meleḥ ha-olam sheheḥeyanu v'ki'yemanu v'higi'anu lazman hazeh.

We praise You, *Adonai* our God, Ruler of the Universe, who has kept us alive and well so that we can celebrate this special time.

Some people cover their tables with a white cloth and wear white clothing as a symbol of purity. Some also refrain from wearing leather shoes, as is dictated in the *Mishnah*.

It is also customary to bless the children in the family. The traditional blessings are:

For girls:

יְשִׂימֵךְ אֱלֹהִים כְּשָׂרָה,
רִבְקָה, לֵאָה וְרָחֵל.

Y'simeiḥ Elohim k'Sarah,
Rivkah, Le'ah v'Raḥel.

May you be like Sarah, Rebecca, Leah and Rachel.

For boys:

יְשִׂימְךָ אֱלֹהִים
כְּאֶפְרַיִם וְכִמְנַשֶּׁה.

Y'simḥa Elohim
k'Efrayim v'ḥiM'nasheh.

May you be like Ephraim and Menasseh.

It is also appropriate for parents to add their own wishes and blessings.

Parents conclude blessing all children with the threefold blessing:

יְבָרֶכְךָ יְיָ וְיִשְׁמְרֶךָ.
Y'vareḥeḥa Adonai v'yish'mereḥa.

יָאֵר יְיָ פָּנָיו אֵלֶיךָ וִיחֻנֶּךָּ.
Ya'er Adonai panav eileḥa viḥuneka.

יִשָּׂא יְיָ פָּנָיו אֵלֶיךָ
וְיָשֵׂם לְךָ שָׁלוֹם.
Yisa Adonai panav eileḥa
v'yasem l'ḥa shalom.

May *Adonai* bless and protect you.
May *Adonai* shine upon you with graciousness.
May *Adonai* look upon you with favor and grant you peace.

Thoughts in Preparation for *Yom Kippur*

***Y**om Kippur* is called *Shabbat Shabbaton* (the Sabbath of Sabbaths) to tell us that it is the most holy of all days.

If you've ever been in a long race, you know how much energy it takes. *Yom Kippur* is like a long race that requires great energy and concentration. We pray almost non-stop to ask for forgiveness.

Why do adults fast on *Yom Kippur*?

- to realize how much we depend on God;
- to put aside our body's need for food and concentrate on improving our heart;
- to show that we are all equal and have the same needs.

The *Yom Kippur* fast is from sunset until dark the following day.

Children do not fast on *Yom Kippur* until they are of age (boys at 13, girls at 12). However, a year or two before, children can begin preparing themselves to fast by not eating for part of the day. If you are not old enough to fast, you can eat a little less food than you normally do or at least not eat desserts or snack foods. Talk to your parents first about this.

When there was a cholera epidemic in 1848, Rabbi Israel Salanter ate a roll in front of his congregation on the day of *Yom Kippur*. This was so that they would see and follow his example. We are to "live by the commandments," not die by them.

The service for *Yom Kippur* is the same as for *Rosh haShanah* until this point. See pages 5-28.

THE *AMIDAH*

(We rise as the ark is opened.)

Adonai, open my lips and my mouth shall praise You.

בָּרוּךְ אַתָּה יְיָ אֱלֹהֵינוּ וֵאלֹהֵי אֲבוֹתֵינוּ, אֱלֹהֵי אַבְרָהָם
אֱלֹהֵי יִצְחָק וֵאלֹהֵי יַעֲקֹב, הָאֵל הַגָּדוֹל הַגִּבּוֹר וְהַנּוֹרָא
אֵל עֶלְיוֹן גּוֹמֵל חֲסָדִים טוֹבִים וְקוֹנֵה הַכֹּל, וְזוֹכֵר חַסְדֵי
אָבוֹת וּמֵבִיא גוֹאֵל לִבְנֵי בְנֵיהֶם לְמַעַן שְׁמוֹ בְּאַהֲבָה.

זָכְרֵנוּ לְחַיִּים מֶלֶךְ חָפֵץ בַּחַיִּים,
וְכָתְבֵנוּ בְּסֵפֶר הַחַיִּים לְמַעַנְךָ אֱלֹהִים חַיִּים.
מֶלֶךְ עוֹזֵר וּמוֹשִׁיעַ וּמָגֵן. בָּרוּךְ אַתָּה יְיָ מָגֵן אַבְרָהָם.

אַתָּה גִּבּוֹר לְעוֹלָם אֲדֹנָי מְחַיֵּה מֵתִים אַתָּה רַב לְהוֹשִׁיעַ.
מְכַלְכֵּל חַיִּים בְּחֶסֶד מְחַיֵּה מֵתִים בְּרַחֲמִים רַבִּים, סוֹמֵךְ
נוֹפְלִים וְרוֹפֵא חוֹלִים וּמַתִּיר אֲסוּרִים וּמְקַיֵּם אֱמוּנָתוֹ
לִישֵׁנֵי עָפָר. מִי כָמוֹךָ בַּעַל גְּבוּרוֹת וּמִי דּוֹמֶה לָּךְ, מֶלֶךְ
מֵמִית וּמְחַיֶּה וּמַצְמִיחַ יְשׁוּעָה.

מִי כָמוֹךָ אַב הָרַחֲמִים, זוֹכֵר יְצוּרָיו לְחַיִּים בְּרַחֲמִים.

וְנֶאֱמָן אַתָּה לְהַחֲיוֹת מֵתִים. בָּרוּךְ אַתָּה יְיָ מְחַיֵּה הַמֵּתִים.

Zoḥrenu l'ḥayim Meleḥ ḥafetz b'ḥayim,
v'ḥotveinu b'sefer haḥayim, l'ma'anḥa Elohim ḥayim.

Blessed are You, *Adonai,* our God and God of our ancestors,
God of Abraham, Isaac and Jacob.
Supreme God Who responds with kindness,
You remember the good deeds of our ancestors and
lovingly bring help to us.

On this day, we ask You for mercy.
Remember us for life, God Who delights in life.

Blessed are You, *Adonai,* Who protects Abraham.

You are the Source of life Who grants us healing and strength.

There is none as great and powerful as You.

We who are Your creation, *Adonai,* ask to be remembered for life.

Blessed are You, Source of life.

Continued on page 113.

THE *AMIDAH*

(We rise as the ark is opened.)

Adonai, open my lips and my mouth shall praise You.

בָּרוּךְ אַתָּה יְיָ אֱלֹהֵינוּ וֵאלֹהֵי אֲבוֹתֵינוּ, אֱלֹהֵי אַבְרָהָם
אֱלֹהֵי יִצְחָק וֵאלֹהֵי יַעֲקֹב, אֱלֹהֵי שָׂרָה אֱלֹהֵי רִבְקָה
אֱלֹהֵי רָחֵל וֵאלֹהֵי לֵאָה, הָאֵל הַגָּדוֹל הַגִּבּוֹר וְהַנּוֹרָא אֵל
עֶלְיוֹן גּוֹמֵל חֲסָדִים טוֹבִים וְקוֹנֵה הַכֹּל, וְזוֹכֵר חַסְדֵי
אָבוֹת וּמֵבִיא גוֹאֵל לִבְנֵי בְנֵיהֶם לְמַעַן שְׁמוֹ בְּאַהֲבָה.

זָכְרֵנוּ לְחַיִּים מֶלֶךְ חָפֵץ בַּחַיִּים,
וְכָתְבֵנוּ בְּסֵפֶר הַחַיִּים לְמַעַנְךָ אֱלֹהִים חַיִּים.

מֶלֶךְ עוֹזֵר וּפֹקֵד וּמוֹשִׁיעַ וּמָגֵן. בָּרוּךְ אַתָּה יְיָ מָגֵן
אַבְרָהָם וּפֹקֵד שָׂרָה.

אַתָּה גִּבּוֹר לְעוֹלָם אֲדֹנָי מְחַיֵּה מֵתִים אַתָּה רַב לְהוֹשִׁיעַ.
מְכַלְכֵּל חַיִּים בְּחֶסֶד מְחַיֵּה מֵתִים בְּרַחֲמִים רַבִּים, סוֹמֵךְ
נוֹפְלִים וְרוֹפֵא חוֹלִים וּמַתִּיר אֲסוּרִים וּמְקַיֵּם אֱמוּנָתוֹ
לִישֵׁנֵי עָפָר. מִי כָמוֹךָ בַּעַל גְּבוּרוֹת וּמִי דוֹמֶה לָּךְ, מֶלֶךְ
מֵמִית וּמְחַיֶּה וּמַצְמִיחַ יְשׁוּעָה.

מִי כָמוֹךָ אַב הָרַחֲמִים, זוֹכֵר יְצוּרָיו לְחַיִּים בְּרַחֲמִים.

וְנֶאֱמָן אַתָּה לְהַחֲיוֹת מֵתִים. בָּרוּךְ אַתָּה יְיָ מְחַיֵּה הַמֵּתִים.

Zoḥrenu l'ḥayim Meleḥ ḥafetz b'ḥayim,
v'ḥotveinu b'sefer haḥayim, l'ma'anḥa Elohim ḥayim.

Blessed are You, *Adonai,* our God and God of our ancestors,
God of Abraham, Isaac and Jacob,
God of Sarah, Rebecca, Leah and Rachel.
Supreme God Who responds with kindness,
You remember the good deeds of our ancestors and
lovingly bring help to us.

On this day, we ask You for mercy.
Remember us for life, God Who delights in life.

Blessed are You, *Adonai,* Who protects Abraham and
remembers Sarah.

You are the Source of life Who grants us healing and strength.

There is none as great and powerful as You.

We who are Your creation, *Adonai,* ask to be remembered for life.

Blessed are You, Source of life.

> **Silent Devotion**
>
> On *Yom Kippur*, an eight-year-old boy, seated next to his father in the synagogue, was reading the prayers very softly. His father gently whispered to him:
>
> "Son, I can't hear you praying."
>
> "I wasn't talking to you," the boy replied in a firm voice.

אֵל נָא, אַתָּה הוּא אֱלֹהֵינוּ

בַּשָּׁמַיִם וּבָאָרֶץ גִּבּוֹר וְנַעֲרָץ.

דָּגוּל מֵרְבָבָה הוּא שָׂח וַיֶּהִי.

צַדִּיק וְיָשָׁר קָרוֹב לְקוֹרְאָיו בֶּאֱמֶת.

רָם וּמִתְנַשֵּׂא שׁוֹכֵן שְׁחָקִים.

תּוֹלֶה אֶרֶץ עַל בְּלִימָה.

חַי וְקַיָּם נוֹרָא וּמָרוֹם וְקָדוֹשׁ.

Countless people declare Your greatness, for You spoke and the world was created, assuring Your everlasting fame. Though You are mighty, You are close to all who call for guidance.

The Hebrew word *nora* (find it in the above prayer) means that God fills us with awe (we feel amazed and excited).

We may not know all we want to know about God, but we can feel that God is near us. Here are some times people have said they felt God close to them:

-at the sea shore
-in the middle of a storm
-after accomplishing a hard task
-when their parent kisses them good night
-upon seeing a new baby

Can you tell about a time when you felt God close to you?

לְאֵל עוֹרֵךְ דִּין
לְבוֹחֵן לְבָבוֹת בְּיוֹם דִּין, לְגוֹלֶה עֲמֻקּוֹת בַּדִּין.
לְדוֹבֵר מֵישָׁרִים בְּיוֹם דִּין, לְהוֹגֶה דֵעוֹת בַּדִּין.
לְיוֹדֵעַ מַחֲשָׁבוֹת בְּיוֹם דִּין, לְכוֹבֵשׁ כַּעְסוֹ בַּדִּין.
לְלוֹבֵשׁ צְדָקוֹת בְּיוֹם דִּין, לְמוֹחֵל עֲוֹנוֹת בַּדִּין.
לְרַחֵם עַמּוֹ בְּיוֹם דִּין, לְשׁוֹמֵר אוֹהֲבָיו בַּדִּין.
לְתוֹמֵךְ תְּמִימָיו בְּיוֹם דִּין.

God searches our hearts on the
Day of Judgment and examines us.

God is dressed in righteousness on the
Day of Judgment and pardons us.

God shows mercy on the
Day of Judgment and remembers us.

The ark is closed. We recite the *Kedushah* while standing.
The congregation chants the indented lines.

נַעֲרִיצְךָ וְנַקְדִּישְׁךָ כְּסוֹד שִׂיחַ שַׂרְפֵי־קֹֽדֶשׁ הַמַּקְדִּישִׁים שִׁמְךָ
בַּקֹּֽדֶשׁ, כַּכָּתוּב עַל יַד נְבִיאֶֽךָ, וְקָרָא זֶה אֶל זֶה וְאָמַר:

קָדוֹשׁ קָדוֹשׁ קָדוֹשׁ יְיָ צְבָאוֹת, מְלֹא כָל־הָאָֽרֶץ כְּבוֹדוֹ.

כְּבוֹדוֹ מָלֵא עוֹלָם, מְשָׁרְתָיו שׁוֹאֲלִים זֶה לָזֶה אַיֵּה מְקוֹם
כְּבוֹדוֹ, לְעֻמָּתָם בָּרוּךְ יֹאמֵֽרוּ:

בָּרוּךְ כְּבוֹד יְיָ מִמְּקוֹמוֹ.

מִמְּקוֹמוֹ הוּא יִֽפֶן בְּרַחֲמִים וְיָחֹן עַם הַמְיַחֲדִים שְׁמוֹ עֶֽרֶב
וָבֹֽקֶר בְּכָל־יוֹם תָּמִיד פַּעֲמַֽיִם בְּאַהֲבָה שְׁמַע אוֹמְרִים:

שְׁמַע יִשְׂרָאֵל יְיָ אֱלֹהֵֽינוּ יְיָ אֶחָד.

הוּא אֱלֹהֵֽינוּ הוּא אָבִֽינוּ הוּא מַלְכֵּֽנוּ הוּא מוֹשִׁיעֵֽנוּ, וְהוּא
יַשְׁמִיעֵֽנוּ בְּרַחֲמָיו שֵׁנִית לְעֵינֵי כָּל־חָי, לִהְיוֹת לָכֶם לֵאלֹהִים:

אֲנִי יְיָ אֱלֹהֵיכֶם.

אַדִּיר אַדִּירֵֽנוּ יְיָ אֲדוֹנֵֽינוּ, מָה אַדִּיר שִׁמְךָ בְּכָל־הָאָֽרֶץ.
וְהָיָה יְיָ לְמֶֽלֶךְ עַל כָּל־הָאָֽרֶץ, בַּיּוֹם הַהוּא יִהְיֶה יְיָ אֶחָד
וּשְׁמוֹ אֶחָד. וּדְבְרֵי קָדְשְׁךָ כָּתוּב לֵאמֹר:

יִמְלֹךְ יְיָ לְעוֹלָם אֱלֹהַֽיִךְ צִיּוֹן לְדֹר וָדֹר, הַלְלוּיָהּ.

לְדוֹר וָדוֹר נַגִּיד גָּדְלֶךָ, וּלְנֵצַח נְצָחִים קְדֻשָּׁתְךָ נַקְדִּישׁ, וְשִׁבְחֲךָ אֱלֹהֵינוּ מִפִּינוּ לֹא יָמוּשׁ לְעוֹלָם וָעֶד כִּי אֵל מֶלֶךְ גָּדוֹל וְקָדוֹשׁ אָתָּה.

We will declare God's holiness here on earth as we imagine heavenly angels do above:

> Holy, holy, holy — the whole world is filled with God's glory.

And we, the Jewish people, declare:

> *Shema Yisrael* — Hear, O Israel: The Lord Our God, the Lord is One.
>
> God shall be Ruler over all.

In every generation we will speak of God's greatness and forever declare God's holiness.

וּבְכֵן תֵּן פַּחְדְּךָ יְיָ אֱלֹהֵינוּ עַל
כָּל־מַעֲשֶׂיךָ וְאֵימָתְךָ
עַל־כָּל־מַה־שֶּׁבָּרָאתָ, וְיִירָאוּךָ
כָּל־הַמַּעֲשִׂים וְיִשְׁתַּחֲווּ לְפָנֶיךָ
כָּל־הַבְּרוּאִים, וְיֵעָשׂוּ כֻלָּם
אֲגֻדָּה אַחַת לַעֲשׂוֹת רְצוֹנְךָ בְּלֵבָב שָׁלֵם.

וּבְכֵן תֵּן כָּבוֹד יְיָ לְעַמֶּךָ תְּהִלָּה לִירֵאֶיךָ וְתִקְוָה
לְדוֹרְשֶׁיךָ וּפִתְחוֹן פֶּה לַמְיַחֲלִים לָךְ, שִׂמְחָה לְאַרְצֶךָ
וְשָׂשׂוֹן לְעִירֶךָ וּצְמִיחַת קֶרֶן לְדָוִד עַבְדֶּךָ וַעֲרִיכַת נֵר
לְבֶן־יִשַׁי מְשִׁיחֶךָ בִּמְהֵרָה בְיָמֵינוּ.

וּבְכֵן צַדִּיקִים יִרְאוּ וְיִשְׂמָחוּ וִישָׁרִים יַעֲלֹזוּ וַחֲסִידִים
בְּרִנָּה יָגִילוּ, וְעוֹלָתָה תִּקְפָּץ־פִּיהָ וְכָל־הָרִשְׁעָה כֻּלָּהּ
כְּעָשָׁן תִּכְלֶה כִּי תַעֲבִיר מֶמְשֶׁלֶת זָדוֹן מִן הָאָרֶץ. בָּרוּךְ
אַתָּה יְיָ הַמֶּלֶךְ הַקָּדוֹשׁ.

Let all creatures feel awe in Your presence and join together to follow Your will.

Grant honor to Your people and glory to all who have faith in You. Grant joy to Israel and gladness to Jerusalem. Answer our prayers and bring a time when we all share our blessings with each other.

When You remove cruel governments and wickedness from the world, then the righteous will be glad and the faithful ones will celebrate in song.

Blessed are You, *Adonai,* the holy Ruler.

Beruriah and the Robbers

There were once some robbers who lived in Rabbi Meir's neighborhood. Because they caused so much trouble, Rabbi Meir prayed that they would die. His wise and learned wife, Beruriah, told him that this kind of prayer should not be permitted. "It is better to pray that these wicked people change their ways," she said, "and then there won't be wickedness." Rabbi Meir did pray for them and they stopped their wickedness.

You have called us to Your service through the *mitzvot* and chosen us to celebrate special, holy days.

(On *Shabbat* add the words in brackets)

אַתָּה בְחַרְתָּנוּ מִכָּל־הָעַמִּים, אָהַבְתָּ אוֹתָנוּ וְרָצִיתָ בָּנוּ
וְרוֹמַמְתָּנוּ מִכָּל־הַלְּשׁוֹנוֹת וְקִדַּשְׁתָּנוּ בְּמִצְוֹתֶיךָ וְקֵרַבְתָּנוּ
מַלְכֵּנוּ לַעֲבוֹדָתֶךָ וְשִׁמְךָ הַגָּדוֹל וְהַקָּדוֹשׁ עָלֵינוּ קָרָאתָ.

וַתִּתֶּן־לָנוּ יְיָ אֱלֹהֵינוּ בְּאַהֲבָה אֶת־יוֹם (הַשַּׁבָּת הַזֶּה
לִקְדֻשָּׁה וְלִמְנוּחָה וְאֶת־יוֹם) הַכִּפּוּרִים הַזֶּה לִמְחִילָה
וְלִסְלִיחָה וּלְכַפָּרָה וְלִמְחׇל־בּוֹ אֶת־כׇּל־עֲוֹנוֹתֵינוּ (בְּאַהֲבָה)
מִקְרָא קֹדֶשׁ, זֵכֶר לִיצִיאַת מִצְרָיִם.

וַיִּקְרָא בְשֵׁם יְיָ. וַיַּעֲבֹר יְיָ עַל פָּנָיו וַיִּקְרָא:

יְיָ יְיָ אֵל רַחוּם וְחַנּוּן, אֶרֶךְ אַפַּיִם וְרַב חֶסֶד וֶאֱמֶת
נֹצֵר חֶסֶד לָאֲלָפִים נֹשֵׂא עָוֺן וָפֶשַׁע וְחַטָּאָה, וְנַקֵּה.

S'LIḤOT

Adonai, Adonai, merciful and patient God,
You remember our kind acts for a thousand generations.
You accept our shortcomings and pardon our sins.

We rise.

שְׁמַע קוֹלֵנוּ, יְיָ אֱלֹהֵינוּ, חוּס וְרַחֵם עָלֵינוּ,
וְקַבֵּל בְּרַחֲמִים וּבְרָצוֹן אֶת־תְּפִלָּתֵנוּ.
הֲשִׁיבֵנוּ יְיָ אֵלֶיךָ וְנָשׁוּבָה, חַדֵּשׁ יָמֵינוּ כְּקֶדֶם.

אַל תַּשְׁלִיכֵנוּ לְעֵת זִקְנָה, כִּכְלוֹת כֹּחֵנוּ אַל תַּעַזְבֵנוּ.
אַל תַּעַזְבֵנוּ, יְיָ אֱלֹהֵינוּ, אַל תִּרְחַק מִמֶּנּוּ.

Hear our voices, *Adonai,* our God,
And answer our prayers with Your lovingkindness.
Do not turn from us and be distant.

Do not let us feel all alone in old age.

A THOUGHT ON OUR ELDERS

God, may all people grow old with dignity and may we have the wisdom to help them do so. May we always show respect, love and appreciation to our elders.

In this prayer, we ask God not to forget us when we are old. What is different about old age that can make some old people feel especially helpless? What fears do you think old people have? How can we help to make their lives better?

In His Own Way

There was once a farmer who had a son who could not tell a *resh* from a *lamed.* Since he could not recite a single prayer, his father did not even take him to the synagogue. "Why bother," he would say. "It is a waste of time for such a child to pray."

One *Yom Kippur*, when the son had turned thirteen, the farmer became concerned that if the boy were left at home, he might eat by mistake, so he brought him along to the synagogue. In his pocket, the boy carried the little silver flute that he played when he tended his father's sheep.

As the boy listened to the sad, soulful melodies during the service, he longed to play a tune on his flute. However, when he asked his father's permission, the farmer scolded him and told him it was forbidden to do such a thing on *Yom Kippur*.

All day long, the young boy tried to restrain himself, but as the service was drawing to a close, he could not resist the urge to take out his flute and blow one long powerful note. The congregation became still as the horrified father tried to grab the flute from the boy.

The rabbi, the great *Baal Shem Tov,* broke the silence with these words, "Don't be angry or embarrassed. The lad spoke to God in his own way. So strong was his desire to pray that his prayer on the flute not only went straight to the Holy One but also carried our prayers up to the gates of heaven."

How can we put our own feelings into the prayers "set out" in our prayer books?

אֱלֹהֵינוּ וֵאלֹהֵי אֲבוֹתֵינוּ, סְלַח לָנוּ, מְחַל לָנוּ, כַּפֶּר־לָנוּ.

כִּי אָנוּ עַמֶּךָ וְאַתָּה אֱלֹהֵינוּ, אָנוּ בָנֶיךָ וְאַתָּה אָבִינוּ.
אָנוּ עֲבָדֶיךָ וְאַתָּה אֲדוֹנֵנוּ, אָנוּ קְהָלֶךָ וְאַתָּה חֶלְקֵנוּ.
אָנוּ נַחֲלָתֶךָ וְאַתָּה גוֹרָלֵנוּ, אָנוּ צֹאנֶךָ וְאַתָּה רוֹעֵנוּ.
אָנוּ כַרְמֶךָ וְאַתָּה נוֹטְרֵנוּ, אָנוּ פְעֻלָּתֶךָ וְאַתָּה יוֹצְרֵנוּ.
אָנוּ רַעְיָתֶךָ וְאַתָּה דוֹדֵנוּ, אָנוּ סְגֻלָּתֶךָ וְאַתָּה קְרוֹבֵנוּ.
אָנוּ עַמֶּךָ וְאַתָּה מַלְכֵּנוּ, אָנוּ מַאֲמִירֶךָ וְאַתָּה מַאֲמִירֵנוּ.

We are Your people — And You are our God.
We are Your children — And You are our Parent.
We are Your flock — And You are our Shepherd.
We are Your vineyard — And You are our Keeper.
We are Your creation — And You are our Creator.
We are Your loved ones — And You are our Beloved.

Ki anu ameḥa v'atah Eloheinu,
Anu vaneḥa v'atah avinu.
Anu avadeḥa v'atah adoneinu,
Anu k'haleḥa v'atah ḥelkeinu.
Anu naḥalateḥa v'atah goraleinu,
Anu tzoneḥa v'atah roeinu.

"...I think there's a God somewhere, but He's not like we might think He is; I mean, He may be different — and that's about all I know! Maybe it's fun for God to keep us all guessing! It's probably better for us, too. We're on our toes, and we're not falling asleep. God wouldn't want all His people dozing half the time!"

These words were spoken by a boy named Avrum. Do you agree with him?

A THOUGHT ON SAYING THAT WE HAVE DONE WRONG

Our God and God of our ancestors, let our prayers reach You and not be ignored. We are not so bold or foolish to think that we have been perfect and have not made mistakes. To be honest, we must admit we have missed the mark, sinned.

"Kol Yisrael areivim zeh lazeh — All Jews are responsible for one another." We confess our sins as a group to show that we all must take responsibility for each other.

We stand, confess our wrongdoings and ask for God's forgiveness.

אָשַׁמְנוּ, בָּגַדְנוּ, גָּזַלְנוּ, דִּבַּרְנוּ דֹפִי. הֶעֱוִינוּ, וְהִרְשַׁעְנוּ,
זַדְנוּ, חָמַסְנוּ, טָפַלְנוּ שֶׁקֶר. יָעַצְנוּ רָע, כִּזַּבְנוּ, לַצְנוּ,
מָרַדְנוּ, נִאַצְנוּ, סָרַרְנוּ, עָוִינוּ, פָּשַׁעְנוּ, צָרַרְנוּ, קִשִּׁינוּ עֹרֶף.
רָשַׁעְנוּ, שִׁחַתְנוּ, תִּעַבְנוּ, תָּעִינוּ, תִּעְתָּעְנוּ.

We have been cruel.
We have teased.
We have lied.
We have acted violently.
We have cheated.
We have boasted exceedingly.
We have been false.

We have mocked.
We have gossiped.
We have acted wickedly.
We have quarrelled.
We have been unjust.
We have acted selfishly.
We have not remembered Zion.

We remain standing.

Ashamnu, bagadnu, gazalnu, dibarnu dofi; he'evinu, v'hirshanu,
zadnu, ḥamasnu, tafalnu shaker; ya'atznu ra, kizavnu, latznu,
maradnu, ni'atznu, sararnu, avinu, pashanu, tzararnu, kishinu oref;
rashanu, shiḥatnu, ti'avnu, ta'inu, titanu.

In the *Ashamnu* prayer that we just said, we recite a list of sins in alphabetical order. In this English version of the prayer each letter of the alphabet was used at least once. Can you find each one?

Did you ever hear anyone say, "I've tried everything from A to Z"? Since A is the start of the alphabet and Z is the finish, this expression means that a wide range of things have been done. By using the whole alphabet in the Hebrew, we admit that we have done every possible wrongdoing from *alef* to *tav,* A to Z — maybe not each of us individually, but as a community. By saying "we have sinned," we hold ourselves responsible for what happens in our communities.

Yom Kippur can bring forgiveness for the wrongs we have done to God, but it cannot bring forgiveness for the wrongs we have done to family and friends. We must seek out those with whom we've quarreled or those we have hurt and ask their forgiveness.

We must be forgiving to all who have hurt or angered us during the past year. Why? Because...

- we realize that we all are human. Everyone makes mistakes.
- we don't want anyone to feel guilty because of us.
- we accept the commandment to love our neighbors as ourselves.

עַל חֵטְא שֶׁחָטָאנוּ לְפָנֶיךָ בְּאֹנֶס וּבְרָצוֹן,

וְעַל חֵטְא שֶׁחָטָאנוּ לְפָנֶיךָ בִּבְלִי דָעַת.

עַל חֵטְא שֶׁחָטָאנוּ לְפָנֶיךָ בְּזִלְזוּל הוֹרִים וּמוֹרִים,

וְעַל חֵטְא שֶׁחָטָאנוּ לְפָנֶיךָ בְּחֹזֶק יָד.

עַל חֵטְא שֶׁחָטָאנוּ לְפָנֶיךָ בְּטֻמְאַת שְׂפָתָיִם.

וְעַל כֻּלָּם אֱלוֹהַּ סְלִיחוֹת, סְלַח לָנוּ, מְחַל לָנוּ, כַּפֶּר־לָנוּ.

עַל חֵטְא שֶׁחָטָאנוּ לְפָנֶיךָ בְּכַחַשׁ וּבְכָזָב,
וְעַל חֵטְא שֶׁחָטָאנוּ לְפָנֶיךָ בְּלָצוֹן.
עַל חֵטְא שֶׁחָטָאנוּ לְפָנֶיךָ בְּשִׂיחַ שִׂפְתוֹתֵינוּ,
וְעַל חֵטְא שֶׁחָטָאנוּ לְפָנֶיךָ בְּעֵינַיִם רָמוֹת.
עַל חֵטְא שֶׁחָטָאנוּ לְפָנֶיךָ בְּקַלּוּת רֹאשׁ,
וְעַל חֵטְא שֶׁחָטָאנוּ לְפָנֶיךָ בְּרִיצַת רַגְלַיִם לְהָרַע.

וְעַל כֻּלָּם אֱלוֹהַּ סְלִיחוֹת, סְלַח לָנוּ, מְחַל לָנוּ, כַּפֶּר־לָנוּ.

V'al kulam Eloha s'liḥot, s'laḥ lanu, m'ḥal lanu, kaper lanu.

The Hebrew word *ḥet* is usually translated as "sin." A more correct translation is "missing the mark." Think of a target. Plan to hit more "bulls'-eyes" next year.

May it be Your will, *Adonai,* the God of our ancestors, to forgive our sins and grant us a new beginning, for we have missed the mark.

For the sin we have sinned against You...

by acting selfishly.
by hurting others.
by not respecting parents and teachers.
by lying.
by being greedy.
by gossiping.
by acting irresponsibly.
by cheating.
by rushing to do evil.

Add your own words here...

For all these sins, God of forgiveness, forgive us,
pardon us, and grant us a new beginning.

We are seated.

An Angel's *Teshuvah*

An angel once disobeyed God. When she was brought before the throne of judgment, she begged for forgiveness. "Give me a chance to do *teshuvah*," she pleaded. "Your *teshuvah*," the Holy One announced, "will be to return to earth to find the most precious thing in the world and then bring it back to Me."

For three years, the angel patiently roamed the earth. Finally, on a battlefield, she heard a dying soldier call out for water. Then she saw his wounded friend crawl to him to give him a drink from his canteen. When the last drop of water touched his parched lips, the angel seized the canteen and brought it to the Holy One.

God said to the angel, "This is very precious but it is not the most precious thing in the world."

The angel returned to earth and roamed the world for another three years until she came to a hospital where a doctor lay dying of a disease she had gotten caring for a patient. The angel caught her last breath and brought it to the Holy One.

Again God said to the angel, "This is very precious but it is not the most precious thing in the world."

The angel returned to earth to continue the search. Suddenly, she saw a mean-looking man holding a sword. He was walking to the house of his enemy to kill him. A light was on in the house so the man peered inside. He saw his enemy's wife putting her little son to sleep. She was teaching him to say the bedtime prayers. As he watched them, the man's heart melted. He remembered how his own mother had cared for him and taught him these same prayers. When a tear fell from his eyes, the angel caught it and flew directly to the Holy One.

God smiled and spoke. "Indeed, this is the most precious thing in the world. *Teshuvah* opens the gates of heaven."

The Rabbis teach: "Who is truly mighty? The one who makes an enemy a friend."

בָּרוּךְ אַתָּה יְיָ מֶלֶךְ מוֹחֵל וְסוֹלֵחַ לַעֲוֺנוֹתֵינוּ וְלַעֲוֺנוֹת עַמּוֹ
בֵּית יִשְׂרָאֵל וּמַעֲבִיר אַשְׁמוֹתֵינוּ בְּכָל־שָׁנָה וְשָׁנָה, מֶלֶךְ עַל
כָּל־הָאָרֶץ מְקַדֵּשׁ (הַשַּׁבָּת וְ)יִשְׂרָאֵל וְיוֹם הַכִּפּוּרִים.

Praised are You, *Adonai*
  Who pardons and forgives our sins,
  and the sins of all the people Israel,
Who rules the earth and sanctifies [the *Shabbat*], the people Israel and *Yom Kippur*.

May God look upon us and our prayers with favor. May we soon sense God's presence in Zion.

רְצֵה יְיָ אֱלֹהֵינוּ בְּעַמְּךָ יִשְׂרָאֵל וּבִתְפִלָּתָם וְהָשֵׁב
אֶת־הָעֲבוֹדָה לִדְבִיר בֵּיתֶךָ וּתְפִלָּתָם בְּאַהֲבָה תְקַבֵּל
בְּרָצוֹן וּתְהִי לְרָצוֹן תָּמִיד עֲבוֹדַת יִשְׂרָאֵל עַמֶּךָ. וְתֶחֱזֶינָה
עֵינֵינוּ בְּשׁוּבְךָ לְצִיּוֹן בְּרַחֲמִים. בָּרוּךְ אַתָּה יְיָ הַמַּחֲזִיר
שְׁכִינָתוֹ לְצִיּוֹן.

מוֹדִים אֲנַחְנוּ לָךְ שָׁאַתָּה הוּא יְיָ אֱלֹהֵינוּ וֵאלֹהֵי אֲבוֹתֵינוּ לְעוֹלָם
וָעֶד, צוּר חַיֵּינוּ מָגֵן יִשְׁעֵנוּ אַתָּה הוּא. לְדוֹר וָדוֹר נוֹדֶה לְּךָ
וּנְסַפֵּר תְּהִלָּתֶךָ עַל חַיֵּינוּ הַמְּסוּרִים בְּיָדֶךָ וְעַל נִשְׁמוֹתֵינוּ
הַפְּקוּדוֹת לָךְ וְעַל נִסֶּיךָ שֶׁבְּכָל־יוֹם עִמָּנוּ וְעַל נִפְלְאוֹתֶיךָ
וְטוֹבוֹתֶיךָ שֶׁבְּכָל־עֵת עֶרֶב וָבֹקֶר וְצָהֳרָיִם. הַטּוֹב כִּי לֹא כָלוּ
רַחֲמֶיךָ וְהַמְרַחֵם כִּי לֹא תַמּוּ חֲסָדֶיךָ מֵעוֹלָם קִוִּינוּ לָךְ.

וְעַל כֻּלָּם יִתְבָּרַךְ וְיִתְרוֹמַם שִׁמְךָ מַלְכֵּנוּ תָּמִיד לְעוֹלָם וָעֶד.

וּכְתֹב לְחַיִּים טוֹבִים כָּל־בְּנֵי בְרִיתֶךָ.

וְכֹל הַחַיִּים יוֹדוּךָ סֶּלָה וִיהַלְלוּ אֶת־שִׁמְךָ בֶּאֱמֶת הָאֵל
יְשׁוּעָתֵנוּ וְעֶזְרָתֵנוּ סֶלָה. בָּרוּךְ אַתָּה יְיָ הַטּוֹב שִׁמְךָ וּלְךָ
נָאֶה לְהוֹדוֹת.

How grateful we are to You, God of our ancestors, the Eternal One. You are the source of our strength just as You have been the protecting shield of each generation.

We thank You for our lives which are in Your hands and our souls which are in Your care. We thank You for Your miracles which surround us all the time and the wondrous acts of kindness that we experience each morning, noon and night.

You are the source of never-ending lovingkindness. You are our hope forever.

May we all look forward to a good year of life.

Blessed are You,
Adonai, Ruler of the Universe,
Who deserves our praise.

אֱלֹהֵינוּ וֵאלֹהֵי אֲבוֹתֵינוּ, בָּרְכֵנוּ בַבְּרָכָה הַמְשֻׁלֶּשֶׁת בַּתּוֹרָה הַכְּתוּבָה עַל יְדֵי מֹשֶׁה עַבְדֶּךָ, הָאֲמוּרָה מִפִּי אַהֲרֹן וּבָנָיו כֹּהֲנִים עַם קְדוֹשֶׁךָ, כָּאָמוּר:

יְבָרֶכְךָ יְיָ וְיִשְׁמְרֶךָ. כֵּן יְהִי רָצוֹן.
יָאֵר יְיָ פָּנָיו אֵלֶיךָ וִיחֻנֶּךָּ. כֵּן יְהִי רָצוֹן.
יִשָּׂא יְיָ פָּנָיו אֵלֶיךָ וְיָשֵׂם לְךָ שָׁלוֹם. כֵּן יְהִי רָצוֹן.

שִׂים שָׁלוֹם בָּעוֹלָם, טוֹבָה וּבְרָכָה חֵן וָחֶסֶד וְרַחֲמִים עָלֵינוּ וְעַל כָּל־יִשְׂרָאֵל עַמֶּךָ. בָּרְכֵנוּ אָבִינוּ כֻּלָּנוּ כְּאֶחָד בְּאוֹר פָּנֶיךָ, כִּי בְאוֹר פָּנֶיךָ נָתַתָּ לָּנוּ יְיָ אֱלֹהֵינוּ תּוֹרַת חַיִּים וְאַהֲבַת חֶסֶד וּצְדָקָה וּבְרָכָה וְרַחֲמִים וְחַיִּים וְשָׁלוֹם. וְטוֹב בְּעֵינֶיךָ לְבָרֵךְ אֶת־עַמְּךָ יִשְׂרָאֵל בְּכָל־עֵת וּבְכָל־שָׁעָה בִּשְׁלוֹמֶךָ.

Congregation and Leader:

בְּסֵפֶר חַיִּים בְּרָכָה וְשָׁלוֹם וּפַרְנָסָה טוֹבָה נִזָּכֵר וְנִכָּתֵב לְפָנֶיךָ אֲנַחְנוּ וְכָל־עַמְּךָ בֵּית יִשְׂרָאֵל לְחַיִּים טוֹבִים וּלְשָׁלוֹם.

בָּרוּךְ אַתָּה יְיָ עוֹשֵׂה הַשָּׁלוֹם.

Let peace, prosperity, happiness, and lovingkindness come to our world, to us, and to all the Jewish people. Bless us all, Holy One, with Your light, for by that light You have given the Torah to guide us. May it please You to bless the Jewish people in every season and at all times with goodness and peace.

May we and all the Jewish people be remembered and recorded in Your book for a good and peaceful life.

Praised are You, *Adonai,* Source of peace.

(We omit on *Shabbat.*)
The ark is opened and we rise.

אָבִינוּ מַלְכֵּנוּ, חָטָאנוּ לְפָנֶיךָ.
אָבִינוּ מַלְכֵּנוּ, אֵין לָנוּ מֶלֶךְ אֶלָּא אָתָּה.
אָבִינוּ מַלְכֵּנוּ, עֲשֵׂה עִמָּנוּ לְמַעַן שְׁמֶךָ.
אָבִינוּ מַלְכֵּנוּ, חַדֵּשׁ עָלֵינוּ שָׁנָה טוֹבָה.
אָבִינוּ מַלְכֵּנוּ, כָּתְבֵנוּ בְּסֵפֶר חַיִּים טוֹבִים.
אָבִינוּ מַלְכֵּנוּ, כָּתְבֵנוּ בְּסֵפֶר גְּאֻלָּה וִישׁוּעָה.
אָבִינוּ מַלְכֵּנוּ, כָּתְבֵנוּ בְּסֵפֶר פַּרְנָסָה וְכַלְכָּלָה.
אָבִינוּ מַלְכֵּנוּ, כָּתְבֵנוּ בְּסֵפֶר זְכֻיּוֹת.
אָבִינוּ מַלְכֵּנוּ, כָּתְבֵנוּ בְּסֵפֶר סְלִיחָה וּמְחִילָה.

Avinu Malkeinu, our Holy Parent and Ruler
We have sinned before You,
You Who are our only God.
Still, grant us a good new year
and write us in Your Book of Forgiveness.

Avinu Malkeinu,
Answer our prayers.
Treat us with mercy.

We all join in singing.

אָבִינוּ מַלְכֵּנוּ, חָנֵּנוּ וַעֲנֵנוּ, כִּי אֵין בָּנוּ מַעֲשִׂים,
עֲשֵׂה עִמָּנוּ צְדָקָה וָחֶסֶד וְהוֹשִׁיעֵנוּ.

Avinu Malkeinu, ḥoneinu va'aneinu, ki ein banu ma'asim,
aseh imanu tzedakah vaḥesed v'hoshi'einu.

The ark is closed and we are seated.

For some ancient peoples, God as a parent meant that She/He was really the physical parent of the human race. Judaism speaks of God as parent to teach us that we should behave as if we are all children of God.

The prophet Malaḥai says "Have we not all the same parent? Has not one God created us?" This means that if God is the parent of us all, we are all brothers and sisters — all equal and important in God's eyes.

Where in the world are people not treated as equals? Are there people in your local community who are not being treated as if they are children of God?

KADDISH SHALEM

Full *Kaddish* קַדִּישׁ שָׁלֵם

Leader:

יִתְגַּדַּל וְיִתְקַדַּשׁ שְׁמֵהּ רַבָּא. בְּעָלְמָא דִּי בְרָא כִרְעוּתֵהּ,
וְיַמְלִיךְ מַלְכוּתֵהּ בְּחַיֵּיכוֹן וּבְיוֹמֵיכוֹן וּבְחַיֵּי דְכָל־בֵּית
יִשְׂרָאֵל בַּעֲגָלָא וּבִזְמַן קָרִיב, וְאִמְרוּ אָמֵן.

Congregation and Leader answer:

יְהֵא שְׁמֵהּ רַבָּא מְבָרַךְ לְעָלַם וּלְעָלְמֵי עָלְמַיָּא.

Y'hai shmai rabbah m'varaḥ l'olam u'l'olmei almay'ya.

Leader:

יִתְבָּרַךְ וְיִשְׁתַּבַּח וְיִתְפָּאַר וְיִתְרוֹמַם וְיִתְנַשֵּׂא וְיִתְהַדַּר
וְיִתְעַלֶּה וְיִתְהַלַּל שְׁמֵהּ דְּקֻדְשָׁא

Congregation and Leader answer:

בְּרִיךְ הוּא.

B'riḥ hu.

Leader:

לְעֵלָּא לְעֵלָּא מִכָּל־בִּרְכָתָא וְשִׁירָתָא תֻּשְׁבְּחָתָא וְנֶחֱמָתָא
דַּאֲמִירָן בְּעָלְמָא, וְאִמְרוּ אָמֵן.

תִּתְקַבֵּל צְלוֹתְהוֹן וּבָעוּתְהוֹן דְּכָל־יִשְׂרָאֵל קֳדָם אֲבוּהוֹן
דִּי בִשְׁמַיָּא, וְאִמְרוּ אָמֵן.

יְהֵא שְׁלָמָא רַבָּא מִן שְׁמַיָּא וְחַיִּים עָלֵינוּ וְעַל כָּל־יִשְׂרָאֵל,
וְאִמְרוּ אָמֵן.

עוֹשֶׂה שָׁלוֹם בִּמְרוֹמָיו הוּא יַעֲשֶׂה שָׁלוֹם עָלֵינוּ וְעַל
כָּל־יִשְׂרָאֵל, וְאִמְרוּ אָמֵן.

אֵין כָּמְוֹךָ בָאֱלֹהִים אֲדֹנָי
וְאֵין כְּמַעֲשֶׂיךָ.

Ein ka'moḥa va'Elohim Adonai
v'ein k'ma'aseḥa.

מַלְכוּתְךָ מַלְכוּת כָּל־עֹלָמִים
וּמֶמְשַׁלְתְּךָ בְּכָל־דּוֹר וָדֹר.

Malḥut'ḥa malḥut kol olamim,
umem'shalt'ḥa b'ḥol dor va'dor.

יְיָ מֶלֶךְ, יְיָ מָלָךְ,
יְיָ יִמְלֹךְ לְעֹלָם וָעֶד.

Adonai Meleḥ, Adonai malaḥ,
Adonai yimloḥ l'olam va'ed.

יְיָ עֹז לְעַמּוֹ יִתֵּן,
יְיָ יְבָרֵךְ אֶת־עַמּוֹ בַשָּׁלוֹם.

Adonai oz l'amo yiten,
Adonai y'vareḥ et amo va'shalom.

We rise.

The ark is opened.

וַיְהִי בִּנְסֹעַ הָאָרֹן
Vay'hi binso'a ha'aron,

וַיֹּאמֶר מֹשֶׁה:
vay'yomer Mosheh:

קוּמָה יְיָ וְיָפֻצוּ אֹיְבֶיךָ
Kuma Adonai v'yafutzu oyveḥa,

וְיָנֻסוּ מְשַׂנְאֶיךָ מִפָּנֶיךָ.
v'yanusu m'saneḥa mipaneḥa.

כִּי מִצִּיּוֹן תֵּצֵא תוֹרָה
Ki mitziyon teitzei Torah,

וּדְבַר יְיָ מִירוּשָׁלָיִם.
u'd'var Adonai mirushalayim.

בָּרוּךְ שֶׁנָּתַן תּוֹרָה לְעַמּוֹ
Baruḥ shenatan Torah l'amo

יִשְׂרָאֵל בִּקְדֻשָּׁתוֹ.
Yisrael bik'dushato.

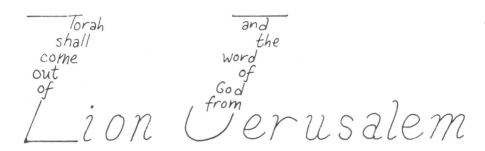

Torah shall come out of Zion and the word of God from Jerusalem

Blessed is the One Who gave the Torah to the people of Israel.

We omit on *Shabbat*.

יְיָ יְיָ אֵל רַחוּם וְחַנּוּן, אֶרֶךְ אַפַּיִם וְרַב חֶסֶד וֶאֱמֶת
נֹצֵר חֶסֶד לָאֲלָפִים נֹשֵׂא עָוֹן וָפֶשַׁע וְחַטָּאָה, וְנַקֵּה.

וַאֲנִי תְפִלָּתִי לְךָ יְיָ עֵת רָצוֹן, אֱלֹהִים בְּרָב־חַסְדֶּךָ, עֲנֵנִי
בֶּאֱמֶת יִשְׁעֶךָ.

Adonai, Adonai, merciful and patient God
You remember our kind acts for a thousand generations
You accept our shortcomings and pardon our sins.

May the words I say today be acceptable to You, *Adonai*.
Show me kindness and answer the prayers of my heart.

Adonai, Adonai, El raḥum v'ḥanun,
ereḥ apayim v'rav ḥesed ve'emet.
Notzer ḥesed la'alafim,
nosei avon vafesha v'ḥata'ah v'nakeh.

Va'ani t'filati l'ḥa Adonai et ratzon.
Elohim b'rov ḥasdeḥa aneini be'emet yish'eḥa.

My Prayer

We pray together for it gives us comfort and strength. We pray together to be a part of the Jewish people. But we also need time to be alone with our thoughts. We need time to say the prayers of our own hearts.

Below are some words to help you begin and create your own prayer.

On this day, God, before Your holy ark,

I feel...
I regret that...
I want to...
I'm thankful for...
Please...

May all our prayers be answered.

The Torah is taken and held.
Leader and then congregation say:

שְׁמַע יִשְׂרָאֵל יְיָ אֱלֹהֵינוּ יְיָ אֶחָד.

Hear, O Israel: The Lord our God, the Lord is One.
Shema Yisrael, Adonai Eloheinu Adonai eḥad.

Leader and then congregation say:

אֶחָד אֱלֹהֵינוּ גָּדוֹל אֲדוֹנֵינוּ קָדוֹשׁ וְנוֹרָא שְׁמוֹ.

Our God is One, Great and Holy.
Eḥad Eloheinu, gadol adoneinu, kadosh v'nora shemo.

Leader:

גַּדְּלוּ לַייָ אִתִּי, וּנְרוֹמְמָה שְׁמוֹ יַחְדָּו.

Join me in proclaiming God's greatness.
Together, let us praise God.

As the Torah is carried around the congregation,
we kiss the Torah and all sing:

לְךָ יְיָ הַגְּדֻלָּה וְהַגְּבוּרָה וְהַתִּפְאֶרֶת וְהַנֵּצַח וְהַהוֹד, כִּי כֹל
בַּשָּׁמַיִם וּבָאָרֶץ, לְךָ יְיָ הַמַּמְלָכָה וְהַמִּתְנַשֵּׂא לְכֹל לְרֹאשׁ.

רוֹמְמוּ יְיָ אֱלֹהֵינוּ וְהִשְׁתַּחֲווּ לַהֲדֹם רַגְלָיו, קָדוֹשׁ הוּא.
רוֹמְמוּ יְיָ אֱלֹהֵינוּ וְהִשְׁתַּחֲווּ לְהַר קָדְשׁוֹ, כִּי קָדוֹשׁ יְיָ אֱלֹהֵינוּ.

Yours, *Adonai,* is the greatness, power and splendor.
Yours is the triumph and the majesty.
For all in heaven and on earth is Yours.
You rule over all.

Praise *Adonai,* the Holy One. Worship at God's holy mountain,
for there is none like *Adonai,* our God.

L'ḥa Adonai hag'dulah v'hag'vurah v'hatiferet v'hanetzaḥ v'hahod.
Ki ḥol bashamayim uva'aretz,
L'ḥa Adonai hamamlaḥa v'hamitnasei l'ḥol l'rosh.
Romemu Adonai Eloheinu v'hishtaḥavu lahadom raglav, kadosh hu.
Romemu Adonai Eloheinu v'hishtaḥavu l'har kod'sho,
Ki kadosh Adonai Eloheinu.

For some additional Torah songs for everyone to sing, see page 47.

Congregants are honored by being called up to the *bimah* (platform) to bless the Torah before and after each selection. This is called an *aliyah* (meaning "going up").

If *Yom Kippur* is on a weekday, there are six selections for the Torah that are read aloud. If *Yom Kippur* is on a *Shabbat*, seven selections are read.

Because each section for an *aliyah* should contain at least three verses, we have selected a few more than twenty-one verses for the Torah reading.

At a children's service, if there is a small group or if only one selection is to be read, an alternative is to have a group *aliyah* where the blessings before and after the Torah reading are recited together.

If you are going to read less than six/seven sections, we recommend that you choose: *Shlishi* (on *Shabbat: Shevi'i*).

TORAH BLESSINGS

The one(s) being honored say(s):

בָּרְכוּ אֶת־יְיָ הַמְבֹרָךְ.

Praise *Adonai,* Source of all blessing.

The congregation answers:

בָּרוּךְ יְיָ הַמְבֹרָךְ לְעוֹלָם וָעֶד.

Praise *Adonai,* Source of all blessing, forever and ever.

The one(s) being honored repeat(s) the above line and continue(s):

בָּרוּךְ אַתָּה יְיָ אֱלֹהֵינוּ מֶלֶךְ הָעוֹלָם אֲשֶׁר בָּחַר בָּנוּ
מִכָּל־הָעַמִּים וְנָתַן לָנוּ אֶת־תּוֹרָתוֹ. בָּרוּךְ אַתָּה יְיָ נוֹתֵן הַתּוֹרָה.

Praised are You, *Adonai,* Ruler of the universe, Who has chosen us with the gift of the Torah. Praised are You, *Adonai,* Giver of the Torah.

After the Torah is read, the one(s) being honored say(s):

בָּרוּךְ אַתָּה יְיָ אֱלֹהֵינוּ מֶלֶךְ הָעוֹלָם אֲשֶׁר נָתַן לָנוּ תּוֹרַת
אֱמֶת וְחַיֵּי עוֹלָם נָטַע בְּתוֹכֵנוּ. בָּרוּךְ אַתָּה יְיָ נוֹתֵן הַתּוֹרָה.

Praised are You, *Adonai,* Ruler of the universe, Who has given us the Torah of truth, a guide forever. Praised are You, *Adonai,* Giver of the Torah.

TORAH READING

Leviticus, Chapter 16

The Torah reading for today describes a unique service that took place in ancient times. The Torah speaks of the time the Israelites wandered in the desert, of Aaron the first *kohen* (priest) and of the portable Sanctuary. The service which it describes became part of the Temple service in Jerusalem on *Yom Kippur*. Aaron, the High Priest, dressed in a white robe and head covering, confessed not only his own sins but also the sins of his household and the entire people of Israel. He also performed an unusual ceremony involving two goats.

One goat he declared "for *Adonai*" and gave it as an offering. The other goat was a "scapegoat." The people imagined that their sins were placed on the goat and it was sent off into the wilderness, carrying their sins away. This was done as a sign that they truly wanted to get rid of their sins and turn to God.

Today's Torah portion also includes these verses about the observance of *Yom Kippur*:

> On the tenth day of the month you shall fast and do no work. This law is meant for both the citizen and the stranger who lives in your area. For on that day, atonement will be made, so that you will be cleansed of your sins before *Adonai*. It will be a Sabbath of Sabbaths for you and all the generations to come. (Lev. 16:29-31)

Today when we think of a scapegoat, we usually mean someone who is blamed for someone else's problems. A scapegoat can be a person or an entire people. Were you or someone you know ever made a scapegoat? Tell how it felt. Can you give examples of times when the Jewish people were scapegoats? How is the scapegoat in the Torah the same as a scapegoat today? How is it different? What can we do to avoid unjustly putting the blame on someone?

TORAH READING

Leviticus, Chapter 16 **וַיִּקְרָא טז**

Kohen

וְנָתַ֧ן אַהֲרֹ֛ן עַל־שְׁנֵ֥י הַשְּׂעִירִ֖ם גֹּֽרָל֑וֹת גּוֹרָ֤ל אֶחָד֙ לַֽיהוָ֔ה וְגוֹרָ֥ל אֶחָ֖ד
לַעֲזָאזֵֽל׃ וְהִקְרִ֤יב אַהֲרֹן֙ אֶת־הַשָּׂעִ֔יר אֲשֶׁ֨ר עָלָ֥ה עָלָ֛יו הַגּוֹרָ֖ל
לַיהוָ֑ה וְעָשָׂ֖הוּ חַטָּֽאת׃ וְהַשָּׂעִ֗יר אֲשֶׁר֩ עָלָ֨ה עָלָ֤יו הַגּוֹרָל֙ לַעֲזָאזֵ֔ל
יָֽעֳמַד־חַ֛י לִפְנֵ֥י יְהוָ֖ה לְכַפֵּ֣ר עָלָ֑יו לְשַׁלַּ֥ח אֹת֛וֹ לַעֲזָאזֵ֖ל הַמִּדְבָּֽרָה׃
On Shabbat: Levi וְהִקְרִ֨יב אַהֲרֹ֜ן אֶת־פַּ֤ר הַֽחַטָּאת֙ אֲשֶׁר־ל֔וֹ וְכִפֶּ֥ר
בַּעֲד֖וֹ וּבְעַ֣ד בֵּית֑וֹ וְשָׁחַ֛ט אֶת־פַּ֥ר הַחַטָּ֖את אֲשֶׁר־לֽוֹ׃ וְלָקַ֣ח
מְלֹֽא־הַ֠מַּחְתָּה גַּֽחֲלֵי־אֵ֞שׁ מֵעַ֤ל הַמִּזְבֵּ֙חַ֙ מִלִּפְנֵ֣י יְהוָ֔ה וּמְלֹ֣א חָפְנָ֔יו
קְטֹ֥רֶת סַמִּ֖ים דַּקָּ֑ה וְהֵבִ֖יא מִבֵּ֥ית לַפָּרֹֽכֶת׃ וְנָתַ֧ן אֶֽת־הַקְּטֹ֛רֶת
עַל־הָאֵ֖שׁ לִפְנֵ֣י יְהוָ֑ה וְכִסָּ֣ה ׀ עֲנַ֣ן הַקְּטֹ֗רֶת אֶת־הַכַּפֹּ֛רֶת אֲשֶׁ֥ר
עַל־הָעֵד֖וּת וְלֹ֥א יָמֽוּת׃

Levi On Shabbat: Shlishi

וְלָקַח֙ מִדַּ֣ם הַפָּ֔ר וְהִזָּ֧ה בְאֶצְבָּע֛וֹ עַל־פְּנֵ֥י הַכַּפֹּ֖רֶת קֵ֑דְמָה וְלִפְנֵ֣י
הַכַּפֹּ֗רֶת יַזֶּ֧ה שֶֽׁבַע־פְּעָמִ֛ים מִן־הַדָּ֖ם בְּאֶצְבָּעֽוֹ׃ וְשָׁחַ֞ט אֶת־שְׂעִ֤יר
הַֽחַטָּאת֙ אֲשֶׁ֣ר לָעָ֔ם וְהֵבִיא֙ אֶת־דָּמ֔וֹ אֶל־מִבֵּ֖ית לַפָּרֹ֑כֶת וְעָשָׂ֣ה
אֶת־דָּמ֗וֹ כַּאֲשֶׁ֤ר עָשָׂה֙ לְדַ֣ם הַפָּ֔ר וְהִזָּ֥ה אֹת֛וֹ עַל־הַכַּפֹּ֖רֶת וְלִפְנֵ֥י
הַכַּפֹּֽרֶת׃ וְכִפֶּ֣ר עַל־הַקֹּ֗דֶשׁ מִטֻּמְאֹת֙ בְּנֵ֣י יִשְׂרָאֵ֔ל וּמִפִּשְׁעֵיהֶ֖ם לְכָל־
חַטֹּאתָ֑ם וְכֵ֤ן יַעֲשֶׂה֙ לְאֹ֣הֶל מוֹעֵ֔ד הַשֹּׁכֵ֣ן אִתָּ֔ם בְּת֖וֹךְ טֻמְאֹתָֽם׃

Shlishi On Shabbat: R'vi'i

וְכָל־אָדָ֞ם לֹא־יִהְיֶ֣ה ׀ בְּאֹ֣הֶל מוֹעֵ֗ד בְּבֹא֛וֹ לְכַפֵּ֥ר בַּקֹּ֖דֶשׁ עַד־צֵאת֑וֹ
וְכִפֶּ֤ר בַּעֲדוֹ֙ וּבְעַ֣ד בֵּית֔וֹ וּבְעַ֖ד כָּל־קְהַ֥ל יִשְׂרָאֵֽל׃ וְיָצָ֗א
אֶל־הַמִּזְבֵּ֛חַ אֲשֶׁ֥ר לִפְנֵֽי־יְהוָ֖ה וְכִפֶּ֣ר עָלָ֑יו וְלָקַ֞ח מִדַּ֤ם הַפָּר֙ וּמִדַּ֣ם

הַשָּׂעִיר וְנָתַן עַל־קַרְנוֹת הַמִּזְבֵּחַ סָבִיב׃ וְהִזָּה עָלָיו מִן־הַדָּם
בְּאֶצְבָּעוֹ שֶׁבַע פְּעָמִים וְטִהֲרוֹ וְקִדְּשׁוֹ מִטֻּמְאֹת בְּנֵי יִשְׂרָאֵל׃

R'vi'i   On Shabbat: Ḥamishi

וְכִלָּה מִכַּפֵּר אֶת־הַקֹּדֶשׁ וְאֶת־אֹהֶל מוֹעֵד וְאֶת־הַמִּזְבֵּחַ וְהִקְרִיב
אֶת־הַשָּׂעִיר הֶחָי׃ וְסָמַךְ אַהֲרֹן אֶת־שְׁתֵּי יָדָו עַל־רֹאשׁ הַשָּׂעִיר
הַחַי וְהִתְוַדָּה עָלָיו אֶת־כָּל־עֲוֺנֹת בְּנֵי יִשְׂרָאֵל וְאֶת־כָּל־פִּשְׁעֵיהֶם
לְכָל־חַטֹּאתָם וְנָתַן אֹתָם עַל־רֹאשׁ הַשָּׂעִיר וְשִׁלַּח בְּיַד־אִישׁ עִתִּי
הַמִּדְבָּרָה׃ וְנָשָׂא הַשָּׂעִיר עָלָיו אֶת־כָּל־עֲוֺנֹתָם אֶל־אֶרֶץ גְּזֵרָה
וְשִׁלַּח אֶת־הַשָּׂעִיר בַּמִּדְבָּר׃ וּבָא אַהֲרֹן אֶל־אֹהֶל מוֹעֵד וּפָשַׁט
אֶת־בִּגְדֵי הַבָּד אֲשֶׁר לָבַשׁ בְּבֹאוֹ אֶל־הַקֹּדֶשׁ וְהִנִּיחָם שָׁם׃

Ḥamishi   On Shabbat: Shishi

וְרָחַץ אֶת־בְּשָׂרוֹ בַמַּיִם בְּמָקוֹם קָדוֹשׁ וְלָבַשׁ אֶת־בְּגָדָיו וְיָצָא
וְעָשָׂה אֶת־עֹלָתוֹ וְאֶת־עֹלַת הָעָם וְכִפֶּר בַּעֲדוֹ וּבְעַד הָעָם׃ וְאֵת
חֵלֶב הַחַטָּאת יַקְטִיר הַמִּזְבֵּחָה׃ וְהַמְשַׁלֵּחַ אֶת־הַשָּׂעִיר לַעֲזָאזֵל
יְכַבֵּס בְּגָדָיו וְרָחַץ אֶת־בְּשָׂרוֹ בַּמָּיִם וְאַחֲרֵי־כֵן יָבוֹא אֶל־הַמַּחֲנֶה׃

Shishi   On Shabbat: Sh'vi'i

וְאֵת פַּר הַחַטָּאת וְאֵת ׀ שְׂעִיר הַחַטָּאת אֲשֶׁר הוּבָא אֶת־דָּמָם
לְכַפֵּר בַּקֹּדֶשׁ יוֹצִיא אֶל־מִחוּץ לַמַּחֲנֶה וְשָׂרְפוּ בָאֵשׁ אֶת־עֹרֹתָם
וְאֶת־בְּשָׂרָם וְאֶת־פִּרְשָׁם׃ וְהַשֹּׂרֵף אֹתָם יְכַבֵּס בְּגָדָיו וְרָחַץ
אֶת־בְּשָׂרוֹ בַּמָּיִם וְאַחֲרֵי־כֵן יָבוֹא אֶל־הַמַּחֲנֶה׃ וְהָיְתָה לָכֶם לְחֻקַּת
עוֹלָם בַּחֹדֶשׁ הַשְּׁבִיעִי בֶּעָשׂוֹר לַחֹדֶשׁ תְּעַנּוּ אֶת־נַפְשֹׁתֵיכֶם
וְכָל־מְלָאכָה לֹא תַעֲשׂוּ הָאֶזְרָח וְהַגֵּר הַגָּר בְּתוֹכְכֶם׃ כִּי־בַיּוֹם
הַזֶּה יְכַפֵּר עֲלֵיכֶם לְטַהֵר אֶתְכֶם מִכֹּל חַטֹּאתֵיכֶם לִפְנֵי יְהוָה
תִּטְהָרוּ׃ שַׁבַּת שַׁבָּתוֹן הִיא לָכֶם וְעִנִּיתֶם אֶת־נַפְשֹׁתֵיכֶם חֻקַּת
עוֹלָם׃

We stand as we raise the Torah and all say:

וְזֹאת הַתּוֹרָה אֲשֶׁר שָׂם מֹשֶׁה לִפְנֵי בְּנֵי יִשְׂרָאֵל עַל פִּי יְיָ בְּיַד מֹשֶׁה.

This is the Torah of God, given through Moses who presented it to the people of Israel.

V'zot haTorah asher sam Mosheh lifnei b'nei Yisrael al pi Adonai b'yad Mosheh.

MAFTIR

The *maftir* (Numbers 29:7-11) which is read from a second Torah scroll in adult congregations instructs the people of Israel to observe a sacred fast day on the tenth day of the seventh month. On this day (of *Yom Kippur*) no work should be done. It should be a time of offering sacrifices to atone for sins.

HAFTARAH

Isaiah 57:14-58:14

Cry out and raise your voice like a *shofar* to tell my people of their sins. They have tried to be close and to follow my ways but they have not been sincere. They fasted while treating their workers unfairly. They fasted while fighting with their neighbors. Thus, I will not listen to their voices.

The fast I desire must go along with good deeds. Therefore, free the oppressed. Remove the poverty that is all around you. Give bread to the hungry, clothes to the needy and shelter to the homeless.

Then you will be healed and the glory of God will be with you to guide you and give you strength. Your gloom will be gone and you will feel satisfied. You will be like a watered garden, like a never-failing spring. You will then repair and rebuild what we began together long ago. (based on Isaiah 58:1-12)

To think about ...

The *haftarah* teaches us that the real meaning of *Yom Kippur* is not just in following the rules of this day. The rules are meant to help us think about how we can make ourselves and the world better. Fasting, for example, may be important, but feeding the hungry is more important. Our day of prayer and fasting must lead us to acts of kindness that help others. All of our praying and all of our fasting are not enough unless we do good in the world.

The Prophet Isaiah's message in the *haftarah* for *Yom Kippur* reminds us of our responsibility of caring for the hungry. We do this by bringing food to the synagogue for distribution to the hungry in our community and by contributing to organizations such as Mazon, A Jewish Response to Hunger. Conservative synagogues, based on today's *haftarah,* call their year-round program to feed the hungry Operation Isaiah. In many congregations the custom has been established of people bringing food for distribution at the beginning of the fast when they arrive for *Yom Kippur*. By doing this, we remind ourselves of Isaiah's message that we have an obligation to help those in need all year round.

Does your congregation have a program to feed the hungry? If not, perhaps you can discuss the possibility with your rabbi.

THE *HAFTARAH*

This blessing is said before reading the *haftarah*.

בָּרוּךְ אַתָּה יְיָ אֱלֹהֵינוּ מֶלֶךְ הָעוֹלָם אֲשֶׁר בָּחַר בִּנְבִיאִים
טוֹבִים וְרָצָה בְדִבְרֵיהֶם הַנֶּאֱמָרִים בֶּאֱמֶת. בָּרוּךְ אַתָּה יְיָ
הַבּוֹחֵר בַּתּוֹרָה וּבְמֹשֶׁה עַבְדּוֹ וּבְיִשְׂרָאֵל עַמּוֹ וּבִנְבִיאֵי
הָאֱמֶת וָצֶדֶק.

The *haftarah* is read.

FROM THE HAFTARAH

Isaiah 58: 5-8

ישעיה נח: ה-ח

הֲכָזֶ֗ה יִֽהְיֶה֙ צ֣וֹם אֶבְחָרֵ֔הוּ י֛וֹם עַנּ֥וֹת אָדָ֖ם נַפְשׁ֑וֹ
הֲלָכֹ֨ף כְּאַגְמֹ֜ן רֹאשׁ֗וֹ וְשַׂ֤ק וָאֵ֙פֶר֙ יַצִּ֔יעַ הֲלָזֶה֙ תִּקְרָא־צ֔וֹם
וְי֥וֹם רָצ֖וֹן לַיהוָֽה׃ הֲל֣וֹא זֶ֗ה צ֚וֹם אֶבְחָרֵ֔הוּ פַּתֵּ֙חַ֙
חַרְצֻבּ֣וֹת רֶ֔שַׁע הַתֵּ֖ר אֲגֻדּ֣וֹת מוֹטָ֑ה וְשַׁלַּ֤ח רְצוּצִים֙
חָפְשִׁ֔ים וְכָל־מוֹטָ֖ה תְּנַתֵּֽקוּ׃ הֲל֨וֹא פָרֹ֤ס לָֽרָעֵב֙ לַחְמֶ֔ךָ
וַעֲנִיִּ֥ים מְרוּדִ֖ים תָּ֣בִיא בָ֑יִת כִּֽי־תִרְאֶ֤ה עָרֹם֙ וְכִסִּית֔וֹ
וּמִבְּשָׂרְךָ֖ לֹ֥א תִתְעַלָּֽם׃ אָ֣ז יִבָּקַ֤ע כַּשַּׁ֙חַר֙ אוֹרֶ֔ךָ וַאֲרֻכָתְךָ֖
מְהֵרָ֣ה תִצְמָ֑ח וְהָלַ֤ךְ לְפָנֶ֙יךָ֙ צִדְקֶ֔ךָ כְּב֥וֹד יְהוָ֖ה יַאַסְפֶֽךָ׃

These blessings are said after the *haftarah* is read.
(On *Shabbat* add the words in brackets.)

בָּרוּךְ אַתָּה יְיָ אֱלֹהֵינוּ מֶלֶךְ הָעוֹלָם, צוּר כָּל־הָעוֹלָמִים, צַדִּיק בְּכָל־הַדּוֹרוֹת, הָאֵל הַנֶּאֱמָן הָאוֹמֵר וְעוֹשֶׂה הַמְדַבֵּר וּמְקַיֵּם, שֶׁכָּל־דְּבָרָיו אֱמֶת וָצֶדֶק. נֶאֱמָן אַתָּה הוּא יְיָ אֱלֹהֵינוּ וְנֶאֱמָנִים דְּבָרֶיךָ, וְדָבָר אֶחָד מִדְּבָרֶיךָ אָחוֹר לֹא יָשׁוּב רֵיקָם, כִּי אֵל מֶלֶךְ נֶאֱמָן וְרַחֲמָן אָתָּה. בָּרוּךְ אַתָּה יְיָ הָאֵל הַנֶּאֱמָן בְּכָל־דְּבָרָיו.

רַחֵם עַל צִיּוֹן כִּי הִיא בֵּית חַיֵּינוּ. וְלַעֲלוּבַת נֶפֶשׁ תּוֹשִׁיעַ בִּמְהֵרָה בְיָמֵינוּ. בָּרוּךְ אַתָּה יְיָ מְשַׂמֵּחַ צִיּוֹן בְּבָנֶיהָ.

שַׂמְּחֵנוּ יְיָ אֱלֹהֵינוּ בְּאֵלִיָּהוּ הַנָּבִיא עַבְדֶּךָ וּבְמַלְכוּת בֵּית דָּוִד מְשִׁיחֶךָ. בִּמְהֵרָה יָבוֹא וְיָגֵל לִבֵּנוּ, עַל כִּסְאוֹ לֹא יֵשֶׁב זָר וְלֹא יִנְחֲלוּ עוֹד אֲחֵרִים אֶת־כְּבוֹדוֹ, כִּי בְשֵׁם קָדְשְׁךָ נִשְׁבַּעְתָּ לוֹ שֶׁלֹּא יִכְבֶּה נֵרוֹ לְעוֹלָם וָעֶד. בָּרוּךְ אַתָּה יְיָ מָגֵן דָּוִד.

עַל הַתּוֹרָה וְעַל הָעֲבוֹדָה וְעַל הַנְּבִיאִים (וְעַל יוֹם הַשַּׁבָּת הַזֶּה) וְעַל יוֹם הַכִּפּוּרִים הַזֶּה שֶׁנָּתַתָּ לָּנוּ יְיָ אֱלֹהֵינוּ (לִקְדֻשָּׁה וְלִמְנוּחָה) לִמְחִילָה וְלִסְלִיחָה וּלְכַפָּרָה לְכָבוֹד וּלְתִפְאָרֶת. עַל הַכֹּל יְיָ אֱלֹהֵינוּ אֲנַחְנוּ מוֹדִים לָךְ, וּמְבָרְכִים אוֹתָךְ. יִתְבָּרַךְ שִׁמְךָ בְּפִי כָּל־חַי תָּמִיד לְעוֹלָם וָעֶד. וּדְבָרְךָ אֱמֶת וְקַיָּם לָעַד. בָּרוּךְ אַתָּה יְיָ מֶלֶךְ מוֹחֵל וְסוֹלֵחַ לַעֲוֹנוֹתֵינוּ וְלַעֲוֹנוֹת עַמּוֹ בֵּית יִשְׂרָאֵל, וּמַעֲבִיר אַשְׁמוֹתֵינוּ בְּכָל־שָׁנָה וְשָׁנָה, מֶלֶךְ עַל כָּל־הָאָרֶץ מְקַדֵּשׁ (הַשַּׁבָּת וְ)יִשְׂרָאֵל וְיוֹם הַכִּפּוּרִים.

Happy are those who dwell in Your house, for they will continually praise You. Happy is the people whose God is *Adonai*.

אַשְׁרֵי יוֹשְׁבֵי בֵיתֶךָ, עוֹד יְהַלְלוּךָ סֶּלָה.
אַשְׁרֵי הָעָם שֶׁכָּכָה לּוֹ, אַשְׁרֵי הָעָם שֶׁיְיָ אֱלֹהָיו.

תְּהִלָּה לְדָוִד.

אֲרוֹמִמְךָ אֱלוֹהַי הַמֶּלֶךְ וַאֲבָרְכָה שִׁמְךָ לְעוֹלָם וָעֶד.
בְּכָל־יוֹם אֲבָרְכֶךָּ וַאֲהַלְלָה שִׁמְךָ לְעוֹלָם וָעֶד.
גָּדוֹל יְיָ וּמְהֻלָּל מְאֹד וְלִגְדֻלָּתוֹ אֵין חֵקֶר.
דּוֹר לְדוֹר יְשַׁבַּח מַעֲשֶׂיךָ וּגְבוּרֹתֶיךָ יַגִּידוּ.
הֲדַר כְּבוֹד הוֹדֶךָ וְדִבְרֵי נִפְלְאֹתֶיךָ אָשִׂיחָה.
וֶעֱזוּז נוֹרְאֹתֶיךָ יֹאמֵרוּ וּגְדוּלָּתְךָ אֲסַפְּרֶנָּה.
זֵכֶר רַב טוּבְךָ יַבִּיעוּ וְצִדְקָתְךָ יְרַנֵּנוּ.
חַנּוּן וְרַחוּם יְיָ, אֶרֶךְ אַפַּיִם וּגְדָל־חָסֶד.
טוֹב יְיָ לַכֹּל וְרַחֲמָיו עַל כָּל־מַעֲשָׂיו.
יוֹדוּךָ יְיָ כָּל־מַעֲשֶׂיךָ וַחֲסִידֶיךָ יְבָרְכוּכָה.
כְּבוֹד מַלְכוּתְךָ יֹאמֵרוּ וּגְבוּרָתְךָ יְדַבֵּרוּ.
לְהוֹדִיעַ לִבְנֵי הָאָדָם גְּבוּרֹתָיו וּכְבוֹד הֲדַר מַלְכוּתוֹ.
מַלְכוּתְךָ מַלְכוּת כָּל־עֹלָמִים וּמֶמְשַׁלְתְּךָ בְּכָל־דּוֹר וָדֹר.
סוֹמֵךְ יְיָ לְכָל־הַנֹּפְלִים וְזוֹקֵף לְכָל־הַכְּפוּפִים.
עֵינֵי כֹל אֵלֶיךָ יְשַׂבֵּרוּ וְאַתָּה נוֹתֵן לָהֶם אֶת־אָכְלָם בְּעִתּוֹ.

פּוֹתֵחַ אֶת־יָדֶךָ וּמַשְׂבִּיעַ לְכָל־חַי רָצוֹן.
צַדִּיק יְיָ בְּכָל־דְּרָכָיו וְחָסִיד בְּכָל־מַעֲשָׂיו.
קָרוֹב יְיָ לְכָל־קֹרְאָיו, לְכֹל אֲשֶׁר יִקְרָאֻהוּ בֶאֱמֶת.
רְצוֹן יְרֵאָיו יַעֲשֶׂה וְאֶת־שַׁוְעָתָם יִשְׁמַע וְיוֹשִׁיעֵם.
שׁוֹמֵר יְיָ אֶת־כָּל־אֹהֲבָיו וְאֵת כָּל־הָרְשָׁעִים יַשְׁמִיד.
תְּהִלַּת יְיָ יְדַבֶּר־פִּי וִיבָרֵךְ כָּל־בָּשָׂר שֵׁם קָדְשׁוֹ לְעוֹלָם וָעֶד.
וַאֲנַחְנוּ נְבָרֵךְ יָהּ מֵעַתָּה וְעַד עוֹלָם. הַלְלוּיָהּ.

A Prayersong of David (selections)

I glorify You, my God, my Ruler, and I will praise Your name forever.

God is to be praised though there are not adequate words to describe God's greatness.

One generation tells the next about Your acts.

They speak of Your wonders and Your majesty.

They tell of Your goodness and sing about Your love for us.

Adonai is close to all who pray with a sincere heart.

We shall praise *Adonai,* now and always, Halleluyah!

Everyone stands as the Torah is lifted up and returned to the ark.
As the Torah is carried around the congregation, the leader sings:

יְהַלְלוּ אֶת־שֵׁם יְיָ כִּי נִשְׂגָּב שְׁמוֹ לְבַדּוֹ.

The congregation sings:

הוֹדוֹ עַל אֶרֶץ וְשָׁמָיִם. וַיָּרֶם קֶרֶן לְעַמּוֹ
תְּהִלָּה לְכָל־חֲסִידָיו, לִבְנֵי יִשְׂרָאֵל עַם קְרֹבוֹ. הַלְלוּיָהּ.

Hodo al eretz v'shamayim.
Va'yarem keren l'amo, t'hilah l'ḥol ḥasidav,
liv'nei Yisrael am k'rovo, haleluyah.

We sing this only on *Shabbat:*

מִזְמוֹר לְדָוִד. הָבוּ לַיְיָ בְּנֵי אֵלִים, הָבוּ לַיְיָ כָּבוֹד וָעֹז.
הָבוּ לַיְיָ כְּבוֹד שְׁמוֹ, הִשְׁתַּחֲווּ לַיְיָ בְּהַדְרַת קֹדֶשׁ.
קוֹל יְיָ עַל הַמָּיִם, אֵל הַכָּבוֹד הִרְעִים, יְיָ עַל מַיִם רַבִּים.
קוֹל יְיָ בַּכֹּחַ, קוֹל יְיָ בֶּהָדָר.
קוֹל יְיָ שֹׁבֵר אֲרָזִים וַיְשַׁבֵּר יְיָ אֶת־אַרְזֵי הַלְּבָנוֹן.
וַיַּרְקִידֵם כְּמוֹ עֵגֶל, לְבָנוֹן וְשִׂרְיוֹן כְּמוֹ בֶן־רְאֵמִים.
יְיָ עֹז לְעַמּוֹ יִתֵּן, יְיָ יְבָרֵךְ אֶת־עַמּוֹ בַשָּׁלוֹם.

We sing this on weekdays.

לְדָוִד מִזְמוֹר. לַיְיָ הָאָרֶץ וּמְלוֹאָהּ, תֵּבֵל וְיֹשְׁבֵי בָהּ. כִּי
הוּא עַל יַמִּים יְסָדָהּ, וְעַל נְהָרוֹת יְכוֹנְנֶהָ. מִי יַעֲלֶה בְהַר
יְיָ, וּמִי יָקוּם בִּמְקוֹם קָדְשׁוֹ. נְקִי כַפַּיִם וּבַר לֵבָב,
אֲשֶׁר לֹא נָשָׂא לַשָּׁוְא נַפְשִׁי, וְלֹא נִשְׁבַּע לְמִרְמָה.

The Torah is placed in the ark.

וּבְנֻחֹה יֹאמַר: שׁוּבָה יְיָ, רִבְבוֹת אַלְפֵי יִשְׂרָאֵל. קוּמָה יְיָ
לִמְנוּחָתֶךָ, אַתָּה וַאֲרוֹן עֻזֶּךָ. כֹּהֲנֶיךָ יִלְבְּשׁוּ־צֶדֶק,
וַחֲסִידֶיךָ יְרַנֵּנוּ. בַּעֲבוּר דָּוִד עַבְדֶּךָ, אַל תָּשֵׁב פְּנֵי
מְשִׁיחֶךָ. כִּי לֶקַח טוֹב נָתַתִּי לָכֶם, תּוֹרָתִי אַל תַּעֲזֹבוּ.

עֵץ חַיִּים הִיא לַמַּחֲזִיקִים בָּהּ, וְתֹמְכֶיהָ מְאֻשָּׁר.
דְּרָכֶיהָ דַרְכֵי־נֹעַם, וְכָל־נְתִיבוֹתֶיהָ שָׁלוֹם.
הֲשִׁיבֵנוּ יְיָ אֵלֶיךָ וְנָשׁוּבָה, חַדֵּשׁ יָמֵינוּ כְּקֶדֶם.

The Torah is a tree of life to those who live by its teachings.
Its ways are ways of pleasantness
and its paths are paths of peace.
Guide us back to You, *Adonai*.
Renew our glory as in days of old.

Etz ḥayim hi lamaḥazikim bah,
V'tomḥeha m'ushar.
D'raḥeha darḥei noam v'ḥol n'tivoteḥa shalom.
Hashiveinu Adonai eileḥa v'nashuvah,
ḥadesh yameinu k'kedem.

ḤATZI KADDISH

Short *Kaddish* חֲצִי קַדִּישׁ

Leader:

יִתְגַּדַּל וְיִתְקַדַּשׁ שְׁמֵהּ רַבָּא בְּעָלְמָא דִּי בְרָא כִרְעוּתֵהּ,
וְיַמְלִיךְ מַלְכוּתֵהּ בְּחַיֵּיכוֹן וּבְיוֹמֵיכוֹן וּבְחַיֵּי דְכָל־בֵּית
יִשְׂרָאֵל בַּעֲגָלָא וּבִזְמַן קָרִיב, וְאִמְרוּ אָמֵן.

Congregation and leader answer:

יְהֵא שְׁמֵהּ רַבָּא מְבָרַךְ לְעָלַם וּלְעָלְמֵי עָלְמַיָּא.

Y'hai shmai rabbah m'varaḥ l'olam u'l'olmei almay'ya.

Leader:

יִתְבָּרַךְ וְיִשְׁתַּבַּח וְיִתְפָּאַר וְיִתְרוֹמַם וְיִתְנַשֵּׂא וְיִתְהַדַּר
וְיִתְעַלֶּה וְיִתְהַלַּל שְׁמֵהּ דְּקֻדְשָׁא

Congregation and leader answer:

בְּרִיךְ הוּא.

B'riḥ hu.

Leader:

לְעֵלָּא לְעֵלָּא מִכָּל־בִּרְכָתָא וְשִׁירָתָא תֻּשְׁבְּחָתָא וְנֶחֱמָתָא
דַּאֲמִירָן בְּעָלְמָא, וְאִמְרוּ אָמֵן.

The version of the first blessing which speaks of our forefathers is found on page 149. The version which includes both the forefathers and mothers is found on page 151.

MUSAF

THE *AMIDAH*

(We rise as the Ark is opened.)

Adonai, open my lips and my mouth shall praise You.

בָּרוּךְ אַתָּה יְיָ אֱלֹהֵינוּ וֵאלֹהֵי אֲבוֹתֵינוּ, אֱלֹהֵי אַבְרָהָם
אֱלֹהֵי יִצְחָק וֵאלֹהֵי יַעֲקֹב, הָאֵל הַגָּדוֹל הַגִּבּוֹר וְהַנּוֹרָא
אֵל עֶלְיוֹן גּוֹמֵל חֲסָדִים טוֹבִים וְקוֹנֵה הַכֹּל, וְזוֹכֵר חַסְדֵי
אָבוֹת וּמֵבִיא גוֹאֵל לִבְנֵי בְנֵיהֶם לְמַעַן שְׁמוֹ בְּאַהֲבָה.

זָכְרֵנוּ לְחַיִּים מֶלֶךְ חָפֵץ בַּחַיִּים,
וְכָתְבֵנוּ בְּסֵפֶר הַחַיִּים לְמַעַנְךָ אֱלֹהִים חַיִּים.

מֶלֶךְ עוֹזֵר וּמוֹשִׁיעַ וּמָגֵן. בָּרוּךְ אַתָּה יְיָ מָגֵן אַבְרָהָם.

אַתָּה גִּבּוֹר לְעוֹלָם אֲדֹנָי מְחַיֵּה מֵתִים אַתָּה רַב לְהוֹשִׁיעַ.
מְכַלְכֵּל חַיִּים בְּחֶסֶד מְחַיֵּה מֵתִים בְּרַחֲמִים רַבִּים, סוֹמֵךְ
נוֹפְלִים וְרוֹפֵא חוֹלִים וּמַתִּיר אֲסוּרִים וּמְקַיֵּם אֱמוּנָתוֹ
לִישֵׁנֵי עָפָר. מִי כָמוֹךָ בַּעַל גְּבוּרוֹת וּמִי דּוֹמֶה לָּךְ, מֶלֶךְ
מֵמִית וּמְחַיֶּה וּמַצְמִיחַ יְשׁוּעָה.

מִי כָמוֹךָ אַב הָרַחֲמִים, זוֹכֵר יְצוּרָיו לְחַיִּים בְּרַחֲמִים.

וְנֶאֱמָן אַתָּה לְהַחֲיוֹת מֵתִים. בָּרוּךְ אַתָּה יְיָ מְחַיֵּה הַמֵּתִים.

Zoḥrenu l'ḥayim Meleḥ ḥafetz b'ḥayim,
v'ḥotveinu b'sefer haḥayim, l'ma'anḥa Elohim ḥayim.

Blessed are You, *Adonai,* our God and God of our ancestors,
God of Abraham, Isaac and Jacob.
Supreme God Who responds with kindness,
You remember the good deeds of our ancestors and
lovingly bring help to us.

On this day, we ask You for mercy.
Remember us for life, God Who delights in life.

Blessed are You, *Adonai,* Who protects Abraham.

You are the Source of life Who grants us healing and strength.

There is none as great and powerful as You.

We who are Your creation, *Adonai,* ask to be remembered for life.

Blessed are You, Source of life.

Continue on page 153.

MUSAF

THE *AMIDAH*

(We rise as the ark is opened.)

Adonai, open my lips and my mouth shall praise You.

בָּרוּךְ אַתָּה יְיָ אֱלֹהֵינוּ וֵאלֹהֵי אֲבוֹתֵינוּ, אֱלֹהֵי אַבְרָהָם
אֱלֹהֵי יִצְחָק וֵאלֹהֵי יַעֲקֹב, אֱלֹהֵי שָׂרָה אֱלֹהֵי רִבְקָה
אֱלֹהֵי רָחֵל וֵאלֹהֵי לֵאָה, הָאֵל הַגָּדוֹל הַגִּבּוֹר וְהַנּוֹרָא אֵל
עֶלְיוֹן גּוֹמֵל חֲסָדִים טוֹבִים וְקוֹנֵה הַכֹּל, וְזוֹכֵר חַסְדֵי
אָבוֹת וּמֵבִיא גוֹאֵל לִבְנֵי בְנֵיהֶם לְמַעַן שְׁמוֹ בְּאַהֲבָה.

זָכְרֵנוּ לְחַיִּים מֶלֶךְ חָפֵץ בַּחַיִּים,
וְכָתְבֵנוּ בְּסֵפֶר הַחַיִּים לְמַעַנְךָ אֱלֹהִים חַיִּים.

מֶלֶךְ עוֹזֵר וּפֹקֵד וּמוֹשִׁיעַ וּמָגֵן. בָּרוּךְ אַתָּה יְיָ מָגֵן
אַבְרָהָם וּפֹקֵד שָׂרָה.

אַתָּה גִּבּוֹר לְעוֹלָם אֲדֹנָי מְחַיֵּה מֵתִים אַתָּה רַב לְהוֹשִׁיעַ.
מְכַלְכֵּל חַיִּים בְּחֶסֶד מְחַיֵּה מֵתִים בְּרַחֲמִים רַבִּים, סוֹמֵךְ
נוֹפְלִים וְרוֹפֵא חוֹלִים וּמַתִּיר אֲסוּרִים וּמְקַיֵּם אֱמוּנָתוֹ
לִישֵׁנֵי עָפָר. מִי כָמוֹךָ בַּעַל גְּבוּרוֹת וּמִי דּוֹמֶה לָּךְ, מֶלֶךְ
מֵמִית וּמְחַיֶּה וּמַצְמִיחַ יְשׁוּעָה.

מִי כָמוֹךָ אַב הָרַחֲמִים, זוֹכֵר יְצוּרָיו לְחַיִּים בְּרַחֲמִים.

וְנֶאֱמָן אַתָּה לְהַחֲיוֹת מֵתִים. בָּרוּךְ אַתָּה יְיָ מְחַיֵּה הַמֵּתִים.

Zoḥrenu l'ḥayim Meleḥ ḥafetz b'ḥayim,
v'ḥotveinu b'sefer haḥayim, l'ma'anḥa Elohim ḥayim.

Blessed are You, *Adonai,* our God and God of our ancestors,
God of Abraham, Isaac and Jacob,
God of Sarah, Rebecca, Leah and Rachel.
Supreme God Who responds with kindness,
You remember the good deeds of our ancestors and
lovingly bring help to us.

On this day, we ask You for mercy.
Remember us for life, God Who delights in life.

Blessed are You, *Adonai,* Who protects Abraham and
remembers Sarah.

You are the Source of life Who grants us healing and strength.

There is none as great and powerful as You.

We who are Your creation, *Adonai,* ask to be remembered for life.

Blessed are You, Source of life.

וּנְתַנֶּה תֹּקֶף קְדֻשַּׁת הַיּוֹם כִּי הוּא נוֹרָא וְאָיֹם. וּבוֹ תִנַּשֵּׂא
מַלְכוּתֶךָ וְיִכּוֹן בְּחֶסֶד כִּסְאֶךָ וְתֵשֵׁב עָלָיו בֶּאֱמֶת. אֱמֶת כִּי
אַתָּה הוּא דַיָּן וּמוֹכִיחַ וְיוֹדֵעַ וָעֵד, וְכוֹתֵב וְחוֹתֵם וְסוֹפֵר
וּמוֹנֶה, וְתִזְכֹּר כָּל־הַנִּשְׁכָּחוֹת, וְתִפְתַּח אֶת־סֵפֶר הַזִּכְרוֹנוֹת,
וּמֵאֵלָיו יִקָּרֵא וְחוֹתַם יַד כָּל־אָדָם בּוֹ.

וּבְשׁוֹפָר גָּדוֹל יִתָּקַע וְקוֹל דְּמָמָה דַקָּה יִשָּׁמַע. וּמַלְאָכִים
יֵחָפֵזוּן וְחִיל וּרְעָדָה יֹאחֵזוּן וְיֹאמְרוּ הִנֵּה יוֹם הַדִּין.
לִפְקֹד עַל צְבָא מָרוֹם בַּדִּין כִּי לֹא יִזְכּוּ בְעֵינֶיךָ בַּדִּין,
וְכָל־בָּאֵי עוֹלָם יַעַבְרוּן לְפָנֶיךָ כִּבְנֵי מָרוֹן. כְּבַקָּרַת
רוֹעֶה עֶדְרוֹ מַעֲבִיר צֹאנוֹ תַּחַת שִׁבְטוֹ, כֵּן תַּעֲבִיר וְתִסְפֹּר
וְתִמְנֶה וְתִפְקֹד נֶפֶשׁ כָּל־חָי, וְתַחְתֹּךְ קִצְבָה לְכָל־בְּרִיָּה
וְתִכְתֹּב אֶת־גְּזַר דִּינָם.

Let us declare the greatness of this day of holiness! It is a day that acknowledges You, God, as our Judge. Today we pass before You like sheep. Each is precious to You and none goes unnoticed.

Help us to look into our hearts to judge ourselves. Give us the strength and courage to improve in the coming year.

בְּרֹאשׁ הַשָּׁנָה יִכָּתֵבוּן וּבְיוֹם צוֹם כִּפּוּר יֵחָתֵמוּן.

B'rosh hashanah yikateivun,
U'vyom tzom kippur yeiḥateimun.

We know, too, that our days on earth are precious. Only You can predict our future. But only we can decide how to live our lives.

Through prayer, charitable deeds and turning to God for forgiveness, we can make our lives better. May You soften our judgment, God, for You are the God of life.

Teshuvah, tefillah and *tzedakah* can change our lives.

וּתְשׁוּבָה וּתְפִלָּה וּצְדָקָה
מַעֲבִירִין אֶת־רֹעַ הַגְּזֵרָה.

U'teshuvah u'tefillah u'tzedakah ma'avirin et ro'a ha'g'zerah.

A Lesson at the Doorway

Rabbi Elijah spent much time trying to persuade the rich people in Lodz to help the poor people in that town. Sadly, some had to be coaxed to donate money.

One bitter winter, there were many poor people who could not afford to buy coal to keep warm. Rabbi Elijah decided he would pay a visit to Kalman Poznansky, the richest Jew in Lodz.

Kalman Poznansky was not pleased to hear that Rabbi Elijah was at his door. He guessed that the rabbi wanted a donation and Kalman was not eager to part with his money. Still, he felt it was his duty to greet the rabbi.

As soon as Kalman Poznansky opened the door, Rabbi Elijah began to talk non-stop about every topic under the sun. On and on he went as Kalman shivered from the cold temperature and freezing wind.

Finally, when his teeth began to chatter, Kalman asked the rabbi if they could continue the discussion inside. When they were seated, Kalman Poznansky then asked Rabbi Elijah why he wanted to talk to him at the doorway instead of in his comfortable warm house.

The rabbi explained that he had indeed come to ask for *tzedakah.* If he had made his request inside, Kalman would not have understood about the sufferings of the poor.

Kalman said to himself, "I have been in the freezing cold for only a few minutes. Imagine how hard it is for those who have to endure this cold all winter." And so, he gave Rabbi Elijah an extra-generous donation.

The ark is closed. We recite the *Kedushah* while standing.
The congregation chants the indented lines.

עֲשֵׂה לְמַעַן שְׁמֶֽךָ וְקַדֵּשׁ אֶת־שִׁמְךָ עַל מַקְדִּישֵׁי שְׁמֶֽךָ,
בַּעֲבוּר כְּבוֹד שִׁמְךָ הַנַּעֲרָץ וְהַנִּקְדָּשׁ כְּסוֹד שִֽׂיחַ
שַׂרְפֵי־קֹֽדֶשׁ הַמַּקְדִּישִׁים שְׁמֶךָ בַּקֹּֽדֶשׁ, דָּרֵי מַֽעְלָה עִם דָּרֵי
מַֽטָּה כַּכָּתוּב עַל יַד נְבִיאֶֽךָ, וְקָרָא זֶה אֶל זֶה וְאָמַר:

קָדוֹשׁ קָדוֹשׁ קָדוֹשׁ יְיָ צְבָאוֹת, מְלֹא כָל־הָאָֽרֶץ כְּבוֹדוֹ.

כְּבוֹדוֹ מָלֵא עוֹלָם, מְשָׁרְתָיו שׁוֹאֲלִים זֶה לָזֶה אַיֵּה מְקוֹם
כְּבוֹדוֹ, לְעֻמָּתָם בָּרוּךְ יֹאמֵֽרוּ:

בָּרוּךְ כְּבוֹד יְיָ מִמְּקוֹמוֹ.

מִמְּקוֹמוֹ הוּא יִֽפֶן בְּרַחֲמִים וְיָחֹן עַם הַמְיַחֲדִים שְׁמוֹ עֶֽרֶב
וָבֹֽקֶר בְּכָל־יוֹם תָּמִיד פַּעֲמַֽיִם בְּאַהֲבָה שְׁמַע אוֹמְרִים:

שְׁמַע יִשְׂרָאֵל יְיָ אֱלֹהֵֽינוּ יְיָ אֶחָד.

הוּא אֱלֹהֵֽינוּ הוּא אָבִֽינוּ הוּא מַלְכֵּֽנוּ הוּא מוֹשִׁיעֵֽנוּ, וְהוּא
יַשְׁמִיעֵֽנוּ בְּרַחֲמָיו שֵׁנִית לְעֵינֵי כָּל־חָי, לִהְיוֹת לָכֶם
לֵאלֹהִים:

אֲנִי יְיָ אֱלֹהֵיכֶם.

אַדִּיר אַדִּירֵֽנוּ יְיָ אֲדוֹנֵֽינוּ, מָה אַדִּיר שִׁמְךָ בְּכָל־הָאָֽרֶץ.
וְהָיָה יְיָ לְמֶֽלֶךְ עַל כָּל־הָאָֽרֶץ, בַּיּוֹם הַהוּא יִהְיֶה יְיָ אֶחָד
וּשְׁמוֹ אֶחָד. וּבְדִבְרֵי קָדְשְׁךָ כָּתוּב לֵאמֹר:

יִמְלֹךְ יְיָ לְעוֹלָם אֱלֹהַיִךְ צִיּוֹן לְדֹר וָדֹר, הַלְלוּיָהּ.

לְדוֹר וָדוֹר נַגִּיד גָּדְלֶךָ, וּלְנֵצַח נְצָחִים קְדֻשָּׁתְךָ נַקְדִּישׁ,
וְשִׁבְחֲךָ אֱלֹהֵינוּ מִפִּינוּ לֹא יָמוּשׁ לְעוֹלָם וָעֶד כִּי אֵל מֶלֶךְ
גָּדוֹל וְקָדוֹשׁ אָתָּה.

We imagine heavenly angels, together with us on earth, singing the praises of God. They call to one another:

> Holy, holy, holy — the whole world is filled with God's glory.

And we, the Jewish people, declare:

> *Shema Yisrael* — Hear, O Israel: The Lord Our God, the Lord is One.

In every generation we will speak of God's greatness and forever declare God's holiness.

וּבְכֵן תֵּן פַּחְדְּךָ יְיָ אֱלֹהֵינוּ עַל כָּל-מַעֲשֶׂיךָ וְאֵימָתְךָ
עַל-כָּל-מַה-שֶּׁבָּרָאתָ, וְיִירָאוּךָ כָּל-הַמַּעֲשִׂים וְיִשְׁתַּחֲווּ
לְפָנֶיךָ כָּל-הַבְּרוּאִים, וְיֵעָשׂוּ כֻלָּם אֲגֻדָּה אַחַת לַעֲשׂוֹת
רְצוֹנְךָ בְּלֵבָב שָׁלֵם.

Let all creatures feel awe in Your presence and join together to follow Your will.

Why does the world begin with Adam and Eve?

In order that no person can say: "My parents were more important than yours."

וּבְכֵן תֵּן כָּבוֹד יְיָ לְעַמֶּךָ תְּהִלָּה לִירֵאֶיךָ וְתִקְוָה
לְדוֹרְשֶׁיךָ וּפִתְחוֹן פֶּה לַמְיַחֲלִים לָךְ, שִׂמְחָה לְאַרְצֶךָ
וְשָׂשׂוֹן לְעִירֶךָ וּצְמִיחַת קֶרֶן לְדָוִד עַבְדֶּךָ וַעֲרִיכַת נֵר
לְבֶן־יִשַׁי מְשִׁיחֶךָ בִּמְהֵרָה בְיָמֵינוּ.

וּבְכֵן צַדִּיקִים יִרְאוּ וְיִשְׂמָחוּ וִישָׁרִים יַעֲלֹזוּ וַחֲסִידִים
בְּרִנָּה יָגִילוּ, וְעוֹלָתָה תִּקְפָּץ־פִּיהָ וְכָל־הָרִשְׁעָה כֻּלָּהּ
כְּעָשָׁן תִּכְלֶה כִּי תַעֲבִיר מֶמְשֶׁלֶת זָדוֹן מִן הָאָרֶץ.

בָּרוּךְ אַתָּה יְיָ הַמֶּלֶךְ הַקָּדוֹשׁ.

Grant honor to our people and glory to all who have faith in You.

May the day come when all wickedness will end.

Blessed are You, *Adonai,* the holy Ruler.

You have called us to Your service through Your *mitzvot* and chosen us to celebrate special holy days.

אַתָּה בְחַרְתָּנוּ מִכָּל־הָעַמִּים, אָהַבְתָּ אוֹתָנוּ וְרָצִיתָ בָּנוּ
וְרוֹמַמְתָּנוּ מִכָּל־הַלְּשׁוֹנוֹת וְקִדַּשְׁתָּנוּ בְּמִצְוֹתֶיךָ וְקֵרַבְתָּנוּ
מַלְכֵּנוּ לַעֲבוֹדָתֶךָ וְשִׁמְךָ הַגָּדוֹל וְהַקָּדוֹשׁ עָלֵינוּ קָרָאתָ.

On *Shabbat* add the words in brackets:

וַתִּתֶּן־לָֽנוּ יְיָ אֱלֹהֵֽינוּ בְּאַהֲבָה אֶת־יוֹם (הַשַּׁבָּת הַזֶּה
לִקְדֻשָּׁה וְלִמְנוּחָה וְאֶת־יוֹם) הַכִּפּוּרִים הַזֶּה לִמְחִילָה
וְלִסְלִיחָה וּלְכַפָּרָה וְלִמְחָל־בּוֹ אֶת־כָּל־עֲוֹנוֹתֵֽינוּ (בְּאַהֲבָה)
מִקְרָא קֹֽדֶשׁ זֵֽכֶר לִיצִיאַת מִצְרָֽיִם.

On *Shabbat* only, we say:

יִשְׂמְחוּ בְמַלְכוּתְךָ שׁוֹמְרֵי שַׁבָּת וְקֽוֹרְאֵי עֹֽנֶג. עַם מְקַדְּשֵׁי
שְׁבִיעִי כֻּלָּם יִשְׂבְּעוּ וְיִתְעַנְּגוּ מִטּוּבֶֽךָ. וְהַשְּׁבִיעִי רָצִֽיתָ בּוֹ
וְקִדַּשְׁתּוֹ, חֶמְדַּת יָמִים אוֹתוֹ קָרָֽאתָ זֵֽכֶר לְמַעֲשֵׂה בְרֵאשִׁית.

We all rise.

It is for us to praise the Ruler of all and to glorify the Creator of the world for giving us a special heritage and a unique destiny.

Before our Supreme Ruler we bend the knee and bow in devotion.

As it is written in the Torah, "Accept this day with both mind and heart. Know that God's presence fills all of creation."

Because we believe in You, we hope for the day when Your majesty will triumph and all the world will accept Your reign.

For it is written in the Torah, "*Adonai* shall rule for ever and ever."

Adonai shall rule forever and ever.

It is for us to praise the Ruler of all and to glorify the Creator of the World, for giving us a special heritage and a unique destiny. Before our Supreme Ruler we bend the knee and bow in devotion. As it is written in the Torah, "Accept this day with both mind and heart. Know that God's presence fills creation." Because we believe in You, we hope for the day when Your majesty will triumph and all the world will accept Your reign. For it is written in the Torah, "Adonai shall rule f o r e v e r a n d e v e r."

עָלֵינוּ לְשַׁבֵּחַ לַאֲדוֹן הַכֹּל, לָתֵת גְּדֻלָּה לְיוֹצֵר בְּרֵאשִׁית,
שֶׁלֹּא עָשָׂנוּ כְּגוֹיֵי הָאֲרָצוֹת וְלֹא שָׂמָנוּ כְּמִשְׁפְּחוֹת הָאֲדָמָה,
שֶׁלֹּא שָׂם חֶלְקֵנוּ כָּהֶם וְגוֹרָלֵנוּ כְּכָל־הֲמוֹנָם.

וַאֲנַחְנוּ כּוֹרְעִים וּמִשְׁתַּחֲוִים וּמוֹדִים לִפְנֵי מֶלֶךְ מַלְכֵי
הַמְּלָכִים הַקָּדוֹשׁ בָּרוּךְ הוּא,

שֶׁהוּא נוֹטֶה שָׁמַיִם וְיוֹסֵד אָרֶץ וּמוֹשַׁב יְקָרוֹ בַּשָּׁמַיִם
מִמַּעַל וּשְׁכִינַת עֻזּוֹ בְּגָבְהֵי מְרוֹמִים. הוּא אֱלֹהֵינוּ אֵין
עוֹד. אֱמֶת מַלְכֵּנוּ אֶפֶס זוּלָתוֹ, כַּכָּתוּב בְּתוֹרָתוֹ: וְיָדַעְתָּ
הַיּוֹם וַהֲשֵׁבֹתָ אֶל לְבָבֶךָ כִּי יְיָ הוּא הָאֱלֹהִים בַּשָּׁמַיִם
מִמַּעַל וְעַל הָאָרֶץ מִתָּחַת, אֵין עוֹד.

We are seated.

S'LIḤOT

יְיָ יְיָ אֵל רַחוּם וְחַנּוּן, אֶרֶךְ אַפַּיִם וְרַב חֶסֶד וֶאֱמֶת
נֹצֵר חֶסֶד לָאֲלָפִים נֹשֵׂא עָוֹן וָפֶשַׁע וְחַטָּאָה, וְנַקֵּה.

וְסָלַחְתָּ לַעֲוֹנֵנוּ וּלְחַטָּאתֵנוּ, וּנְחַלְתָּנוּ.

Adonai, Adonai, merciful and patient God,
You forgive our wrongdoings and our sins.

Adonai, answer our prayers with Your lovingkindness.

AVODAH SERVICE

In the days of the *Beit Mikdash* (Temple) in Jerusalem, a special service was held on *Yom Kippur*. On this day alone, the High Priest entered the room known as the Holy of Holies in which the Ark was placed. On this day alone, he also uttered the holy name of God. This was the name God told Moses at the burning bush. How this name was actually pronounced was never written down, so we don't know how to say it today. After the Temple was destroyed, the High Priest's prayers of confession became a part of our *Yom Kippur* service. They remind us to be devoted to God in both word and deed.

The High Priest used to say: Answer me, God, for I and my whole family have sinned before You. Forgive us. For it is written in Your holy Torah: "On this day I will grant you a new beginning and forgive all your sins."

Then, when the priests and all the people standing in the courtyard of the Temple heard the special name of God, they would bow and kneel. They would shout out the words, "Praised be God's glorious reign for ever and ever."

Then the High Priest would say these words from the Torah: "You shall be cleansed." After which he prayed: "And You, *Adonai,* in Your kindness, forgive Your devoted priest." Finally, the High Priest confessed his own sins as well as those of his household and all Israel.

This is a time to think about what we have done wrong and promise to improve our behavior.

EILEH EZKERAH

"These I remember with great sadness...."

On this holy day, we remember those martyrs who lost their lives because of their Jewish beliefs.

The ancient Roman court forbad us to study or teach the Torah. Many rabbis ignored this decree, though it meant torture and death. We remember Rabbi Ishmael, Rabbi Shimon and Rabbi Akiba. We remember Rabbi Judah ben Bava and Rabbi Ḥaninah.

When the Romans caught Rabbi Ḥaninah teaching Torah in public, they wrapped him in a *sefer* Torah (a Torah scroll) and set him on fire. As he was dying, he called to his students, "The parchment is burning but the letters are flying free!" He taught us that ideas can never be killed and truth will always live on.

To honor the memory of these martyrs, we pledge to study and follow the Torah.

On this holy day, we also remember those martyrs who lost their lives simply because they were Jewish.

The Nazis murdered six million innocent Jews. The Nazis believed Hitler's evil idea that the Jews were less than human and in their rush to do evil, the Nazis forgot that all are God's children, that all are equal and are cherished.

To honor the memory of these martyrs we pledge to protect Jews all over the world and to continue the Jewish way of life.

Adonai, answer our prayers with Your lovingkindness.

שְׁמַע קוֹלֵנוּ, יְיָ אֱלֹהֵינוּ, חוּס וְרַחֵם עָלֵינוּ,
וְקַבֵּל בְּרַחֲמִים וּבְרָצוֹן אֶת־תְּפִלָּתֵנוּ.
הֲשִׁיבֵנוּ יְיָ אֵלֶיךָ וְנָשׁוּבָה, חַדֵּשׁ יָמֵינוּ כְּקֶדֶם.

God has given us a gift — the opportunity to be able to ask for forgiveness and start over with a clean slate.

If we refuse to ask for forgiveness, we are insulting God who is waiting to forgive us.

By saying "**We** have sinned," we hold ourselves responsible for what happens in our communities.

אָשַׁמְנוּ, בָּגַדְנוּ, גָּזַלְנוּ, דִּבַּרְנוּ דֹפִי. הֶעֱוִינוּ, וְהִרְשַׁעְנוּ,
זַדְנוּ, חָמַסְנוּ, טָפַלְנוּ שֶׁקֶר. יָעַצְנוּ רָע, כִּזַּבְנוּ, לַצְנוּ,
מָרַדְנוּ, נִאַצְנוּ, סָרַרְנוּ, עָוִינוּ, פָּשַׁעְנוּ, צָרַרְנוּ, קִשִּׁינוּ עֹרֶף.
רָשַׁעְנוּ, שִׁחַתְנוּ, תִּעַבְנוּ, תָּעִינוּ, תִּעְתָּעְנוּ.

We have been cruel.
We have teased.
We have lied.
We have acted violently.
We have cheated.
We have boasted exceedingly.
We have been false.
We have mocked.
We have gossiped.
We have acted wickedly.
We have quarrelled.
We have been unjust.
We have acted selfishly.
We have not remembered Zion.

Ashamnu, bagadnu, gazalnu, dibarnu dofi;
he'evinu, v'hirshanu, zadnu, ḥamasnu, tafalnu shaker;
ya'atznu ra, kizavnu, latznu, maradnu, ni'atznu,
sararnu, avinu, pashanu, tzararnu, kishinu oref;
rashanu, shiḥatnu, ti'avnu, ta'inu, titanu.

We miss opportunities to do what is required of us. The following is a list in the Talmud of very important *mitzvot,* deeds that bring us closer to God:

honoring parents
visiting the sick
caring for guests
doing deeds of lovingkindness
trying to understand prayer
studying Torah
making peace between two people

Here are some opportunities to do *mitzvot:*

Inviting a new student to your house.

Calling someone in your class who is out sick to find out how they are feeling.

Helping your parents clean up around the house.

Helping an elderly person do yard work.

Thinking about what you are trying to do in synagogue during the High Holy Days.

Helping someone understand how they bother someone else.

Talking with your parents about something you learned in your synagogue school.

עַל חֵטְא שֶׁחָטָאנוּ לְפָנֶיךָ בְּאִמּוּץ הַלֵּב,
וְעַל חֵטְא שֶׁחָטָאנוּ לְפָנֶיךָ בְּבִטּוּי שְׂפָתָיִם.
עַל חֵטְא שֶׁחָטָאנוּ לְפָנֶיךָ בַּגָּלוּי וּבַסָּתֶר,
וְעַל חֵטְא שֶׁחָטָאנוּ לְפָנֶיךָ בְּדִבּוּר פֶּה.
עַל חֵטְא שֶׁחָטָאנוּ לְפָנֶיךָ בְּהַרְהוֹר הַלֵּב,
וְעַל חֵטְא שֶׁחָטָאנוּ לְפָנֶיךָ בְּחִלּוּל הַשֵּׁם.
עַל חֵטְא שֶׁחָטָאנוּ לְפָנֶיךָ בְּטִפְּשׁוּת פֶּה,
וְעַל חֵטְא שֶׁחָטָאנוּ לְפָנֶיךָ בְּיוֹדְעִים וּבְלֹא יוֹדְעִים.

וְעַל כֻּלָּם אֱלוֹהַּ סְלִיחוֹת, סְלַח לָנוּ, מְחַל לָנוּ, כַּפֶּר־לָנוּ.

עַל חֵטְא שֶׁחָטָאנוּ לְפָנֶיךָ בְּמַאֲכָל וּבְמִשְׁתֶּה,
וְעַל חֵטְא שֶׁחָטָאנוּ לְפָנֶיךָ בִּנְטִיַּת גָּרוֹן.
עַל חֵטְא שֶׁחָטָאנוּ לְפָנֶיךָ בְּשִׂקּוּר עָיִן,
וְעַל חֵטְא שֶׁחָטָאנוּ לְפָנֶיךָ בִּרְכִילוּת.
עַל חֵטְא שֶׁחָטָאנוּ לְפָנֶיךָ בְּשִׂנְאַת חִנָּם.

וְעַל כֻּלָּם אֱלוֹהַּ סְלִיחוֹת, סְלַח לָנוּ, מְחַל לָנוּ, כַּפֶּר־לָנוּ.

V'al kulam Eloha s'liḥot, s'laḥ lanu, m'ḥal lanu, kaper lanu.

Our God and God of our ancestors, let our prayers reach You and not be ignored. We are not so bold or foolish to think that we have been perfect and have not made mistakes. To be honest, we must admit we have sinned — missed the mark.

We have missed the mark

by not trying our best.
by not being loyal to friends.
by not being kind to animals.
by gossiping.
by not standing up for what is right.
by fighting and being mean.
by wasting time.
by giving up hope.

Add your own words.

For all these sins, God of forgiveness, forgive us, pardon us and grant us a new beginning.

Why do we say that God is the "Ruler who pardons and forgives our sins" when we are not truly certain if God will forgive us? Rabbi Elimeleḥ of Rudnik answered this question with a story:

Once a father brought home some delicious smelling apples. His son desperately wanted to have one but knew that they had been bought for guests who would soon be arriving. The boy's desire was so strong that he came up with a plan. In a loud voice so his father could hear, the son recited the blessing for fruit. Not wishing the child's blessing to be wasted, the father handed him an apple. So, too, when we say "Praised are You, *Adonai,* Who pardons and forgives our sins," we hope God will not want our blessing to be wasted.

בָּרוּךְ אַתָּה יְיָ מֶלֶךְ מוֹחֵל וְסוֹלֵחַ לַעֲוֹנוֹתֵינוּ וְלַעֲוֹנוֹת עַמּוֹ
בֵּית יִשְׂרָאֵל וּמַעֲבִיר אַשְׁמוֹתֵינוּ בְּכָל־שָׁנָה וְשָׁנָה, מֶלֶךְ עַל
כָּל־הָאָרֶץ מְקַדֵּשׁ (הַשַּׁבָּת וְ)יִשְׂרָאֵל וְיוֹם הַכִּפּוּרִים.

Praised are You, *Adonai,*
Who pardons and forgives our sins
and the sins of all the people Israel,
Who rules the earth and sanctifies [the *Shabbat*], the people Israel and *Yom Kippur*.

רְצֵה יְיָ אֱלֹהֵינוּ בְּעַמְּךָ יִשְׂרָאֵל וּבִתְפִלָּתָם וְהָשֵׁב
אֶת־הָעֲבוֹדָה לִדְבִיר בֵּיתֶךָ וּתְפִלָּתָם בְּאַהֲבָה תְקַבֵּל
בְּרָצוֹן וּתְהִי לְרָצוֹן תָּמִיד עֲבוֹדַת יִשְׂרָאֵל עַמֶּךָ. וְתֶחֱזֶינָה
עֵינֵינוּ בְּשׁוּבְךָ לְצִיּוֹן בְּרַחֲמִים. בָּרוּךְ אַתָּה יְיָ הַמַּחֲזִיר
שְׁכִינָתוֹ לְצִיּוֹן.

May God look upon us and our prayers with favor.
May we witness the return of Your glory to Zion.

מוֹדִים אֲנַחְנוּ לָךְ שָׁאַתָּה הוּא יְיָ אֱלֹהֵינוּ וֵאלֹהֵי אֲבוֹתֵינוּ
לְעוֹלָם וָעֶד, צוּר חַיֵּינוּ מָגֵן יִשְׁעֵנוּ אַתָּה הוּא. לְדוֹר וָדוֹר
נוֹדֶה לְּךָ וּנְסַפֵּר תְּהִלָּתֶךָ עַל חַיֵּינוּ הַמְּסוּרִים בְּיָדֶךָ וְעַל
נִשְׁמוֹתֵינוּ הַפְּקוּדוֹת לָךְ וְעַל נִסֶּיךָ שֶׁבְּכָל־יוֹם עִמָּנוּ וְעַל
נִפְלְאוֹתֶיךָ וְטוֹבוֹתֶיךָ שֶׁבְּכָל־עֵת עֶרֶב וָבֹקֶר וְצָהֳרָיִם.
הַטּוֹב כִּי לֹא כָלוּ רַחֲמֶיךָ וְהַמְרַחֵם כִּי לֹא תַמּוּ חֲסָדֶיךָ
מֵעוֹלָם קִוִּינוּ לָךְ.

וְעַל כֻּלָּם יִתְבָּרַךְ וְיִתְרוֹמַם שִׁמְךָ מַלְכֵּנוּ תָּמִיד לְעוֹלָם וָעֶד.

וּכְתֹב לְחַיִּים טוֹבִים כָּל־בְּנֵי בְרִיתֶךָ.

וְכֹל הַחַיִּים יוֹדוּךָ סֶּלָה וִיהַלְלוּ אֶת־שִׁמְךָ בֶּאֱמֶת הָאֵל
יְשׁוּעָתֵנוּ וְעֶזְרָתֵנוּ סֶלָה. בָּרוּךְ אַתָּה יְיָ הַטּוֹב שִׁמְךָ וּלְךָ
נָאֶה לְהוֹדוֹת.

We are grateful, God, for all the wonderful and good things that are part of our daily lives.

May we look forward to a good year of life.
Blessed are You, *Adonai,*
Ruler of the Universe,
Who deserves our praise.

THE PRIESTLY BLESSING

אֱלֹהֵינוּ וֵאלֹהֵי אֲבוֹתֵינוּ, בָּרְכֵנוּ בַבְּרָכָה הַמְשֻׁלֶּשֶׁת
בַּתּוֹרָה הַכְּתוּבָה עַל יְדֵי מֹשֶׁה עַבְדֶּךָ, הָאֲמוּרָה מִפִּי
אַהֲרֹן וּבָנָיו כֹּהֲנִים עַם קְדוֹשֶׁךָ, כָּאָמוּר:

Leader:	Congregation answers:
יְבָרֶכְךָ יְיָ וְיִשְׁמְרֶךָ.	כֵּן יְהִי רָצוֹן.
יָאֵר יְיָ פָּנָיו אֵלֶיךָ וִיחֻנֶּךָּ.	כֵּן יְהִי רָצוֹן.
יִשָּׂא יְיָ פָּנָיו אֵלֶיךָ וְיָשֵׂם לְךָ שָׁלוֹם.	כֵּן יְהִי רָצוֹן.

God of our ancestors, bless us with the threefold blessing recited by the priests of old:

May *Adonai* bless and protect you,

May *Adonai* shine upon you with graciousness,

May *Adonai* look upon you with favor and grant you peace.

שִׂים שָׁלוֹם בָּעוֹלָם, טוֹבָה וּבְרָכָה חֵן וָחֶסֶד וְרַחֲמִים
עָלֵינוּ וְעַל כָּל־יִשְׂרָאֵל עַמֶּךָ. בָּרְכֵנוּ אָבִינוּ כֻּלָּנוּ כְּאֶחָד
בְּאוֹר פָּנֶיךָ, כִּי בְאוֹר פָּנֶיךָ נָתַתָּ לָּנוּ יְיָ אֱלֹהֵינוּ תּוֹרַת
חַיִּים וְאַהֲבַת חֶסֶד וּצְדָקָה וּבְרָכָה וְרַחֲמִים וְחַיִּים וְשָׁלוֹם.
וְטוֹב בְּעֵינֶיךָ לְבָרֵךְ אֶת־עַמְּךָ יִשְׂרָאֵל בְּכָל־עֵת
וּבְכָל־שָׁעָה בִּשְׁלוֹמֶךָ.

בְּסֵפֶר חַיִּים בְּרָכָה וְשָׁלוֹם וּפַרְנָסָה טוֹבָה נִזָּכֵר וְנִכָּתֵב
לְפָנֶיךָ אֲנַחְנוּ וְכָל־עַמְּךָ בֵּית יִשְׂרָאֵל לְחַיִּים טוֹבִים וּלְשָׁלוֹם.

Let peace, prosperity, happiness and lovingkindness come to our world, to us and to all the Jewish people. Bless us all, Holy One, with Your light, for by that light You have given the Torah to guide us. May it please You to bless the Jewish people in every season and at all times with goodness and peace.

May we and all the Jewish people be remembered and recorded in Your book for a good and peaceful life.

The ark is opened and we rise.

Leader:	Congregation answers:
הַיּוֹם תְּאַמְּצֵנוּ.	אָמֵן.
הַיּוֹם תְּבָרְכֵנוּ.	אָמֵן.
הַיּוֹם תְּגַדְּלֵנוּ.	אָמֵן.
הַיּוֹם תִּדְרְשֵׁנוּ לְטוֹבָה.	אָמֵן.
הַיּוֹם תִּכְתְּבֵנוּ לְחַיִּים טוֹבִים.	אָמֵן.

Leader:	Congregation answers:
Hayom t'amtzeinu.	*Amen.*
Hayom t'varḥeinu.	*Amen.*
Hayom t'gadleinu.	*Amen.*
Hayom tidr'sheinu l'tovah.	*Amen.*
Hayom tiḥt'veinu l'ḥayim tovim.	*Amen.*

בָּרוּךְ אַתָּה יְיָ עוֹשֵׂה הַשָּׁלוֹם.

Praised are You, *Adonai,* Source of peace.

The ark is closed and we are seated.

אֵין כֵּאלֹהֵינוּ, אֵין כַּאדוֹנֵינוּ, אֵין כְּמַלְכֵּנוּ, אֵין כְּמוֹשִׁיעֵנוּ.

מִי כֵאלֹהֵינוּ, מִי כַאדוֹנֵינוּ, מִי כְמַלְכֵּנוּ, מִי כְמוֹשִׁיעֵנוּ.

נוֹדֶה לֵאלֹהֵינוּ, נוֹדֶה לַאדוֹנֵינוּ, נוֹדֶה לְמַלְכֵּנוּ, נוֹדֶה לְמוֹשִׁיעֵנוּ.

בָּרוּךְ אֱלֹהֵינוּ, בָּרוּךְ אֲדוֹנֵינוּ, בָּרוּךְ מַלְכֵּנוּ, בָּרוּךְ מוֹשִׁיעֵנוּ.

אַתָּה הוּא אֱלֹהֵינוּ, אַתָּה הוּא אֲדוֹנֵינוּ, אַתָּה הוּא מַלְכֵּנוּ,
אַתָּה הוּא מוֹשִׁיעֵנוּ.

None compares to You
Our God
Our Lord
Ruler
and Deliverer.

Let us praise You for You are
Our God
Our Lord
Ruler
and Deliverer.

Ein keloheinu, Ein kadoneinu, Ein k'malkeinu, Ein k'moshi'einu.

Mi keiloheinu, Mi kadoneinu, Mi k'malkeinu, Mi k'moshi'einu.

Nodeh leloheinu, Nodeh ladoneinu, Nodeh l'malkeinu,
Nodeh l'moshi'einu.

Baruḥ Eloheinu, Baruḥ Adoneinu. Baruḥ Malkeinu, Baruḥ Moshi'einu.

Atah hu Eloheinu, Atah hu Adoneinu, Atah hu Malkeinu,
Atah hu Moshi'einu.

We rise.

עָלֵינוּ לְשַׁבֵּחַ לַאֲדוֹן הַכֹּל, לָתֵת גְּדֻלָּה לְיוֹצֵר בְּרֵאשִׁית,
שֶׁלֹּא עָשָׂנוּ כְּגוֹיֵי הָאֲרָצוֹת וְלֹא שָׂמָנוּ כְּמִשְׁפְּחוֹת הָאֲדָמָה,
שֶׁלֹּא שָׂם חֶלְקֵנוּ כָּהֶם וְגוֹרָלֵנוּ כְּכָל־הֲמוֹנָם. וַאֲנַחְנוּ
כּוֹרְעִים וּמִשְׁתַּחֲוִים וּמוֹדִים לִפְנֵי מֶלֶךְ מַלְכֵי הַמְּלָכִים
הַקָּדוֹשׁ בָּרוּךְ הוּא, שֶׁהוּא נוֹטֶה שָׁמַיִם וְיוֹסֵד אָרֶץ וּמוֹשַׁב
יְקָרוֹ בַּשָּׁמַיִם מִמַּעַל וּשְׁכִינַת עֻזּוֹ בְּגָבְהֵי מְרוֹמִים. הוּא
אֱלֹהֵינוּ אֵין עוֹד. אֱמֶת מַלְכֵּנוּ אֶפֶס זוּלָתוֹ, כַּכָּתוּב
בְּתוֹרָתוֹ: וְיָדַעְתָּ הַיּוֹם וַהֲשֵׁבֹתָ אֶל לְבָבֶךָ כִּי יְיָ הוּא
הָאֱלֹהִים בַּשָּׁמַיִם מִמַּעַל וְעַל הָאָרֶץ מִתָּחַת, אֵין עוֹד.

It is for us to praise the Ruler of all and to glorify the Creator of the world for giving us a special heritage and a unique destiny.

Before our Supreme Ruler we bend the knee and bow in devotion.

As it is written in the Torah, "Accept this day with both mind and heart. Know that God's presence fills creation."

Because we believe in You, we hope for the day when Your majesty will triumph and all will work to mend the world and live according to Your ways.

Aleinu l'shabei'aḥ la'adon hakol,
latet g'dulah l'yotzer b'reishit.
Shelo asanu k'goyei ha'aratzot,
v'lo samanu k'mishp'ḥot ha'adamah.
Shelo sam ḥelkeinu kahem,
v'goraleinu k'ḥol hamonam.

Va'anaḥnu korim umishtaḥavim umodim,
lifnei Meleḥ malḥei ham'laḥim,
hakadosh baruḥ hu.

Anne Frank was a young girl in Amsterdam, Holland, during the time of the Holocaust.

Two weeks before she died, she wrote these words in her diary:

> "It's really a wonder that I haven't dropped all my ideals, because they seem so absurd and impossible to carry out. Yet I keep them, because in spite of everything I still believe that people are really good at heart. I simply can't build my hopes on a foundation of confusion, misery, and death. I see the world gradually being turned into a wilderness. I hear the approaching thunder, I can feel the suffering of millions and yet, if I look up into the heavens, I think that it will all come out right one of these days, that this cruelty will end, and that peace and tranquility will return again. In the meantime, I must hold on to my ideals for perhaps the day will come when I shall be able to carry them out."

עַל כֵּן נְקַוֶּה לְךָ יְיָ אֱלֹהֵינוּ לִרְאוֹת מְהֵרָה בְּתִפְאֶרֶת
עֻזֶּךָ, לְהַעֲבִיר גִּלּוּלִים מִן הָאָרֶץ וְהָאֱלִילִים כָּרוֹת
יִכָּרֵתוּן, לְתַקֵּן עוֹלָם בְּמַלְכוּת שַׁדַּי וְכָל־בְּנֵי בָשָׂר יִקְרְאוּ
בִשְׁמֶךָ, לְהַפְנוֹת אֵלֶיךָ כָּל־רִשְׁעֵי־אָרֶץ. יַכִּירוּ וְיֵדְעוּ
כָּל־יוֹשְׁבֵי תֵבֵל כִּי לְךָ תִּכְרַע כָּל־בֶּרֶךְ תִּשָּׁבַע כָּל־לָשׁוֹן.
לְפָנֶיךָ יְיָ אֱלֹהֵינוּ יִכְרְעוּ וְיִפֹּלוּ וְלִכְבוֹד שִׁמְךָ יְקָר יִתֵּנוּ,
וִיקַבְּלוּ כֻלָּם אֶת־עֹל מַלְכוּתֶךָ וְתִמְלֹךְ עֲלֵיהֶם מְהֵרָה
לְעוֹלָם וָעֶד, כִּי הַמַּלְכוּת שֶׁלְּךָ הִיא וּלְעוֹלְמֵי עַד תִּמְלֹךְ
בְּכָבוֹד, כַּכָּתוּב בְּתוֹרָתֶךָ: יְיָ יִמְלֹךְ לְעֹלָם וָעֶד. וְנֶאֱמַר:
וְהָיָה יְיָ לְמֶלֶךְ עַל כָּל הָאָרֶץ, בַּיּוֹם הַהוּא יִהְיֶה יְיָ אֶחָד
וּשְׁמוֹ אֶחָד.

For it is written in the Torah, *"Adonai* shall rule for ever and ever."

MOURNER'S *KADDISH*

Mourners and those observing a memorial day rise and say:

יִתְגַּדַּל וְיִתְקַדַּשׁ שְׁמֵהּ רַבָּא בְּעָלְמָא דִּי בְרָא כִרְעוּתֵהּ,
וְיַמְלִיךְ מַלְכוּתֵהּ בְּחַיֵּיכוֹן וּבְיוֹמֵיכוֹן וּבְחַיֵּי דְכָל־בֵּית
יִשְׂרָאֵל בַּעֲגָלָא וּבִזְמַן קָרִיב, וְאִמְרוּ אָמֵן.

The congregation says together with the mourners:

יְהֵא שְׁמֵהּ רַבָּא מְבָרַךְ לְעָלַם וּלְעָלְמֵי עָלְמַיָּא.

Y'hai shmai rabbah m'varaḥ l'olam u'l'olmei almay'ya.

Mourners continue:

יִתְבָּרַךְ וְיִשְׁתַּבַּח וְיִתְפָּאַר וְיִתְרוֹמַם וְיִתְנַשֵּׂא וְיִתְהַדַּר
וְיִתְעַלֶּה וְיִתְהַלַּל שְׁמֵהּ דְּקֻדְשָׁא

Congregation together with mourners:

בְּרִיךְ הוּא.

B'riḥ hu.

לְעֵלָּא לְעֵלָּא מִכָּל־בִּרְכָתָא וְשִׁירָתָא תֻּשְׁבְּחָתָא וְנֶחֱמָתָא
דַּאֲמִירָן בְּעָלְמָא, וְאִמְרוּ אָמֵן.

יְהֵא שְׁלָמָא רַבָּא מִן שְׁמַיָּא וְחַיִּים עָלֵינוּ וְעַל כָּל־יִשְׂרָאֵל,
וְאִמְרוּ אָמֵן.

עוֹשֶׂה שָׁלוֹם בִּמְרוֹמָיו הוּא יַעֲשֶׂה שָׁלוֹם עָלֵינוּ וְעַל
כָּל־יִשְׂרָאֵל, וְאִמְרוּ אָמֵן.

אֲדוֹן עוֹלָם אֲשֶׁר מָלַךְ   בְּטֶרֶם כָּל־יְצִיר נִבְרָא.
לְעֵת נַעֲשָׂה בְחֶפְצוֹ כֹּל   אֲזַי מֶלֶךְ שְׁמוֹ נִקְרָא.
וְאַחֲרֵי כִּכְלוֹת הַכֹּל   לְבַדּוֹ יִמְלֹךְ נוֹרָא.
וְהוּא הָיָה וְהוּא הֹוֶה   וְהוּא יִהְיֶה בְּתִפְאָרָה.
וְהוּא אֶחָד וְאֵין שֵׁנִי   לְהַמְשִׁיל לוֹ לְהַחְבִּירָה.
בְּלִי רֵאשִׁית בְּלִי תַכְלִית   וְלוֹ הָעֹז וְהַמִּשְׂרָה.
וְהוּא אֵלִי וְחַי גֹּאֲלִי   וְצוּר חֶבְלִי בְּעֵת צָרָה.
וְהוּא נִסִּי וּמָנוֹס לִי   מְנָת כּוֹסִי בְּיוֹם אֶקְרָא.
בְּיָדוֹ אַפְקִיד רוּחִי   בְּעֵת אִישַׁן וְאָעִירָה.
וְעִם רוּחִי גְּוִיָּתִי   יְיָ לִי וְלֹא אִירָא.

God ruled before the world came to be and will rule at the end of time.
Our days and nights are in God's care.
Because we trust in God, we have no fear.

EILI EILI

These are the words of Ḥanah Senesh, a young woman who was captured by the Nazis when she parachuted into Hungary to save Jewish children and bring them to safety in Palestine.

Ḥanah Senesh left her comfortable home in Budapest, Hungary, at age eighteen to become a pioneer in *Eretz Yisrael*, the Land of Israel. During World War II, she volunteered to become a parachutist. Her mission was to land in Yugoslavia with her companions and make her way to Hungary. They planned to help the Jews escape from there. Sadly, she was captured and killed by the Nazis. Word of her bravery, both in parachuting and while in prison, spread throughout Europe, giving hope and courage to many Jews.

Below is a beautiful poem she wrote after she had arrived in Israel.

Eili, Eili,
O Lord, my God,
I pray that these things never end
The sand and the sea
The rush of the waters
The crash of the heavens
The prayers of the heart.

גְּמַר חֲתִימָה טוֹבָה.

May you be sealed for a good new year!

INTRODUCTION TO THE BOOK OF JONAH

Jonah is normally read during the *minḥah* (afternoon) service for *Yom Kippur*. Although this *Rosh haShanah* and *Yom Kippur mahzor* contains just the morning services, Jonah has been included because it is such a well known story with great appeal. It can be read and discussed at the end of the service or the leader can use it if there is a time in the afternoon when children (or families) get together.

The story teaches about the need we all have — Jew and non-Jew, for God's mercy. Not only do we need God's mercy, but God longs for us to return. It is said that the Holy One waits for the nations of the world in the hope that they do *teshuvah* and be brought under God's wings.

Jonah is also a story that emphasizes that we all can change. *Teshuvah* is possible. As the holy day of *Yom Kippur* ends, it reminds us to face our responsibilities. It is time to do *teshuvah*.

THE BOOK OF JONAH

An abbreviated version

The word of *Adonai* came to Jonah, son of Amitai, saying: "Get up and go to the great city of Nineveh to call their attention to the great wickedness that I see." Jonah, however, ran away from God's service. He went down to Jaffa where he found a ship sailing to Tarshish. He paid the fare and went aboard.

But *Adonai* cast a mighty wind upon the sea. Such a storm arose that the ship was in danger of breaking up and sinking. The sailors were so terrified they called to their gods for protection and then flung the cargo overboard to make the ship lighter. Meanwhile, Jonah had gone down to the hold of the ship where he lay down and fell asleep. The captain approached him and cried out, "How can you be sleeping so soundly? Get up and call upon your god. Perhaps this god will be kind to us and we will not perish."

Next the sailors cast lots to discover who was responsible for their misfortune. The lot fell on Jonah. Jonah replied that he was a Hebrew who worshipped *Adonai,* the God of Heaven, Who made both sea and land. When the sailors heard this, they were very frightened and cried out, "What have you done?" After Jonah told them he was fleeing from the service of *Adonai,* they asked him what they must do to make the sea calm again. Jonah told them to throw him overboard, for surely he was responsible for the terrible storm.

The sailors on board hesitated, for they did not wish to take the life of an innocent man. But as the sea grew even stormier and the sailors could not row to shore, they finally decided to hurl Jonah overboard. Calling out to *Adonai* for forgiveness, they threw Jonah into the waters. The sea stopped raging and grew calm.

Now *Adonai* provided a gigantic fish to swallow Jonah, and Jonah stayed inside the fish's belly for three days and three nights. Jonah prayed to *Adonai* to save him and *Adonai* commanded the fish to throw Jonah up onto dry land.

Adonai then spoke to Jonah a second time and ordered him to go at once to Nineveh. Jonah did as he was told and journeyed for three days until he came to the city.

When he arrived, Jonah prophesied, "In forty days Nineveh will be destroyed!" The people believed in God and proclaimed a fast. Great and small alike put on sackcloth. When the news reached the king, even he took off his royal robe, and dressed in sackcloth and sat in ashes. He decreed that the people turn from their evil ways in the hope that God would change the plan to destroy them. And God saw how they were turning back from their evil ways and so decided against the punishment that was originally planned.

This greatly displeased Jonah. He prayed to God, saying: "*Adonai*, isn't this exactly what I said would happen? This is why I tried to escape to Tarshish for I know that You are a kind and merciful God. Now I wish You'd take my life."

Jonah left Nineveh and stopped at a place east of the city. There he built a booth to sit in while he waited to see what would happen. As he waited, *Adonai* provided a ricinus plant which grew over Jonah to provide shade for his head and make him more comfortable. Jonah was very pleased about this.

But the next day, at dawn, God provided a worm to attack the plant so that it withered. And when the sun rose and beat upon Jonah's head, he felt faint and begged God for death.

God said to Jonah, "You cared so much about a plant that you didn't even grow. It appeared overnight and perished overnight. If so, shouldn't I care about the great city of Nineveh which has more than a hundred and twenty thousand innocent people, and animals as well!"

At times, we all want to run away from our responsibilities. The Book of Jonah teaches us that in the end we must face up to them. We learn that we cannot run away from God.

Some people think that Jonah didn't believe that the willingness of the people of Nineveh to change was real. Others think that he believed they would repent and he would look foolish for predicting their doom. In either case, God teaches Jonah (and us) the need for compassion.

The story of Jonah describes a *teshuvah* success story — an entire city repented and was forgiven! Imagine a world where everyone repents and changes for the better!

ART PROJECTS AND ACTIVITIES FOR HOME OR SCHOOL

PREPARING FOR HIGH HOLY DAYS

•Create decorative cards with your own greetings for the New Year. These can be made with crayons, magic markers or ink rollers. For an extra challenge, learn calligraphy to make your message special.

•With a large piece of butcher paper, make a giant mural of the creation story or the tale of Jonah and the whale.

•Create a booklet about your life. Use one page for each year you've lived. If you like, add pages to show how you picture your life in five years, ten years, twenty-five years and fifty years from now.

•List ten things that have happened or you think will happen in your lifetime. Separate these things into singular events and continuing processes. For example, winning a race or taking a trip to Israel would be a singular event. An ongoing friendship is a continuing process. Make a personal "Life Line," clipping cards with both the events and processes (use a different color for each). Share your Life Line with a partner.

•Write out a question about *Rosh haShanah* or *Yom Kippur* on an index card and the correct answer on another card. Combine your cards with other students' cards and mix them up. Distribute them. The purpose of the game is to have the correct pairs of questions and answers find each other.

•Plan a High Holy Day Bowl. Divide the class into teams. Use questions that students have submitted or use the ones listed in this *maḥzor*. May the best-prepared team win!

•Set up a message board at home or at school where people can write New Year greetings to each other.

•Make your own High Holy Day dictionary. Decorate it with holiday symbols or scenes.

•This is a perfect time to make your own calendar for the New Year. After filling in the dates for each holiday (and family birthdays!) draw a picture to go along with each Hebrew month.

•Bake round *ḥallot* to show that *Rosh haShanah* is the "head" of the year. And why not make a beautiful round *ḥallah* cover to go with it!

•Dip apples into honey or bake honey cake for a sweet year.

•Enjoy other holiday treats like *rugelaḥ* or *taiglaḥ*.

•Consult your synagogue library to learn about other foods that are traditional on *Rosh haShanah* for Sephardic Jews.

•Make a honey pot out of clay. Carve or paint on it the Hebrew word for honey — *d'vash*.

•Bake and enjoy birthday cupcakes to celebrate the birthday of the world.

•Write blessings and wishes for the New Year. Put them in homemade fortune cookies. Read them out loud with family or friends.

•Make a ceramic *tzedakah* plate.

•Make a *tzedakah* box from a metal or cardboard box.

•Choose a *tzedakah* and make a donation.

QUESTIONS FOR A HIGH HOLY DAY BOWL

For School or After Services

1. When are *S'liḥot* services held?
2. Translate "*L'Shanah Tovah Tikateivu.*"
3. *Rosh haShanah* begins what Hebrew month?
4. What birthday does *Rosh haShanah* celebrate?
5. Why do we dip apples into honey?
6. What shape is the *ḥallah* for *Rosh haShanah*?
7. From what animal is a *shofar* made?
8. Give one reason why we sound the *shofar*.
9. Translate "*rosh*" and "*shanah.*"
10. What's *tashliḥ*?
11. Why do the rabbi and cantor wear white garments on the High Holy Days?
12. In the end, why did God tell Abraham *not* to sacrifice Isaac?
13. What is *Shabbat Shuvah*?
14. What are the ten days between *Rosh haShanah* and *Yom Kippur* called?
15. What does "*yom*" and "*kippur*" mean?
16. Why do we light candles after the meal before *Kol Nidre*?
17. Why do we fast on *Yom Kippur*?
18. Name the notes for the *shofar* blowing.
19. Why do we recite the *"al ḥet"* (the prayer listing our sins) as a whole congregation?
20. Tell one thing that the High Priest did to celebrate *Yom Kippur* in ancient times.
21. When do we blow the *shofar* on *Yom Kippur*?
22. Name a prayer we say on *Yom Kippur*.
23. On which of the High Holy Days do we say *Yizkor*, the prayer to remember those who have died?
24. Why is *Yom Kippur* called "Sabbath of Sabbaths"?
25. Translate and explain the words *tzedakah, teshuvah* and *tefillah*.

NOTES

We have adapted for this *maḥzor* stories from legends and folk tales that are found in many different works. For those interested in an expanded version we have indicated a source. The number in ( ) is keyed to the bibliography.

Page viii-xii: *Home Blessing for Erev Rosh haShanah*—The translations for all blessings recited at home are based on translations by Shoshana Silberman in *A Family Haggadah*. Kar-Ben Copies, Inc. (Rockville, MD), 1987.

Page 3: *The Lesson. . .* (11)

Page 4: *Scales, Balance and Rain. . .* (21)

Page 18: *Just as I created. . . Midrash Tehillim* 116:8

Page 21: *Avrum's words. . .* Robert Cole, *The Spiritual Life of Children*, Houghton Mifflin (New York). Pg. 75

Page 23: *Once a student asked. . .* Martin Buber, *Ten Rungs: Hasidic Sayings*. Schocken Books, 1947. Pg. 82.

Page 40: *The Field of Sisterly Love. . .* (8)

Page 62: *Where Was Rabbi David. . .* (11)

Page 76: *Who is a hero. . . Pirkei Avot* 4:1

Page 86: *When you go on a plane. . .* Robert Cole, *The Spiritual Life of Children*. Pg. 145

Page 88: *The Drum. . .* (4)

Page 89: *Where those who do teshuvah. . . Brachot* 34B

Page 90: *The sounds of the shofar. . . Tiferet Uziel* in S.Y. Agnon, *The Days of Awe*. Shocken Books. Pg. 74.

Page 92: *Bird Song. . .* Anonymous child in the Theriesienstadt Concentration Camp. "Bird Song" in *I Never Saw Another Butterfly*.

Page 97: *There was evening. . .* Genesis 1:15

97: *And on the first day. . . Mishnah Rosh HaShanah* 1:1

97: *Head and nerve center. . .* Rabbi Menachem M. Schneerson from a public address 1990.

Page 102: *The Traveler. . .* (9)

Page 104: *The holy one said. . .*

Page 106-107: *Home Blessings. . . A Family Haggadah*. Kar-Ben Copies, Inc.

Page 108: *When there was a cholera. . .* S.Y. Agnon, *Days of Awe*.

Page 113: *Silent Devotion. . .* (10)

Page 118: *Beruriah And The Robbers. . . Brachot* 10A

Page 120: *In His Own Way. . .* (18)

Page 121: *I think there's a God. . .* Robert Cole, *The Spiritual Life of Children*. Pg. 155.

Page 125: *An Angel's* Teshuvah. . . (4)

: *Who is truly mighty?. . . Avot diRabbi Natan*, Ch. 23

Page 130: *Have we not one parent. . . Malachai* 2:10

Page 135: *A Lesson At The Doorway. . .* (13)

Page 157: *Why does the world begin. . . Mishnah Sanhedrin* 4:5

Page 166: *Rabbi Elimelach's Story. . .* (20)

Page 172: *It's really a wonder. . . Anne Frank: The Diary Of A Young Girl*. Random House, Inc. (New York). Pg. 278.

Page 176: *Get up and go. . .* Numbers *Rabbah* 10:1

BIBLIOGRAPHY

1. Agnon, S.Y. *Days of Awe*. Shocken, New York.1965.
2. Arzt, Max. *Justice and Mercy*. Holt, Rinehart and Winston, New York. 1963.
3. Buber, Martin. *Ten Rungs: Chassidic Sayings*. Shocken, New York. 1947.
4. Certner, Simon. *101 Jewish Stories*. Board of Jewish Education of New York, New York. 1983.
5. Coles, Robert. *The Spiritual Life of Children*. Houghton Mifflin, New York. 1990.
6. Fields, Harvey. *A Torah Commentary For Our Time*. Union of American Hebrew Congregations, New York. 1990.
7. Frank, Anne. *Anne Frank: The Diary of a Young Girl*. Random House, Inc. (Modern Library), New York. 1952.
8. Frankel, Ellen. *The Classic Tales*. Jason Aronson, Inc. Northvale, New Jersey. 1989.
9. Goldin, Barbara Diamond. *A Child's Book of Midrash*. Jason Aronson, Northvale, New Jersey. 1989.
10. Goodman, Philip. *Rejoice in Thy Festival.* Bloch Publishing Company, New York. 1956.
11. Goodman, Philip. *The Rosh HaShana Anthology*. The Jewish Publication Society, Philadelphia. 1973.
12. Goodman, Philip. *The Yom Kippur Anthology*. The Jewish Publication Society, Philadelphia. 1971.
13. Harlow, Jules. *Lessons From Our Living Past.* Behrman House, New York. 1972.
14. Idelsohn, A.Z. *Jewish Liturgy*. Shocken, New York. 1972.
15. *I Never Saw Another Butterfly*. Shocken Books, New York.
16. Kimmel, Eric A. *Days of Awe*. Viking Press, New York. 1991.
17. Kitov, Eliyahu. *The Book of Our Heritage*, Vol. I. Feldheim Publishers, Jerusalem/New York. 1978.
18. Ruthen, Gerald C. *Daniel And the Silver Flute.* United Synagogue Commission on Jewish Education. New York. 1986.
19. Scherman, Nasson and Meir Zlotowitz, eds. *Rosh Hashana*. Art Scroll, Mesorah Series, Mesorah Publications Ltd., Brooklyn, New York. 1969.
20. Scherman, Nasson and Meir Zlotowitz, eds. *Yom Kippur*. Art Scroll, Mesorah Series, Mesorah Publications Ltd., Brooklyn, New York. 1969.
21. Schram, Peninah. *Jewish Stories One Generation Tells Another*. Jason Aronson. Northvale, New Jersey. 1987.
22. Strassfeld, Michael. *The Jewish Holidays*. Harper & Row, Publishers, New York, 1985.
23. Waskow, Arthur. *Seasons of Our Joy*. Bantam Books, Inc., New York. 1982.
24. Weinberg, Matis. *Patterns In Time*, Vol. I. Rosh HaShana. Feldheim Publishers, Jerusalem, New York. 1989.